50 Years of Amicizia
(Friendship)

Stefano Breccia

Warren P Aston
General Editor

Copyright 2013

Front Cover image: adapted from original Amicizia photography of a W56 craft provided by Stefano Breccia.

Back Cover image: this photograph taken by Bruno Sammaciccia shows a "Red" being from another dimension. Another image, now lost, showed Bruno standing in the midst of a circle of these beings. The area of the heart was given special emphasis to symbolize that this race cooperated in Friendship with the Akrij aliens and their human allies.

Stefano Breccia

50 Years of *AMICIZIA*
("Friendship")

Stefano Breccia

CONTENTS

Foreword

Warren Aston

It has been a rare privilege to edit Stefano Breccia's second book. This process began before his sudden passing and, at the invitation of his family following his untimely death, has continued. My intent has always been to let Stefano's voice have the priority above all else, even grammatical considerations, so the editing has been light. I believe he would be pleased with these efforts to place his words on record.

Stefano's first book, *Mass Contacts*, was an extraordinary general recounting of the *Amicizia* experience. The book was truly a revelation to Ufologists as much as to the general public, drawing back the curtains on a tableau that has never been described before in our world. Once the reader grasps the essentials of the case, that claim will no longer be seen as extravagant. Despite my decades as a UFO investigator and writer in the field I had never encountered anything like it. Its truth spoke to me clearly and I soon embarked on a correspondence with Stefano that lasted several years.

Mass Contacts remains required, *essential!* reading still for anyone hoping to comprehend the Friendship case. This second book begins to flesh out some of the stories hinted at in the first. It takes us deeper behind the scenes. We see inside the organization that was established in order to spread the concepts of the Akrij visitors. We meet some of its participants and then follow the collapse of the group's cohesion, leading to the dramatic end of the project. The role of the CTR aliens - for me the most difficult aspect of Amicizia to understand - is a constant thread through the story.

In turn, the new book hints at how much more remains to be told. In our correspondence, Stefano began sharing some of these experiences with me, continuing until just days before his sudden passing.

Indeed, the full extent of Amicizia and its implications has yet to be revealed. Although many of its participants have passed on now, others remain in the shadows, living in a state of cognitive dissonance lives that appear conventional, but retaining the memories of their undeniable experiences. Stefano Breccia was the first to step forth publicly and reveal what he experienced. In so doing he also gave a voice to fellow participants and highlighted the even earlier efforts of consul Alberto Perego to have Amicizia's reality recognized. He and those others who have come forth so far deserve our admiration for their moral courage and integrity.

Regardless of how we may categorize them, both of Stefano Breccia's books stand, quite literally, in a league of their own. For more than three decades the author, along with scores of other credible witnesses, *lived* the Amicizia alien contact experience on a daily basis. Fully immersed in the events with its many human and non-human characters, Breccia functioned as both participant and as observer.

His background as a physicist, an engineer and a linguist uniquely qualified Breccia as he participated in the Akrij contacts. He was the confidant and friend of the two men whose experiences with the visitors were the deepest. It was Breccia whom the dying leader of the Italian contacts, theologian Bruno Sammaciccia, asked to record his story; it was Breccia who participated in the experiments and adventures of Bruno's closest friend, the irrepressible Giancarlo de Carlo. The full extent of the latter's adventures remain to be told.

Stefano's books reflect the advantages that his training gave him in understanding these interactions with the peoples of advanced cultures. Sublime concepts about earth's past, about life in the universe, morality, God and about super-technology await the careful reader. Many require repeated reading to fully appreciate. These are not mystical, Shangri-La-type fantasies but are entirely logical, consistent, universal principles that anyone dedicated to the search for Truth will intuitively respond to. Truth has its own eloquence.

These concepts place UFO's into their broader historical context in surprising ways. For those ready to move beyond speculation, fragmented data and disinformation, a much-needed new paradigm for the world of Ufology results. The paradigm reveals an alien presence on earth far beyond any "fifth column" scenario that has ever been proposed before. Breccia, the engineer, also devotes space to explaining the propulsion methods and navigation systems used by the Akrij aliens. The photographs in the book include not only craft in flight, but interior views of one and the dialogue of the crew recorded during a flight. There are further glimpses of some of the visitors themselves.

Most importantly, however, an expanded understanding of earth's place in the cosmos and what it means to be fully *human* emerges with a new clarity. The breathtaking potential of humanity unfolds within this seminal book. It is a future still beyond our ability to fully grasp, but it comes from Friends who, having trodden the path we are now on, already live in it.

It is a future that all right-thinking people will wish for the human family.

We and the "Infiltrators"

Roberto Pinotti
Former President and General Secretary of the CUN

When my old friend Stefano Breccia at the end decided to surrender to my iterated pressures, he resolved to lift the lid off the uneasy and almost unheard-of (with very few exceptions) history of Amicizia, writing out the disconcerting text of his "Contattismi di massa" (later "Mass Contacts"). I was sure that he would not have been able to tell everything on such complex a topic, and so now we have the necessary second part of his tale; I was also sure that his book would have given birth to a virtuous process of gradual revealing, with new details made known by other characters still alive.

It has been shown that I was right and wrong at the same time. I was right because, beyond Gaspare De Lama and Paolo Di Girolamo (who, after my concern, wrote his "We and They", a complement of Stefano's book), some other "survivors" emerged. It has been the case, for instance, of the unknown author of "The History of Amicizia" that, thanks to researcher Nikola Duper I have been able to insert in my "*Alieni: Un incontro annunciato*" (Oscar Mondadori, Milano, 2009): eight pages signed by "One of the pact" that, beyond the anonymity of their author, are nevertheless important because they confirm the whole story, but at the same time reveal the dread (maybe an excessive one) that their author has to expose himself, not to face social and professional problems.

A dread difficult to overcome by the silent characters who are preferring to remain concealed, in an attitude balancing between the wish to tell their experience and a wait-and-see policy. That's why I have also been wrong. A lot of time has passed, and in the meantime the lawyer Franco Saija passed away before being able to tell his story, as he was willing to. What a pity! Others, an E. B. and a B. G., just to quote two of them, from their homes told me that they are minded to remain silent, at least for the moment. It's a legitimate position, also because, to them, the story is over.

But is it really so?

Indeed it isn't. Formally the story is over, even before Bruno Sammaciccia passed away, but it is not necessarily so. Everything makes us believe that the alien "Infiltrators", having assisted to the progressive decaying of the Pescara experience, and to the weakening of Uredda, did not actually go away as they have pretended, but have just broken their relationship with their friends in this country, probably starting new experiences elsewhere, maybe with more reliable interlocutors. In the end, the problem sits with "us", not with "them". So we assist to an unexpected iteration of the Pescara affairs in South America, and probably not only there. That's an important consideration, that makes us believe that the previous interlocutors have been discarded, and may even be deluded.

But it is not as easy as that. In our environment, when it is decided to stop an operative unit that does not respond as expected, usually also the relationship with its more valid components are cut off. And no good soldier would speak of treachery, also because, like it or not, "we" and "they" are not at all at the same level. And so one might expect illogical and contradictor behaviours towards the ones who have not been up to, in order to throw into disorder their expectations.

That does not allow negative considerations, a Manichaean vision in which also the W56-CTR confrontation may be seen as fictitious, but necessary to satisfy our superficial vision of the reality: good and bad, white and black, positive and negative. We cannot speak to primary school pupils like we would to university students. And indeed the reality is composed by an infinity of levels of grey.

In front of a cosmic prospect, our behaviour becomes more indistinct, less defined, giving way to ethical components much more important of our legitimate desire of knowledge and technology: love, loyalty, a calm comprehension of ours and others limitations. These are all elements upon which we might have built a better world since long time, and that "They", within Amicizia, have always taught us to take into account. It is not so easy to succeed in doing so. The ones who, like Gaspare De Lama and his wife Mirella, have profited from the lesson, taking all benefits from it, and becoming better. Not everybody is able to. Once I have been told that friends must be accepted as they are, beyond any defect. That's right, and that's just what "They" have been doing, and continue to do, towards us, beyond any manifestation of our mediocrity. Let's remember that Amicizia has been but one of the various experiences of mass contact implemented up to now, and that others have been dismissed (the Ummo case, for instance).

Cheer up! Maybe one day we'll we able to better interact with "Them", and so our relation with the "Infiltrators (that someone named "Superior Hierarchies") will no longer have the limitations of today.

My opinion

Stefano Breccia

After "Contattismi di massa" and "Mass Contacts", I have been asked to explore, in a deeper detail, the world of Amicizia. Not an easy job at all! Amicizia has lasted so many years, so many people have been involved in it, so immanent has been the presence of our Friends (forgive me if, from now on, I write this word with a capital letter; it's my way of distinguishing W56s from usual friends: it's a tribute I believe they are entitled to). But, in all evidence, what I have presented in my two previous books is far from being exhaustive, therefore some deepening is necessary.

From the other end, there are still too many details that, simply, cannot be made public. The first one is, of course, the list of the involved persons that I am aware of; in public interviews I've stated that I own a list of something more than 120 people, from different countries, who have taken part in this history in one way or another. Many among them have requested me to not quote their names, and I oblige. But I do not feel comfortable in quoting also the other ones, even if many among them have already passed away; therefore this list is going to remain buried inside my computers.

Then, there are topics that, even to-day, are still too "hot": it would be extremely dangerous to enter into certain details, therefore I will not do anything of this sort.

Another dubious argument is illegality; during Amicizia times, the persons involved in it often had to behave, let's say, not so honestly; the most common crimes consisted in smuggling radio-active materials through customs, all over Europe. After thinking a bit about it, I decided to quote the details (at least in part) of this activity. After all, we damaged nobody in doing so, and probably from a legal point of view this crime is no longer prosecutable. Other items, much more serious ones, have been smuggled, but I obviously am not going on speaking about them!

Then, another obvious question: why has no serious evidence been presented? Well, it has been my decision. In my previous books, I've presented many pictures that, due to the times they have been taken, were really difficult to forge, there are also Super 8 mm films, and so on, so a bit of evidence has been presented, both in my books, and in my lectures. More stringent facts could be presented, for instance the involvement of secret services, both American and Soviet ones, one case of which I have personally witnessed: a conversation between two Russian officers, in Rome, who were unaware that I could understand their language... But I prefer that the reader decides whether this story is believable, or merely a very elaborate science fiction tale. It is an escape, after all: at the very beginning, I was totally against writing about it, because it really is a time-bomb; now I am obliging to some requests, and, above all, after having unveiled Amicizia, I feel obliged to depict it in more precise details; but I will not feel offended if someone does not believe me. Even more: I encourage the strictest criticism of what I am going to say. It might even be a very good help, to myself, just to start. Therefore, Amicizia is going to remain a dubious topic, because it is simply impossible to speak clearly and blatantly about it. I hope that I have been sufficient explicit in explaining why certain concepts just cannot get into the open.

On another side, I believe that it may be interesting to explain some details that in my previous books have not been underlined. First of all, the vision our Friends have about morality, cosmology, and the like. Then, some minor anecdotes, minor in the global scenario, but at times with casualties involved and therefore not to be taken too lightly.

When Bruno Sammaciccia asked me to write down his memories, at first I opposed this idea, because to me Amicizia history was too hot a topic to discuss plainly. Then, after his death, I agreed to the prods from my good friend Roberto Pinotti, and later, Paola Harris, so my first two books on Amicizia have been printed. A lot of unexpected events took place after that. Scholars of world-wide renown have been my guests in order to discuss this story, I've been interviewed by Jaime Maussan, who crossed the ocean from Mexico to meet me; Piergiorgio Caria has made a valuable DVD on this story. At the same time, two other Amicizia men, Paolo Di Girolamo and Gaspare De Lama together with his wonderful wife, agreed to reveal themselves, telling their own experiences, that I will quote here in some detail. Unfortunately, most of the other people in my list did nothing like that; on the contrary, they prevented me once again from quoting even their names.

A strange situation arose a couple of years ago, when a Croatian researcher, Nikola Duper, announced a forthcoming book by an unknown member of Amicizia; at the same time Duper, or his unknown author, expressed unkind remarks about my books. The criticism I am ready to accept is that I was too technical, and had not spoken at length about moral problems; I agree, and will try to correct these problems in this book; at the same time I've been waiting for the work of this unknown person (I'm rather sure I know his identity, but that does not matter), because a different point of view should have added a better understanding of this strange phenomenon. Unfortunately, at this very moment, nothing further is known about this new book.

In all evidence, I failed in my purpose of using my books as a bait for convincing other Amicizia people to tell their stories: just a few of them answered my request, and, even considering the number of people who are no longer with us, it is a small result.

On the other hand, my books have solicited a great number of reactions from people who had never heard about Amicizia before, but who nevertheless have been experiencing unusual phenomena relating to this subject. The most unexpected instance took place with an old time friend of mine (after having first refused, now he allows me to quote his name: Damiano D'Alessandro); we know each other since, say, 20 years or so; we are both private pilots (he is a flying instructor), and have spent many hours flying together. Strangely enough, we have never spoken about UFOs during our flights. Then one morning, in Rome, he has been confronted with a man three meters tall, and a few days later he attended, by pure chance, a convention in Montesilvano (Pescara), where, for the first time, I have been speaking about Amicizia in public. Then he came to my home, asking for details, and, after that, he became one among the most valuable heralds of this story, even opening an Internet site to comment it (www.spazioevita.com).

Another unexpected friend has been Warren Aston, from Australia, who, after enquiring at length with me via e-mails, has written interesting articles on Amicizia. Then (in alphabetic order) Sergio Alcayaga from Chile, Piergiorgio Caria, from Italy, Come Carpentier from India, Harry Challenger from the UK, Ernesto De La Fuente Gandarilla from Chile, A. J. Gevaerd from Brazil, Timothy Good from UK, Ernesto Lacalle from Argentina, Jaime Maussan Flota from Mexico, and many, many others, most of which I cannot afford to name. An old friend of mine who has supported my activity since the days Bruno Sammaciccia passed away is eng. Carlo Bolla, from Rome; another one is Teresa Barbatelli, whose study on Kenio's height is presented later on.

Other friends came to my premises to discuss with me their experiences, even friends I had no longer heard of, since when I was just a boy (too many years ago, unfortunately!), together with people that I had never met before. The, let's say, "Amicizia friends group" has grown to an unexpected amount of people, the Rocca Pia in Ascoli Piceno has been visited by numbers of tourists never seen before, and so on. Of course I am glad for that, but I am also sad for the poor reaction from the members of the old Amicizia group. I hope that this story will help even more people to open their minds to a wider view of the Universe and of our role inside it.

I wish to thank all the other persons who have given me their support in this unexpected adventure; among the best known worldwide, Roberto Pinotti, Timothy Good, Robert Girard, Paola Harris, Michael Salla; plus, of course, many more whose names either cannot be quoted, or would anyway be unknown to my readers. I thank everybody, also the few who have expressed unkind opinions on my work, hoping for all of us, and the rest of mankind, a happy future!

Then, let me present here a few lines that Bruno Sammaciccia told me, during one of our meetings:

Now I have only you, and my wife tells me that you, my boy, are going to get tired, because I am exploiting you.
If he's here, I answer, it's because he volunteered to write a book, but she doesn't understand!
I am exhausting you, she states.
Look, I tell her, he too lived such experiences, a fragment of the whole story; it's not by chance that he's got here!

Chapter 1

A bit of history

UFOlogy in Italy has seen many renowned precursors, dating back to millennia ago, to Latin historians, Julius Obsequens being probably the best known among them, but by far not the most important one. Limiting ourselves, for the sake of brevity, to the last century, many cultured men have privately enquired about the presence of beings "from outside"; almost everybody heard about Guglielmo Marconi reporting that he received radio signals from Mars, as reported by J. C. MacBeth, London manager of the Marconi Wireless Telegraph Company Ltd, but I discovered many others who have been discussing the problem in secluded circles, in order to avoid bad publicity. Of course, one can't but wonder how Benito Mussolini, during the war, on a very formal occasion, in the presence of the German ambassador, dared to say:

It is more likely that United States will be invaded
by the apparently very warlike inhabitants from the planet Mars,
who will descend from spaces in flying fortresses which we can't even
imagine, than by soldiers of the Axis's powers.

(Benito Mussolini: Discorso alla Federazione Fascista dell'Urbe)
February 25, 1941

A rather unexpected statement from the leader of a country that was already encountering some problems in its war operations!

After the war, Italians started reading news about UFO in newspapers and magazines, often with a skeptical attitude. But, here and there, some decided that the subject had to be taken seriously. Now let me recognize the major characters who, in Italy, played significant roles in this direction. All of them, unknown to the general public, had been inside Amicizia.

Alberto Perego

Consul Alberto Perego was an Italian pioneer along this road. As a diplomat, once he understood the significance of the presence of flying saucers in our skies, he started writing books (at his own expenses) about what he was considering, above all, a political problem, presenting statesmen all over the world with them, and getting usually only polite acknowledge. But he failed in his effort to force the world nations to take this problem seriously, at least openly, and he became rather angry for that.

In the meantime he had entered Amicizia (it was Alberto who suggested that I get in touch with Bruno Sammaciccia), and he had got confirmations to his ideas; in his last three books he showed pictures derived from Amicizia, always without any reference (often just a caption reading "Pescara"). As the political authorities did not react in the way he had been expecting, Alberto threatened to write a fifth book, titled "Dirò tutto" ("I'll say everything"), but in the last years of his life he understood that it was simply impossible to present mankind with tales of this kind; my previous book ("Contattismi di massa") was the very first to talk explicitly about Amicizia, decades later.

In those years in the Italian UFO groups contactees were not welcome (one of the reasons why Amicizia has been kept secret), therefore Alberto was pushed, little by little, to the outskirts of these organization, so that he felt more and more alone. While I was attending military duties in Rome, I often invited Alberto to have dinner with me, in a restaurant near to his house, in the Parioli area, in Rome. Unfortunately, when he passed away, in 1981, I was in the States, and I learnt of his death only weeks later.

But I am proud to have been the man who, in 2003, lecturing at a convention organized by CUN (the major UFO organization in Italy) in Rome, dared for the first time to remember Alberto Perego's figure, and his role in the birth of UFO studies in Italy, and abroad.

Bruno Ghibaudi

A journalist, and aeronautical expert, he was conducting a TV program on model planes; at the same time the RAI (the Italian public broadcast) asked him to conduct an inquiry about flying saucers, a phenomenon that was being reported more and more frequently. At first, Bruno was very skeptical but, after having interviewed many witnesses, he realized that it was not all a joke; anyway the program he realized on this topic was never aired, perhaps he had been too much in favour of the phenomenon. Giancarlo (Sammaciccia's best friend) noticed this man talking on TV about planes, liked his well-tempered habits and culture, so got in touch with Ghibaudi, and invited him to pay a visit to Sammaciccia. They liked each other, and so also Ghibaudi (whom I refer to as "Bruno minor" to distinguish from "Bruno major", i.e. Bruno Sammaciccia) entered Amicizia.

He soon started to play an important role within the group: as a journalist, he wrote literally hundreds of articles on UFOs, eventually admitting, in some of them, that he had actually met aliens, never quoting, of course, where it had happened, and with whose help. As one of the goals of Amicizia consisted in a get-acquainted program, to convince laymen of the actual significance of the problem, his activity has been a really precious one.

Even more so when the director of the newspaper "Il Tempo" (one of the most widely diffused paper over Italy) asked Bruno minor to write a full-page article of UFOs, one each day, 15 to 17 thousand words per article, during three months in 1963; in practice, the first Italian book on UFOs! Inside "Mass Contact" I recall Bruno minor in several instances, because, together with Alberto Perego, he has been one of the pioneers of UFOlogy in Italy.

Bruno Sammaciccia

Bruno was the man who was the center of the Italian Amicizia activities. A really valuable man, whose biography has been shortly reported inside "Mass Contacts", but also a real friend. He was, in the good and in the bad, the propulsive motor of the Amicizia group. It was Bruno who introduced Alberto Perego and Bruno Ghibaudi into this world, and that would be enough, but it wasn't actually, for he worked a lot in finding people who could be put in touch with this reality, spending almost all of his time (and his money) in this enterprise.

Would I go on describing Bruno's activity, probably half of this book should be required. As usual, with great persons, these few lines will suffice. He was often lecturing, typically on religious topics, and this is a picture I took of him during one of his conferences.

Giancarlo De Carlo

An accountant, he was my companion in a lot of technical adventures, while trying to put into practice some of the ideas derived from the W56s, at times risking our own lives in the process. We spent thousands of work hours, and a huge amount of money in that. He was at the centre of some incredible adventures that I do not dare to tell. Inside the Italian Amicizia group, he was the real manager of the group, because Sammaciccia was flying much higher than the others. While Bruno senior was an idealist, Giancarlo was a very down-to-earth person. He also kept contacts with the Swiss friends, and some among the German people involved. Aurora, his wife, was an exquisite person, a Mathematics teacher in middle classes, used to the extravagancies of her husband, and of his Friends, and of myself, of course!

Giancarlo was really intolerant about the mistakes of our science and our technology. When referring to our first space attempts, he was making use of a vernacular sentence, that could be translated, more or less, as "a huge straw fire". He had also some uncanny capabilities, among them the ability of concentrating, or dispersing, clouds at will. He was saying that they were ingrained with himself since forever, and he could not explain them.

The image above shows Giancarlo on the hill over Pineto; the picture has been given me by another ex-Amicizia fellow, Emilio, who does not allow me to quote his full name, nor to show a picture of him! Giancalo often displayed a very strong feeling for exploring: once he discovered a very huge underground hall, South of Pescara, whose entrance is tens of meters under the sea level. His discovery was a surprise also to our Friends, one of whom wanted to explore it in a rather strange attire; a composite picture, taken of him on the occasion, sits on the cover of "Mass Contacts".

Bruno Sammaccicia was saying that Giancarlo was his best friend, and I may say something similar from my part.

"Dick"

Then, let me add here Dick, Bruno's shepherd dog. It often played important roles in keeping in touch with our Friends; here (the image is a still frame from a very long movie) it appears standing against a window, looking at a saucer flying in the skies of Milano.

The movie, an 8 mm film, is obviously very old, therefore its quality is not so good. Anyway, Dick's magnificent ears are clearly visible!

Emilio

As I have just said, Emilio is one among the people who do not want to get public. But I believe I may enclose a picture of his, with his head concealed; I have shot this image; we had taken Emilio, and other old Amicizia friends, to the Rocca Pia in Ascoli Piceno; to him, seeing again the old castle after so many years was a really touching experience.

I do not know whether he realized that I had shot this picture; if not, this will be a surprise to him! It took place on Jul 24, 2009.

A few days later, I escorted a small group of six former Amicizia people to visit some places in Pescara that had played some role in the story; here we are in front of what had been a house of Sammaciccia's, the "Villino Verde", in Montesilvano.

So many years later, the house has been totally re-built, (it's fortunate that it has not been replaced by a multi-store building!) anyway, it still keeps its charm.

Chapter 2

The W56s

General outline

It is obviously a titanic task to try to depict alien beings, so let me start with some simple and general considerations.

First than all, the W56 are not a single race, a single population. On the contrary, they are a confederation of several different races, each one of them with its history, its language, its habits, its physical complexion. So, in a sense, it is a mistake speaking about them as a unit. It would also be equally wrong maintaining that they are allies to each other: first, there is nothing against which they should ally, and secondly there is not a common project they are pursuing.

They are very ancient people, have got to the highest levels of scientific knowledge, of morality, of consciousness, therefore all of them behave in similar ways, and in this sense we might think of them as a unity. They state that their history is like a very long river, whose mouth is known to everybody, but whose sources are hidden.

They pretend that, in the whole universe, life originated only on fifty planets, that they call "Mother Planets", our Earth among them (that's why they love and respect so much our small planet). Some among them actually originated here, aeons ago, so that they are more terrestrials than we are!

Then, to the contrary of what I have written in the previous lines, they do not make any distinction between themselves and ourselves, between W56s and Earthlings. To them, we are all members of the same community that dwells in this universe (and may be not only it, surely not only in the way it is perceived by Earth scientists), a community with many differences inside it, but a unity in its background. There are differences in races, in physical structures, in the levels of development, but we all share the same *nature* (not the CTRs, but that's a different matter, that I'll discuss later on). Of course, from our (Earthlings') point of view it is difficult not to differentiate, so that I'll go on speaking about "we" and "they", but I want to make it absolutely clear that from their point of view such a difference is but a mere illusion. On the contrary, they do differentiate between the men's community and the CTRs who, although often more similar to Earthlings than most of the W56s, are deeply different in their nature.

Then the name; the word "W56" has been invented by Bruno Sammaciccia; the "W" stands for "V" + "V": they maintain that when one achieves a Victory in some of his actions, he must immediately attain another Victory, this time against himself, to prevent getting too proud because of the first one; then "56" refer to the year this story has started, for Bruno. Our Friends liked this name very much, to the point that it was written everywhere inside their environments, in Latin characters! Of course they do not attribute themselves a name; there is a common term, in their Global language (they speak a lot of different languages, but there is one understood almost by all of them, what I call the "Global language"; its name is "Darcei", "Dahrtchay" for English speaking readers) that might refer to them as a unity; their name is *"Akrij"* (to English speaking readers, it is pronounced like "Ahkreeh"), and it means "The sage ones".

Strangely enough, I was able to find this same name in our oldest languages, with that very same meaning! It is, according to me, a clear example of their presence over this Earth since millennia ago. In Sanskrit it is written like this:

In Egyptian hieroglyphs it is written this way:

It must be noted that, because of the Egyptian grammar, this name is pronounced "Akriiju" ("Ahkreehou" for English readers), because the plural ending is phonetically a "w", represented by the three bars at the lower right side. This hieroglyph writing shows us another concept, that for obvious reasons is lacking in the Sanskrit version: reading from left to right, the first signs have alphabetical meanings: the vulture is "A", the bowl "K", the mouth "R", the two plumes "IJ"; then the chick is "W", a first plural ending, but not a grammatical one, just a phonetic one; then there is a symbol without any phonetic meaning: that peculiar kind of snake represents "Wisdom", by itself; finally we have another plural ending, this time a grammatical one. Therefore, the Egyptian word could mean something like "The beings who, as a whole, represent wisdom". Egyptian language, while mixing together, in a periphrastic way, symbols and verbs, is extremely expressive. By the way, their "Global language" is a totally periphrastic one, just like ancient Egyptian, to the point that they use no names at all. What we call a noun to them is a verb; for instance, a home to them is "Per" (What a chance! The same word in Egyptian!), a verb that is the passive action of "dwelling", "something that is dwelt", "where people dwell".

Their Global language does not make use of hieroglyphs, nor of letters as we know them. It is not even written in "words", as we are used to, at least not in the general case; typically, a set of coloured symbols transmits the global meaning of a whole sentence, but it would be impossible to isolating a single particle in the whole. From this point of view, their writing is a bit reminiscent of the Chinese philosophy of writing, taken to its extreme consequences. An example of their Global writing may be found in pict. no. 61, at page 369 of "Mass Contacts"; unfortunately this image is in grey tones; its colour version is pict. no. 36 at page 413 of "Contattismi di massa".

Getting back to "Akrij", I've found this same word also in classic Arab and Greek; in the former, its meaning refers to a kind of friendship (what a coincidence!), while the Greek term refers to "somebody who sits high". Summing up, at least four among the classic ancient languages over this Earth have this name, roughly with the same meaning (the two oldest ones with the very same meaning). It cannot be a pure chance. And of course I am totally ignorant about many other languages, that therefore I've not examined. In Latin, "Aker" refers to the "bear", that derives directly from its Greek equivalent, not the animal itself, but its totem. What a chance, this word is again to be found in hieroglyphs, but probably it's better to stop here!

Going to more mundane topics, their aspect: the W56s are totally human-like in their complexion, the most evident diversity consisting in their heights, that may go, as I have been told, from 20 cm (some six inches) to 6 m (some 20 feet)! Their skin is in most cases similar to that of our white race, with several exceptions: there are the "Pale" ones, whose skin is almost transparent, the "Blue people", whose skin has a bluish hue, the "Red" ones, the "Green" ones (same considerations), and so on. Their physical structure has been discussed at length in "Mass Contacts", so it is useless to repeat it here.

Much more interesting are their dwelling environments; as I said before, their vision of the universe is profoundly different from that maintained by our scientists; for instance, our university barons lack totally the concept of "levels", that may yet be derived directly from General Relativity. My opinions on General Relativity have been discussed at length in "Mass Contacts", so I am not going to enter again into such considerations. At this point I would only like to remember that we perceive only three dimensions (plus time) from a universe whose number of dimension is much higher than that; in this moment I do not feel like computing it again, but that number sits around 90. If I select any quadruple of dimensions out of these, I find myself in a different "level" that, although co-existing with ours, inside our same universe, is some way distinct from it, and is usually imperceivable from our point of view, although its effects may be easily measured.

For honesty's sake, I must confess here that things are much more complicated than that, but, roughly speaking, without entering Relativistic problems, we might accept something like that.

Just to add a poetical note, they claim that our universe is like the flower of dandelion (*"taraxacum officinalis"*): the outer portions are the dimensions, it's stems the levels, and at the centre there is God.

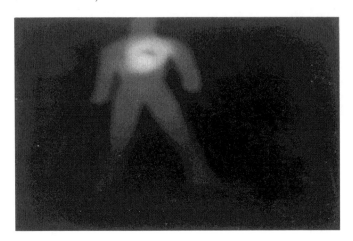

So we have people living on different levels than ours. For instance, a Red race is dwelling a different level (just imagine in how many different ways four numbers may be extracted from 90 or so!). Of course they may, some way, appear in our context, but they look like phantoms, without any apparent consistency. The image above depicts one of these beings, whose consistency is near to nil; the original picture is in colour, and sits on the back cover of this book.

Our universe hosts a huge number of different levels, each one of which is an universe by itself, with its stars, planets, and above all people. The physical structure, stars, planets and the like, may differ very little from level to level, or may be totally different, with physical laws that have nothing to do with the ones we know. Once I have been told that the total number of humans inside this universe is around 10^{20}, a truly terrific number (it means 1, followed by 20 zeroes!), but if we consider how large our universe is, and multiply it for the global number of levels, this figure is no longer as astonishing as it may look.

Then, why are the W56s here? There are several different answers to this question; first, to them, our Earth is a kind of sacred place, it has been one of the very few places where life has started, and many among them originated here. So they want to protect this planet from its present dwellers, who have tried, more than once, to destroy it, at times getting near to reach their goal. Then they want to take care of their small brethren, but of course we should expect no help whatsoever from their part; they only try to protect us from the CTRs and from ourselves. They will never give us a cure for our illnesses, or some kind of low cost energy source, or any other thing we are eager for. First, they state, it would be against cosmic morality, then they are not minded to do so; finally, it would be bad to us. We have to dig our route by ourselves, any help would only make things worse.

And so to the final question: are they going to get openly in contact with us? Quite surely not, for the reasons listed a few lines before, unless some exceptional condition arises, that induces them to do so. What they did, with Sammaciccia *et ali*, has just been a tentative move to sow some enlightened people with the basic concepts of their civilization. Probably, at this very moment, similar operations are taking place nobody knows where, as it has been during the whole of our history.

Then, Friendship: they are totally friendly, to a degree that can't be imagined by people who haven't lived this strange situation. They pretend that friendship is issued and cared for, in every possible community, even (it may sound a bit strange, at first) in a community made by a single person; in this case they mean that one must be a friend to himself, an attitude that seldom takes truly place. To them friendship is both vital, because they live on it, and the concept is impossible to refute, from a philosophic point of view. They can't help being friends to everybody; it is not a choice, but a concept deeply rooted into their morality. Even their hardware is permeated with such concepts, to the point, they maintain, that their machines would destroy themselves if they were not able to avoid damaging somebody. In all evidence, we have a very long road to travel, before getting at their level!

Even their war with the CTRs, in their words is not a war, but just a quarrel with "our enemy brothers"! That's another concept quite outrageous to our own way of thinking. I repeat, their moral behaviour is often really difficult to accept, yet, on the basis of pure logic, it is indeed not easy (I'd say impossible!) to find any mistake in their attitudes. For instance, they "quarrel" with their "enemy brothers", at times killing some of them, or being killed by them, at times with Earthling fatalities involved. These actions are not inherently bad to their way of thinking, so they go on quietly on their road. At the very same time they may share their own facilities with their "enemy brothers", another concept that is hard to be understood by ourselves. Probably they feel a bit obliged towards their "enemy brothers", as I am going to tell in the next chapter, and that's the reason for their strange behaviour.

They state "I am everybody, and everybody is me", this is a very profound sentence, as we are going to see later on; just to summarize here, it means that we all share the same identity, and what we are able to do to strengthen it (friendship) is a help to ourselves first, then to all. It is not just the Christian precept to help the poor, or, to say better, it is not the way it is taught now in our churches. I must be a friend to everybody, rich and poor, friend or enemy, tall or short: it makes no difference at all, because everybody is a part of the global design, to which I too belong.

Then, another typical characteristic of theirs: they are always witty, they like to joke, they enjoy their life, and try to transmit their happiness to everybody around. Remember for one moment Adamski's Masters: very serious people, listened to with awe by their audience. Nothing could be so far away from our Friends: they never teach *ex cathedra*, I'd say that they never teach at all, but try to induce in their friends an attitude that I have named "Maieutics" in "Mass Contacts", because it reflects the Socrates way of teaching.

And, another difference from grave aliens, as literature depicts them, our Friends like our style of living very much, enjoy playing tennis, driving luxury cars, in some cases they have owned private airplanes (once I travelled from Pisa to München, to Pescara, in a plane belonging to them, having one of them as my pilot!). They enjoy eating pizzas, drinking Italian coffee and Italian wines, often with a style that only our eldest countrymen may remember (pouring the wine from the bottle directly into the mouth, without touching the bottle with their lips).

Then their language: while speaking Italian, they are often rather funny: at times they show a heavy accent from Abruzzi, others speak like Fascist leaders, others speak a very pure language, often enriched by rarity; in all evidence, it derives from where and when they have learnt Italian. But obviously they speak also other Earth languages, the most commonly used being English, German, and Russian, but also Latin and Sanskrit.

About Russian, some considerations must be made: in those years, most of the "e-mail" connections were made through IBM 2741 typewriters, those machines with a spherical head jumping crazily all around; it was obviously very difficult (although not impossible at all) to change from a character set to another one, so most of the times, their Russian was written in Latin characters, with all of the ambiguities that could derive from that. Then, who knows why, they like to change language inside a single sentence. An example, already presented in "Mass Contacts" is the sentence:

A VIJ SNAIETE CHTO APUTRA INSANIRE SOLENT.

The first four words are Russian (= "You should know that"), "Aputra" is Sanskrit (= "persons without offspring"), the last two are Latin (= "Often go mad"). Who knows the reasons for this strange habit! Moreover, they are rather surprised that we, Earthlings, do not understand all of the languages spoken over our planet.

Among Bruno's papers, I found a short poem written by Dimpietro, the base commander, in German:

Das will viel heissen, natürlich immer sehr diplomatisch ...
wie vieles andere, aber wenn man genau aufpasst, findet man
doch Alles in den T. , denn wir diskutieren immer über das
Gleiche ... und doch findet man „Stille Hinweise", da und dort ...

Who knows why he had chosen German for praising his friend Bruno; I do not know how many, inside Bruno's group, were able to understand German; I am sure only seven of them: Bruno himself, Giancarlo, Giulio, and the four members of a Swiss family.

About poetry, Sigis, the closest Friend of mine, once had written a long poem in medieval Italian, in the style of the *Carmina Burana*: unfortunately, I remember only the very first stanza:

Un calice di vino
Che mai non si disvuoti!
O nettare divino,
Tu sai quanto tu puoti…

(= *"A glass of wine, that never gets empty! Oh divine nectar, you know how strong you are…"*)

About their behaviour, most of them spend their time inside their underground bases. At times, they may get out, even the ones we would not believe capable to do so, for instance Mr. Dimpietro, 3.5 m (some 12 feet) tall; I had to realize, even from very recent episodes, that we are almost blind, tend not to recognize unusual situations; probably our Friends play an active role in this blindness of ours, who knows? Just a few days ago, a friend of mine told me that, together with his wife, he was confronted, within a crowd, with four people 2.5 meter tall, without anybody noticing!

But, aside Dimpietro running around in his blue and white Citroen DS (probably now he has changed the model!), many of them are living inside our society, playing every possible role inside it. One I met was the Executive Vice President of a TLC multinational company! Another one has played a significant role as the General Manager of an important industry just here in Chieti. A third one was a kind of playboy, going around in a Maserati, being a member of the most exclusive tennis club in Pescara. Others were university professors or researchers, but there was also one who was the owner of a restaurant in Ancona, and, again in Ancona, one was serving as a waitress in a coffee-house! Another one (whose long conversation with myself is reported in "Mass Contacts") was an importer from Germany, and so on. In such cases, they have obviously to create false identities; in those years things were a bit easier than now, because there was the Cold War, and usually they were pretending to be refugees from behind the Iron Curtain, really difficult to be unmasked. Indeed one of them was working at the Soviet Embassy in Rome, pretending to be Russian!

Years later another was employed in a large Siemens facility in Novosibirsk, pretending to be German. When I was visiting Novosibirsk on a regular basis, each time I had to receive an invitation from the university, in order to be granted a visa, and it was a problem, because of the time shift between Rome and Novosibirsk; usually the Russian invitation was sent by fax very late (Rome time), so that the consul in Rome was awoken in the middle of the night (they had not yet an automatic fax machine), and was usually mumbling because of that. I had become a true nightmare for the Russian consul in Rome. He was only slightly relieved because I was paying the really high fares required for business visas. My W56 Friend in Novosibirsk has been the only one to understand this problem, so that he had suggested that a computer be programmed to send a fax in more convenient times, but nobody worked on the idea!

It would look easy to interpret their presence inside our society as a mean to drive it, in a way or another; probably the real reason sits at a much deeper level that I can't even imagine.

At times I've been asked about pets; I really do not know so much, at least nobody has ever told me of finding cats, dogs and the like inside a base. As usual, Dimpietro was an exception, because he was very fond of a pair of parrots he had been presented with, and tried to save their life when they grew too old. On the contrary, I know of some other Friends, living inside our community, who like to have pets with them.

Well, I believe that, as a general introduction, may suffice. Now we are going to enter a much heavier topic, heavy from a philosophic point of view, a topic that I am not so well suited at!

The Concept of Reality

Before entering such a difficult topic, I'd like to quote a letter; it has been written, at the end of 1968, by Franco Saija, a magistrate from Turin, who was within Amicizia, to Count Gian Luigi Zoccoli, from Bologna; both these gentlemen have now passed away. I would like to quote this letter because of the pathos it contains within itself (underlining in the original):

Dear Doctor,

As I promised you, I write this short letter to tell you that, to the contrary of what I was thinking, I do not believe that we may meet shortly, unless you agree to come to Turin, which I do not believe may be too easy to you. Unfortunately my duties prevent me, for the moment, to leave Turin, and I hope that you are not going to disdain me for that.
On the other side, the topic you're so interested at is extremely wide and complex, and nobody, I repeat nobody, not even people who, like me or other people, are aware of some aspects of it, may be able to give satisfying explanations, that might be deep and complete. The principles that direct the life, the morality, the science, and the justice of that world that is fabulous and gigantic, are mainly incomprehensible to us, they are external to our usual points of view, to the way we measure our reality. Their nature is at both times physical and meta-physical, cosmic and ultra-cosmic, at the very same time! To us, even to those who have approached this world, it is not possible to understand it fully. We may only accept the teachings, and the indirect conclusions, coming from it, if we are able to make use of a keen sensibility, an absolute altruism, open mind, deep humbleness, humanity, and INTUITION above all!

Our classical methods of common-day reasoning and our pseudo-cultural and pseudo-scientific ballast are of no use. Believe me, I do not state that in order to discourage you, or to put myself on a pedestal! Since many years, within myself two different visions of life fight and contradict each other, because of an approach, deriving from an egoistic and ridicule science (ours!). I do not believe I have been able to move a single step in the understanding of what we might be able to understand 100,000 years from now! I'd like that this be clear: not I, nor anybody else, may be able to introduce anybody into a world that does not belong to us, a world that is nearly touching us with its sublime fringes, <u>but that is not due to cross its roads with ours, nor now, nor, may be, ever</u>.

Even the ultimate goal and the destiny of this world remain largely mysterious, because they are the goal and the destiny of men who have got to the ultimate end of an immense cycle of evolution and deepening. We are dwarves with respect to their values! We cannot pretend to receive easily what we are meant to conquer day after day as centuries go on, do you understand me? That could not be possible, <u>could not be right</u>. We have to dig our own road; that's the meaning of life, and of human evolution. Only one thing is possible to the ones who have seen and understood something: <u>to witness!</u> To testify that elsewhere the reasons of men's life and universe's life have been understood, the dreadful questions have been answered, the same questions that torment us since ever, and that it has been understood that the right road is a totally different one from ours, and that it must be chosen now, at once, before it is too late. Divine and cosmic laws constitute a titanic wall against which the aberrations of all the negative and abnormal civilizations of the whole universe do break up!

Dear Doctor, in very poor words, this is the world that some among us, touched and trembling, have been able to perceive, in some little, but extremely shining, aspect. Do not ask me why this has taken place, and why to us; I would not be able to answer. Infinite other worlds, and civilizations, exist within the universe, and at times they get to us in their ships, in their disks, with their phenomena, but we are no longer interested in that! We are aware that something exists that is at an extremely superior level, <u>the divine destiny itself of man</u>!

I am sorry: at first this letter was meant to be a short one; forgive me, and accept my warmest and friendly wishes for the incoming Christmas.
Franco Saija

I believe that Dr. Saija explains how far from ours are the W56s points of view, a feeling that I have often experienced myself. At this point, I'd like to present the comment Warren Aston made to this letter:

This is probably the finest piece of writing from an "insider" viewpoint that I have read, succinct and insightful. Thank you for sending it.

Anyway, keeping in mind Saijas words, let's get back to our topic.

Indian philosophers have been maintaining, for millennia, that even if an objective reality existed outside ourselves, we could in no way be able to grasp it. Indeed, they state, we cannot be sure of the messages our senses transmit to us, because we have no way to get outside ourselves to verify their correctness.

How could I be sure that there is a reality outside me, one I learn through my senses? Maybe, on the contrary, what I believe I feel is just an invention of one among the many sub-conscious levels of my ego, that swindles me just like what happens when I am drunk, and my senses transmit me false messages (or my conscious mind is not able to interpret them correctly).

These ancient thinkers go even further with their dissertation: if I have no means to distinguish between a "true" reality, and an invented one, the two hypotheses must be one and the same from my point of view; it's plain logic: if not, I should have some means to discriminate between them, which is against the initial assumption.

Even further: if the two hypotheses are equivalent, whatever statement I make according to one of them, must be equally true (or equally false) also according to the other one. Therefore, let's stay for a moment within the second hypothesis: there is no objective reality, and everything I believe I sense is indeed an unconscious invention of mine.

This computer, my dogs, you, my dear reader, are all inventions, better to say the creations of my unconscious mind. It is myself the one who generates this world, I am the God of my world, the only God of my world because nothing else exists beyond me. Those ancient thinkers had been condensing this concept in the sentence "Tat tvam Asi" (= "You are your God") [2].

As the two hypotheses we started from are equivalent, this concept must be true even if I suppose that indeed an objective reality exists: once again, I am the God of this universe, and the reality is indeed my creation.

Before thinking that I am totally mad, please read back again carefully the previous sentences, examining the logic behind them: are you able to find a mistake in them? Of course not, because they are plain logic.

A first obvious corollary is that I am immortal, or at least something inside me is immortal, beyond my physical body: how could I imagine this universe lacking of my presence?
But there is a second consequence, an even more important one: what is the maximum sacrifice I may make in favour of the apparently existent living beings that, remember, are just my creations? Remember, I am the only existing entity.

What I may do is to take everything up to my level: as the two initial hypotheses are equivalent, it costs me nothing, beside, perhaps, some loss of pride.

Et voilà! Everything turns into existence, even my dogs and you, my dear reader: even more: at least you and I (and billions of similar beings) are all at the very same level: we are all gods of our reality.

After my sacrifice, is there a God remaining? It is no longer myself, because I have abdicated my role. But I can't forget that this new situation has been a consequence of my actions, therefore I cannot be totally deprived of my divine characteristics, that now I share with (at least) the whole of mankind.

And so God emerges anew, in a slightly different profile: unfortunately, I am no philosopher, I am a technician, and often I find it easier to use the language of Mathematics. Mathematically speaking, God is the envelope of all entities, both living and not living [1].

These are the concepts that ancient Indian philosophers have taught us; they are widespread in their classical texts, from the Veda to the Geeta.

The W56s got to the same result, starting from similar initial conditions, but through a totally different reasoning. As I said, they start from roughly the same considerations: I cannot be sure whether an objective reality exists outside of me. The Indians were saying that this is due to my incapacity to verify the truthfulness of the messages my senses are sending me. The W56 approach is more deep-rooted.

It is true that I cannot perceive the reality around me, and that this is an incapacity from my part, but it is due to my inability to tune myself into the truth.

Indeed there are deep relationships that permeate everything, the root of everything is Good. Were I a saint at the topmost level (and probably it would not be enough!) I would be able to perceive the good that permeates everything, but I am not; I continuously depart from good for evil, and this way I get blinded, and perceive false sensations, the more false the more I've abandoned the right path.

That is the main characteristic of living entities, the ability to perceive, in a more or less deep way, the truth, and to act according to good; or departing from it, and getting deluded, in a way or another, about the immanent reality.

Another mistake we make is to think of the reality as a materialistic entity: far from that! The more we tune ourselves in the right direction, the deeper we'll be able to perceive the entity we fancy as being of material nature; matter is just something that is generated when we go in the wrong direction, but it is not the reality, it's a kind of mask added upon it.

Indeed, our Friends maintain that their purpose consists just in overcoming the matter, in abandoning their physical bodies, that are just an obstacle towards the truth. True reality is the set of the means through which good generates itself, and it is a very immanent entity, not just an abstract concept.

Just to lessen one moment the weight of these concepts, let me remember that, to our Friends, the internal cohesion inside a group of people is not an abstract idea, but an actual living entity, that they are calling *Uredda*; the well-being of Uredda is fed by the loyalty of the members of the group to one another, and it is essential to the operations of the W56's hardware. As my friend Gaspare De Lama has put it in an interview, Uredda is a kind of fuel to their machinery!

Getting back to the Indian thinkers I started with, the main difference consists in that we have the potentiality to access the truth (a concept the Indians refuted), but we are prevented from that by our own behaviour.

The universe, by itself, is neither good nor bad: it's a kind of neutral lattice, that gets "polarized" in one direction or another by the behaviour of living entities.

In the first approximation, only *living* entities behave in one way or another, so it is up to them to decide which will be their role inside reality, and that is true from the smallest microbe to the largest whale (just to remain inside our planet!). Whoever acts exerts a will, consciously, and in this way interfaces with the truth.

Of course things are much more complicated than that, according to our Friends, but that is the main idea. Where does God sit in all that?

Obviously it is the good itself, the purest aspect of reality towards which we all should move. And, getting back to our Indian scholars, each living entity participates, more or less, of the entity of God, according to how much good is able to exploit; just while writing these lines I realized that in English God and Good are words very similar to each other; in other languages it is not so, starting with the Sanskrit Deva, through the Greek Theos, to the Latin Deus, to the Italian Dio.

Getting back to theology, every living entity lives at the expenses of other living entity; we kill cattle to eat, kill vegetables to maintain ourselves, and every other living entity does the same. Is that a kind of a sin? Aside from the fact that, according to our Friends' morality, killing is not a sin in itself (and also here the Indian philosophers show that they, somehow, had got in touch with the W56s or similar beings), this is just the way things are going on; were we able to alter the course of such events, it could be a good idea to do so, and then killing cattle would become a sin; for the moment, it is not.

Indeed, sin is a divergence from the right path, a path that nobody can teach us, because it is firmly inherent in ourselves. The W56s are stating that one commits a sin when he abandons his human nature.

Both the Indian and the W56 points of view agree that, in order to do good or evil, it is obviously necessary to have the ability to make a decision, and this can't help but revive the concept of free will. But here a concept rather extraneous to our way of thinking arises, the *Karma*.

Let's start far away; in Christendom, St. Augustin has been debating at length the concept of free will [3]. Briefly speaking, the problem is: if God knows everything in advance, how can it be possible for men to exercise free will? Augustin gave an elegant solution, referring to the concept of Grace, but discussing his ideas here would take us far away from our goals. In short (forgive me for being as rough as that!) he states that, thanks to Grace, we are free to keep God's requirements. Of course, his ideas are by far more complicated than that. But, anyway, there is God's will, that of course is for *good*, and there is the possibility, to men, to act independently from it.

At first glance the Indian concept of Karma is a different thing. It looks as though the fate of everybody is already determined, deriving from his past, and that therefore he can't help but act according to his Karma. This oversimplification is in part true and in part false. The concept of Karma (and, more deeply, that of *Dharma*) does not force our actions; it only changes the meaning of morality in what we do.

For instance, in the "Bhagavad Geeta" (a part of the "Mahabharata"), the lord Arjuna is going to order battle against the enemy army headed by Duryodhana. He asks his charioteer to take him on top of a hill, so that he may be able to examine the battlefield. At this point Arjuna realizes that, when he gives the order to start the battle, he will become at once a sinner, guilty of a fratricidal struggle: relatives, friends, are distributed between the two armies, and the struggle will, of course, disrupt many families, many relationships. Arjuna does not feel able to commit such a sin, and declares that he is not going to give the order of attack. At this point his charioteer reveals himself as the god Krshna (in Sanskrit the "r" is a vowel, so this name may be pronounced, after all!), and, during the whole Geeta, he explains to Arjuna the meaning of Dharma. By the way, at the end of Geeta, the battle starts.

What is Krshna's message? He states that Arjuna's Karma has taken him to be the head of his army, that the destiny of his country depends upon his decision, and that his future sin is a must, that derives from his Karma; it would be a heavier sin to abandon the battlefield. Therefore Arjuna is forced to commit evil (or, to say it better, is free to choose between two different evils), but in his case the first sin (attacking his enemies) should revert to a good action for him.

We learn from this poem that the concept of good and evil is a very relative one: no action is, inherently, good or bad; it depends on the circumstances. In "Mass Contacts" I present a conversation between one among our Friends, and myself; at a certain point, he said: "It is not bad, in itself, to kill a man" ("Mass Contacts", page 274). This sentence, taken away from its context, would look preposterous; on the contrary it is true, in the deepest sense.

The W56s morality is similar, in many aspects, to the Indian one (or, maybe, it would be better to say it the opposite way!). What is missing is the concept of an immutable good that permeates our three major religions. Of course God's will is always absolute, but it does not obey to a standard set of laws. Or, to say it better, no law exists, but only the ability to act according to what each one feels is good.

Once, Dimpietro (the master of the Italian W56 group), was telling about a very wealthy Polish family some centuries ago. Inside this family there were architects, piano players, engineers, and so on; and he was saying that among the artists, one pianist was getting better and better, reaching the topmost ability in his art, then, when he was at his highest level, he started to decrease, he was no longer as clever as he had been before. According to Dimpietro this was due to the attempt, by the player, to maintain his level, to the point that he was worsening just in the effort of keeping his best. Dimpietro was saying: "You see? When one looks after a goal, and spends all his efforts towards it, often he falls down, because he mixes his capabilities with wrong efforts. If one does not let himself to be dominated by vanity, or the like, he will be able to reach his best; on the contrary, when one permits himself to be blinded by the research of his maximum, often he will miss his goal".

From such considerations, it is obvious that our Friends do not have a *corpus jurum*, nor law-courts, lawyers, judges, or the like. As one of them was stating, "lawfulness is not morality, while morality is lawfulness." This means that, from their point of view, no crime can be performed willingly, to them it is simply absurd. The concept itself of crime is totally absent from their minds; they conceive mistakes, that someone may make unwillingly, but not crimes. Equally absurd to them is that some one might think to rise up himself to judge the behaviour of his fellows; such a megalomania is totally foreign to their thinking.

Obviously things are not as simple as that. Another alien group exists, that Bruno had named *UTI* (I do not know the meaning of these initials), that operates at a higher level than the W56s and the CTRs; from a very simplified point of view, UTI people could be thought of as some kind of "cosmic police," that intervene when the former or the latter are trespassing some limits. It appears that there are cosmic laws that at times the W56s (or the CTRs) break, and UTIs get in to punish a kind of a crime.

Indeed it is not so, and things are much more complex than that. UTI people are at an even higher level of consciousness, therefore their vision of the reality is keener, so that they can envisage consequences that escape the vision of both W56s and CTRs. That's why, at times, they intervene, and when they do, they act almost brutally, stopping at once what is going on. I experienced that once; Giancarlo and I had built a device, according to our Friends indications, that was potentially harmful, and made a test. Less than 24 hours later I received the visit of an Austrian gentleman, belonging to the UTI group, who came to my premises and gave me a good telling off, underlying that what we had done was very dangerous, that my designs could be stolen and get into the wrong hands. Of course, he was right, and I acknowledged that, and destroyed my papers relating to that experiment.

Their behaviour

It is usually stated that aliens (the W56s among them) conceal their presence, that they do their best to go unnoticed, and so on. Far from that! It is the very opposite. Some years ago, I presented at the annual CUN Convention in San Marino a paper [1], in which I believe to have statistically demonstrated that the UFO activity is almost always oriented toward its witnesses; that is, that they deliberately behave so that they may be seen. Just the opposite of what is usually maintained.

Aside from statistics, it is not so difficult to realize that things are like that: scouts, flying saucers, or whatever, are mobile labs, even weapons at times; their job does not consist in driving aliens along over our skies, but in performing specific duties. Among them, one very important consists in letting such craft being seen by bystanders.

Have you ever wondered about a flying saucer landing in a secluded place (in France, if I remember well), an alien disembarking, and asking a near-by farmer: "What date is it to-day?"; when he answered, say, "Wednesday", the alien objected "No, it's Thursday!", went back to his craft, and flew away. Is there any logic in that? Or a similar scene, again in France, with the alien addressing a peasant in a language unknown to him, a language that, later on, from his remembrance, was found to have been Russian?

Apart from such examples, that belong to the UFO-lore, there are many other episodes that reflect the deliberate decision from the part of the UFOnauts to be seen. Consider, for instance, the continuous activity against our ICBM nuclear missiles [2]. In hundreds of cases, USA and Soviet ICBM batteries have been reduced to impotence. Such operations could well have been conducted making use of almost-invisible small *aniae*, so that nobody could envisage the cause for the missiles going out of service. On the contrary, practically always, huge UFOs appeared over the silos, often terrorizing local guards, underlining that they were connected to what was going on, a kind of signature on the event. By the way, as far as I know, in many of these operations (if not in all of them) *earthlings* have been employed, according to a point of view that we would consider a bit Pharisaic: they pretend that they cannot interfere <u>directly</u> with our civilization, therefore they cannot actively operate on our missiles; but it's quite OK, to them, giving some Earth people training and means to act in their place! That has been, I believe, the reason why they have trained some people to use flying saucers, that they have actually given small saucers (of the "Maljenkij" kind) to some people, just over-alls to others: to achieve the possibility that they perform duties that are impossible to our Friends, because of their moral constraints. A bit more deeply, they tend to force their Earth friends to take a positive action, giving them the means to do so.

Consider for instance the Roswell accident. I was not there in those days, so I can't say whether it has actually taken place or not. What I am sure about is that flying saucers do not fall from the sky, either because of a radar beam, a

35

lightning, or anything else. If indeed a craft crashed at Roswell, it must have been deliberately sent to ground, in order to give USA top-brass something to wonder about. Probably just an empty skull, devoid of the characteristics that make true saucers almost invulnerable. And, why not, maybe with some biological entities inside (biological robots, of course). In a similar accident, at Aztec, New Mexico, the military have been able to open a port in a crashed flying saucer by inserting a wooden pole through a broken port-hole, and activating this way a switch that was conveniently blinking. Preposterous, if true!

So, probably, somewhere in the States the useless scraps of some pretended crashes are stored, together, may be, with the bodies of presumed aliens, with scientists racking their brains over useless garbage...were they actual flying saucers, I do not believe that our scientists could be able to understand anything in them, because, according to me, retro-engineering is but a myth. Even worse if they are studying just mock ups! Had they been true saucers, probably nobody would have been even able to enter them.

Imagine that, for some trick, someone had parked an SR-71 (the "BlackBird", or the "Sled", as its pilots have named it) in the centre of one of the *fori* of ancient Rome. What my ancestors would have been able to understand of it? Of course nothing at all, and they would have interpreted it as a present from some deity.

Actually, something like that looks to have actually taken place in those times and in that place [3]! A very small saucer, a *clipeum*, named *ancile*, fell from the sky, was interpreted as the buckler shield of Ares, and then it was kept inside a temple together with 11 copies of it, so that nobody could try to steal the original one. This happened during the reign of Numa Pompilius (753-673 BC.).

Now, please consider that the gap between our technology and that of Roman times is infinitely smaller than the one that divides us from the W56s. When I state that their technology is almost magic to our eyes, I mean just that.

Strange behaviour

At times, our Friend exhibited sorcerer-like attitudes, often totally incomprehensible ones. One of the strangest ones, to me, consisted in stating that colours are important to them in acquiring remote control on specific areas: they were maintaining that the presence of red or blue hues (preferably both of them) in the place would facilitate their operations. At the same time yellow-green, or yellow-black hues would favour the CTRs. That's why we became used to avoiding such colour matching in our environments.

Another time they suggested us to wear as much copper as possible, especially when engaged in potentially dangerous activities, so we started buying copper in industrial quantities. Even today, I often wear copper soles inside my shoes, as specifically suggested by them!

36

The false problem of non-contact

Reading through books, magazines, Internet sites devoted to UFOs, a common question is: Why haven't the aliens got in touch with us, or, put in another way "Are they going to do so this year? Next year? In 2014?"

I believe that there questions are badly posed, and for several reasons. First, because the Amicizia case is an example of a contact, one on a rather wide scale. Second, because it shows aliens living within our environment, conducting a perfectly normal life, contacting every kind of people from sunrise to sunset (and may be also the other way!). Third, who should be the actors of an improbable large-scale contact? Politicians? Religious leaders? Members of an improbable occult government?

Let's start from this third point, because the first two are plainly evident, and let's suppose that the W56s (or whoever else) decide to make open contact with a significant part of our society; whom should they address? I repeat, suppose that they choose a significant subset of our civilization, who might we consider sufficiently qualified to speak in the name of all Earthlings?

Before trying to answer this question, allow me to explain my point of view on this subject. I believe that a covert government exists, but not in the terms conspiracists present. I do not believe that, hidden maybe in Shamballa, or wherever, there is an undercover King of the Earth, who manages our lives with us utterly ignorance of his (her? Its?) existence. Maybe it is true, but obviously the effects of such actions must be minimal. Of course there is the elite of top-level sailors in the seas of finance, the oil masters, the manufacturers of weapons, and so on, the results of whose activity cannot be denied at all; we all suffer of the effects of their struggle to keep their roles, and, in a sense, they can be actually depicted as the true rulers of this planet. But they could not be invited to a party organized to welcome our Friends, because they would be the very first ones to get deprived of their privileges, should such a meeting actually take place.

The religious leaders, then? And who? Our Catholic pope (I'm Italian, you know)? Her gracious Queen as the leader of the Anglican church? The Dalai Lama, who unfortunately represents but a very small group of people? Or whoever else? Many religious cults do not even have a formal leader (think, for instance, of the Muslims), and, anyway, choosing a person would be detrimental to a large percentage of mankind. Should we therefore choose a delegation composed by the mot eminent representatives of the major religions? Probably they would disagree with each other's presence, and, obviously, could not act as coherent speakers in the name of all Earthlings.

Our politicians, maybe? Again, who? Remember, please, the movie "The Day the Earth Stood Still"; it was plain fiction, but very near to reality (and, what a chance, it has been shot in 1951, with the W56s already walking our streets, according to them). It would clearly be an impossible mission (just to paraphrase another Sci-Fi title). Each political leader would try to take the aliens onto his side, against the others; it would be a total failure.

It was quite interesting when Mr. Reagan and Mr. Gorbachev agreed, in several occasions, on the need of being able to cooperate against a possible aggression from "outside", but, in all evidence, this was not their real goal, to the point that the Strategic Defence Initiative (SDI, in Italian under the pompous name of "Scudi Stellari", Stellar Shields) started in turbulence (the American ACM – Association for Computer Machines – rightly stated that it was a project without any hope to succeed), and ended in almost complete silence, after some rebuttal by Mr. Putin. Now SDI is just a pale phantom of what it had been devised to be decades before. But, I repeat, SDI was not meant as a defense means from any kind of Aliens, because both the Soviets and the Americans were pretty aware that it could do nothing against them; its goals were, as usual, putting pressure against unwelcome Earth rivals.

But not even the politicians may be regarded as the true masters of this planet, engaged, as they are, to fight each other to keep their lucrative existence.

So, whom should we send to act in our name in front of Aliens pretending to be answered? The military, maybe? Again, which general? And which general would like to surrender to what would be, in all evidence, an invading alien nation?

There is, however, a diffuse power, that I feel evident every day here in Italy, but that I have met, similarly evident, both in the United States and in the Soviet Union (and in today's Russia), and in almost every country I have travelled. It does not exhibit decorations, nor any evident sign of its class, because it doesn't even have a class, it is not an evident elite, but it constitutes, anyway, the real ruling class over this Earth. Its members are from every possible class, from politicians to laymen, and are the true ones who have power.

I mean every-day people, laymen, who are much more interested in their own gain, as small as it may be, than in the success of the society around them; small bureaucrats, lazy teachers, careless magistrates, and so on. Each one of them may produce small effects, but there are a lot of them! Of course politicians produce greater effects, but there is a relatively small amount of them, and the same may be said about the conjurers of finance and the masters of oil (in these last two instances, I am not so sure of my assertion).

But the largest majority consists in the people our Dante Alighieri named "Ignavi"; my dictionaries translate this word with "Indolents", but I am not so sure that it is correct; more promising translations look to be "Quitters", or "Opportunists"; anyway, lacking a reasonable English term, I'll make use of the Italian "Ignavi" (singular: "Ignavo").

Ignavi are the real dominating class all over this planet. The majority of our population is made by such people. People who, at best, think only to themselves, but who, most of times, are not even moved by an egoistic reason, people who live day by day without any peculiar goal in mind. And you may meet them by the dozens in every moment of your daily life. Lazy people, whose only ambition consists in maintaining the *status quo*, and who fear that every change may endanger their present situation.

When the Soviet Union came to an abrupt end, I was in Moscow, and I witnessed really chaotic situations ensuing during several months, with almost nothing working any longer. Then Yeltsin seemed to have taken control of the situation once again, and Communism began to slowly dying. Years later, while talking with *laudatores temporis acti*, that is people grieving because Communism was over, they were telling me that previously they were receiving wages from the State, both if they had been working or not, they had been paying nothing, or very little, for apartment loans, for telephone, for heating (which is why, in full winter, most windows in Moskow flats were usually wide open!) for most of their needs. Now, they were forced to act, in one way or another, in order to manage their daily life. For an Ignavo, this is the most disturbing situation… And, obviously, here I am not underlying only the behaviour of former Soviet people. I repeat, I have met people of this kind all over the world, from clerks to policemen, and so on.

Remaining for a moment in the Soviet Union, the first time I went to Moscow, in full Soviet times, I tried to make a telephone call to a Russian professor I had known via mail, but there was no telephone directory in my hotel room; so I phoned the local exchange, but the girl told me that she could not give me the telephone number of my pen-friend, for a very good reason: "If you know him, you already know his telephone number; if you don't, I can't give you his number". So I went to the TLC ministry, and asked to talk to a manager (in those years, I was rather fluent in Russian). I was taken to an office, with a lady seated at her desk, and asked her if it was possible to consult the Moskow telephone directory. She answered me that such a directory simply did not exist, yet it was, in two volumes, sitting on a secondary desk near by. So I asked her: "What is that?", pointing to the two books, and she calmly answered me: "There is nothing on that desk!". So I missed the opportunity of meeting by person my pen-friend, who, unfortunately, passed away shortly later. Only now I realize that, may be, a $50 note could have solved the problem, but you know, it is difficult to react when somebody denies even what is plainly evident.

Getting back to our aliens, we have not been able, up to now, to answer my previous question about whom should be delegated to talk to them in the name of the whole humanity, but, in the meantime, we have discovered who is really ruling this world (at least, from my point of view). So, let's exchange place, and put ourselves in the alien's shoes: if they wanted to get formally in touch with our mankind, what should they do?

Probably nothing different from what they have already done: getting in touch with single persons who (from reasons we can't understand) look to them particularly promising, or trying to put up an effort involving groups, here and there, and trying to conveying, through them, messages to the rest of mankind.

I do not believe that this year, next year, or any time in the near future, formal contact will take place. And the problem is not with the aliens (what a horrible name!) but with our own part!

Possible battles

In several instance, the skies over Italy and nearby countries have seen huge concentrations of UFOs during periods lasting just one hour or so; the objects were often travelling against each other, and some have been seen exploding, or disintegrating in the air, suggesting possible aerial fights between opposite sides.

I am going to present here some of the best known cases; I must state since all of them have received a formal explanation, involving meteors, or falling artificial satellites; of course the characteristics of the events exclude such mundane explanations.

Then, there has been the well known case of the Adriatic sea that "went mad" during a period that lasted some months. I have been really surprised in finding that almost nobody, outside Italy, had ever heard about that, so in "Mass Contacts" I quoted some newspaper articles. Here I am going to discuss this case at length, also because it "officially" marked the final battle between the W56s and the CTRs, with the defeat of the formers.

In the night between Jul 17 and Jul 18, 1967, not less than 50 sightings took place between 10.00 pm and 2.30 am. These events occurred from Naples up to the Lake Maggiore, but were mainly concentrated in Northern Italy. Unfortunately, it would have been too confusing adding to each arrow on the map an indication of the time of the event, anyway, globally speaking, the whole thing lasted four hours and a half, a bit too long a time for speaking about meteors or the like. Then, once again, the directions contradict any explanation of this kind.

On Aug 10, 1968, in the whole area between Bologna and Firenze several UFOs have been observed, between 10 and half past 11, p.m. The following map shows with arrows the cases when a direction has been reported:

You may see them near to Reggio Emilia (South-East), Bologna (South), between these two towns (South), plus two cases near Firenze (North North-West and East North-East). In addition, 7 other objects have been seen exploding in the air inside that area, but there has been no indication about their directions. These phenomena have been seen also from some astronomers from the Arcetri observatory, in Firenze; they were explained as <u>one</u> brilliant meteor, but the duration of the event and the different directions exclude of course such an explanation.

Then, let's get to 1987; the period goes from October to December, although some events took place also in the following January. Hundreds of UFOs were reported, to the point that the national press started publishing one or more articles per day; the area covered was, roughly speaking, centered between Abruzzi and Marche.

Indeed the psychosis reached dangerous levels, to the point that, being

41

interviewed by the national broadcast, I esteemed it better to charge Venus and Jupiter as the possible culprits! My explanation was only partly correct, because in those days the two planets were very bright at night, but obviously it could not justify most of the events, it was just meant to settle the fright down.

The following image depicts (only in part) the extension of what took place over this area.

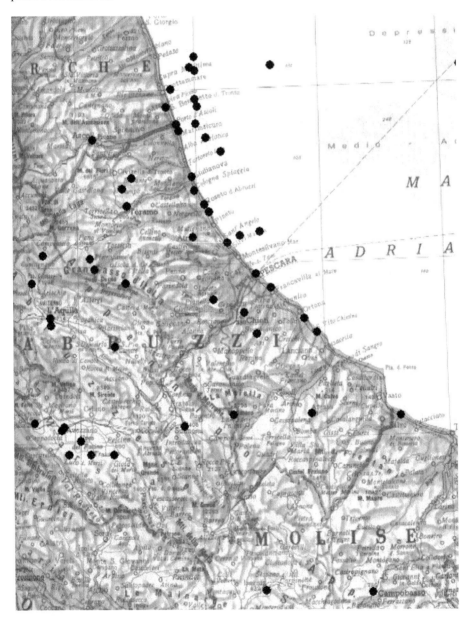

I've marked with black circles the places where some event took place during this period; this drawing is the result of an interactive program I had written to support a presentation; of course looking at a computer screen gives a far better idea of what took place. It also shows the distribution in time, that cannot appear in this image. And, of course, a printed image does not show clearly multiple events over a same place.

The following image shows the distribution in time, together with its global trend:

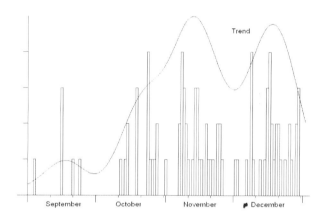

The phenomenon was spread both over land and on the sea. A Police officer in Chieti stated, during an interview, that he had seen, from his office, "… a flying object as big as a three-floors building", so bright that he had to wear his sun-glasses, although it was at night!

Landings were also reported, and it should be quite interesting to quote here the tales of two totally illiterate peasants, who, in strict dialect, reported their (separate) adventures with strange craft. Unfortunately I am not so expert in English to be able to render their tales and their language (maybe George Bernard Shaw should have been necessary, as in his "Pygmalion"!). Nevertheless, I like to present here my poor translation of the two interviews (in the second one, the peasant looks to be more intelligent than the newsman!):

Q: You told you had a near encounter of the third kind?
A: I have just seen them only 20 cm, from their head to their shoulders.
Q: So they were inside their spaceship? How was this spaceship? Round, spherical?
A: It was round.
Q: And there were many of them inside?

A: They were six to seven.

Q: And what did you feel in that moment?

A: Nothing, no fear or anything. I have seen them from three meters away; well, I did not measure it. I looked, and noticed that inside there were men and women.

Q: Were they of a peculiar colour?

A: The women were wonderful, with a complexion like ours, even more beautiful. When I saw it, and perceived that there were people inside, at first I thought that I had gone mad. I remained a quarter of a hour near to it, not touching it, but a meter and a half away.

Q: So you did not feel ill or having seen a vision. You spoke about Martians, males and females, very fine to see. So they were not like this picture, presenting a being with huge brains and a short body?

A: Not at all; women had small heads, I could see only 20 cm of them, and they were laughing at me, while the men were steady.

Q: You told me that you went to sit: what happened?

A: I went to sit beyond a bush, and when I got up, there was nothing left.

Q: Newspapers report that, near a lake, you have seen an extraterrestrial ship.

A: Near to a lake? No, I repeat, I've seen it flying. To say better: I was to bring on my shoulders an oat bale; I took up the bale from the ground, turned toward the cowshed; in that moment I saw this peculiar light, never seen before.

Q: So it is not true that you ran after extraterrestrials waving your pitchfork?

A: No, not true at all. It's a gossip that I don't know where it came from.

Q: Welcoming them with a fork would not be so kind, don't you think so?

A: Welcoming with a fork? I don't know if I would have dared. If something like that happened to me, I do not know if I would dare.

Q: Poets have written poems on the meeting between men and extraterrestrials, and you would assault them with a fork?

A: I repeat, I don't know; if a beast appears, that I have never seen before, I don't know what would I do; sure, if it tries to bite me, I have my fork, and try to do something. Anyway, I don't know.

Of course also fishermen were very upset, because the radar equipment on their ships was often presenting unidentified echoes, and the surface of the Adriatic sea was really mad: water columns erupting all of a sudden, without any apparent reason, rising 10 or even 20 meters high, waters "boiling" and bubbling, UFOs seen everywhere. Then, the night between Oct 14 and 15, 1978, a dramatic change for the worse: the boat of two fishermen from Martinsicuro (North of Pescara) sank without any apparent reason:

Frogmen were later able to find the boat, the "Francesco Padre" sitting straight on the bottom of the sea, at a medium depth, in good conditions; the two fishermen, the brothers Vittorio and Gianfranco De Fulgentiis were found dead on board; subsequent autopsies have not been able to ascertain the cause of their death, certainly they were not drowned.

Many mundane hypotheses have been advanced, but all of them fail to mention an important fact: the Francesco Padre sank at night under the witness of the fishermen on at least two other boats: they all maintain that the lights of the Francesco Padre disappeared at once, without any logical explanation. The boat, indeed, has been found totally intact on the sea bottom, without any apparent reason for its sinking.

Of course, fear spread among fishermen, to the point that at first they pretended to be escorted by the Coast Guard ships (also the military have been witnesses of inexplicable phenomena, both by radar and by sight), then any fishing activity stopped at all for a couple of months. Just think of the economic damage resulting from this halt.

Things started to get slowly back to normality only in the second half of January, 1979.

Notes

The Concept of Reality

1 A continuous set of curves being given, its "envelope" is a new curve that is tangent in every point to one curve of the set.
2 Modern philosophy calls this point of view "solipsism".
3 See "De gratia et libero arbitrio" by St. Augustin from Ippona (418 A.D.).

Their behaviour

1 Stefano Breccia: "Men vs. UFOs" – San Marino International Conference, 1996.
2 Cfr. "Faded Giant" and "UFOs and Nukes", quoted in the Bibliography.
3 Titus Livius: "Ab Urbe Condita", 1:20.

Chapter 3

A tentative study on the strange picture at the end of "Contattismi di Massa"

Teresa Barbatelli
© 2009

The lucky readers of "Contattismi di Massa", by Prof. Stefano Breccia, are going from a *coup-de- theatre* to another, while reading the appealing reconstruction of the contact cases with supposed aliens, not from the part of single earthlings, as we are usually told in most of the literature, but by groups of people who, usually, have preferred to conceal their experiences. He starts from a group of scientists who, in past centuries, have shown intuitions and inventions well in advance of their age, then presents the well-known "Ummo case", with many details unknown up to date, then, in the third chapter, he presents the most astonishing part of his book, the "Amicizia case". At the end of his very detailed story about Amicizia, that went on for more than 30 years, a tale with many details that may be verified even today, mostly focused on the character Bruno Sammaciccia, then the author presents us with the picture of a supposed W56.

The picture is clear and bright (it's incredible to scholars, who have been used to see blurred and out of focus pictures, badly lighted and disputable, when supposed aliens are concerned); it shows a young man in a garden, smiling. He doesn't show anything that might make us think of a being from another world; he looks to be very tall, and the only strangeness consists in his head, which looks a bit too small with respect to his body.

As Prof. Breccia tells about aliens like us, but 2 or even 3 meters tall (Sammaciccia speaks of beings even 6 meters tall), I have been immediately urged to verify whether the boy of the picture was as tall as that; such a discovery would have definitively demonstrated that aliens do exist. It was necessary to go to work.

Unfortunately the picture, although very clear, does not look to show measurable details, therefore no perspective-based computations may be conducted. The plants present in it look to be very young (the lemon plant in the foreground is kept by a small rod), therefore they might have been not too tall, when the picture has been taken.

I was already disappointed in my hope to evaluate how tall the man was, when I noticed, just over his head, what in all evidence were pine-needles; making use of Photoshop, I have taken one needle, and replicated it as many times as to equating the height of the man.

This is the result:

ciuffo di aghi di
pino preso per
riferimento

It's evident that 20 to 21 needles are needed to do the job; moreover, the man is slightly bent to one side.

Now the problem is: how long is a pine-needle?

I must admit I have started to look at all the pine plants that I was meeting along the streets of Rome (I believe there must be millions of them), hoping to meet a plant sufficiently low to permit me to take some needles (contrary to the man of the picture, I'm very short), but I never found one, because they were all very tall, outside my possibilities.

Thankfully, one day a strong wind blow blew a whole branch just to the entrance of my house; under the perplexed look of my house-keeper, I've collected the branch, and taken it home; making use of a photo camera as a witness, I made my measurements.

As it may be seen in my picture, pine-needles are 15-16 cm long, therefore the man should have been 3 meters tall (if we consider only 20 needles, each 15 cm long), or 3.36 (21 needles, 16 cm long).

From 3 to 3.36 meters tall? I must admit that I had a shock! Further enquiries were needed, hopefully with a more detailed copy of the picture. My friend Eng. Carlo Bolla has been able to supply me with a higher resolution copy, so I started to work on my Mac trying to find out details that might be of some help.

My search discovered some railings, almost invisible in the dark, that surround the garden where the picture had been taken.

At the end I had an object, whose dimensions are known, at least with some approximation: railings typically have bars 10 to 15 cm away from each other, and, from these figures, a simple (so to say) geometric projection could have led to the height of the man.

Perspective laws have allowed painters from the past to rendering three dimensions scenes over a bi-dimensional support; this was made making use of a horizon, and a set of straight lines.

They have been generating scenes making use of perspective, I was to do the inverse process, maybe roughly.

Once having taken railings into account, I decided to take the main character away from the picture, in order to better understand the geometry of the railings:

As it may be seen, railings are more evident, but another problem appears: the picture is not vertical: in all evidence, whoever has taken it has not kept the camera in an horizontal attitude, therefore the whole scene looks a bit slanted. In order to make use of perspective laws, the picture was to be straightened up.

After having straightened the picture, whatever horizontal line could have been used as an horizon. In my case, as I was unaware of the height and the reciprocal distance of the bars, I was believing that it should have been sufficient to project the bars unto the ground, so that, estimating a distance between each couple, an unit of measure could be derived, able to allow to compute the dimensions of the other objects present in the picture.

Ringhiera stilizzata:
dieci sbarre di 10 cm ciascuna= 1mt.

The, I stylized the railing, therefore enhancing it. I started supposing a 10 cm distance between each couple of bars, making use of ten of them, therefore over a length of 1 meter. We must obviously remember that usually such distances may be anything between 10 and 15 cm.

I've taken again the character away from the picture, have chosen at random a focal point and a horizon line. The result (10 cm distance between bars) is that the guy is 2.40 meter tall (of course, 12 cm distance would give 2.88 meters, 13 cm 3.12 meters, and so on).

Indeed such absurd figures were disconcerting, they could not be true, and, in the CSICOP style (Author: a group of supposed scientists, usually just debunkers) I started wondering where I was going wrong. I found out that, according to the infinity point I had chosen on the horizon, dimensions could vary considerably.

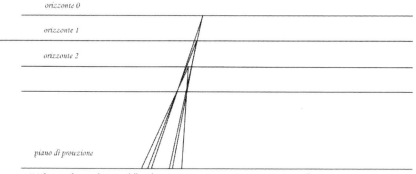

più è lontano il punto di origine delle ombre, più esse si stringono, più è vicino, più esse si allargano.

Therefore it was silly to base oneself on a random horizon line and an infinity point. It was necessary to establish, at least roughly, the point of view of whom had shot the picture, and, above all, it was necessary to find on the ground a grid of lines with two different origins.

Looking at the picture, it seems that who has shot it was, roughly, at the height of the hips of the man. That doesn't mean that the shooter was smaller, because maybe he was kneeling, or maybe the man was on the top of a bounce, and so on.

I was now aware that it was not possible to go on by suppositions, and therefore I started computing the grid, basing myself on an horizon at the height of the man's hips, and on two origins.

In order to find the second origin, I've been forced to extend the railings, again supposing 10 cm of distance between their bars, supposing that they were encircling the garden, and therefore generating a set of squares on the ground, whose sides were 1 meter long by assumption.

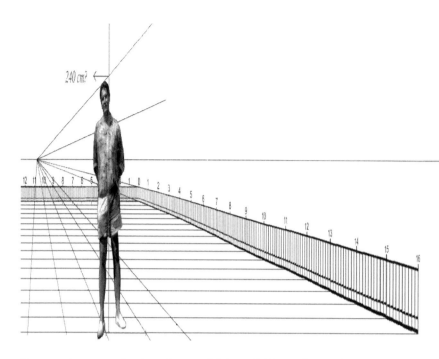

240 cm?

12 11 10 9 8 7 6 5 4 3 2 1 0 1 2 3 4 5 6 7 8 9 10 11 12 13 14 15 16

Once again, supposing bars 1 meter high, and 10 cm distant from one another, the man results to be 2.40 meters tall (the mark is slightly higher, because the man's head is slightly tilted). His height would reach 3.60 meters supposing a 15 cm distance between bars!

According to the point of view of debunkers (if it doesn't look possible, it is impossible) the problem was absurd. Therefore I sought the help of a friend of mine, an architect, without telling him that my goal was to compute the height of a supposed alien. I just asked him: I have a picture of a garden, where some railings are present; how may I compute its planimetry? My friend sighed, and told me that it was a difficult operation, with logarithm-based projections, and I got into despair, because I'm not acquainted with logarithms, after my humanistic studies.

Having tried three different approaches to the problem, I was on the point of giving away, because of my ignorance in mathematics, when I remembered that a very useful software packet exists, Google Sketch Up.

Google Sketch Up may be downloaded from the internet free of charge; it is able to reconstruct three-dimensional structures and to look at them from every possible point of view, rotating and translating them, and so on. It's a software packet that allows three-dimensional architectural de-signs, similar to the ones obtainable from technical experts in this subject.

An interesting feature is that it presents the user with a set of pre-defined objects, for instance sofas, pipes, pianos, and... railings!

Therefore I decided to make a fourth approach: making use of Google Sketch Up, I was to define a plane whatever, put standard railings over it, put the picture from "Contattismi di Massa" on the scene, moving it until the result would match the picture itself. Then, I was only to measure the man's height, making use of the instruments offered by Google Sketch Up.

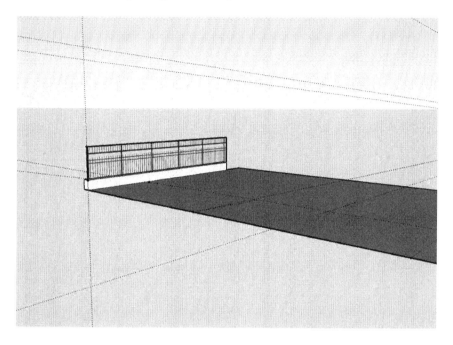

That's an example of a standard railing, given by Google Sketch Up; after the object has been inserted, the whole scene may be rotated, so that one may look at it from every possible point of view.

Then, I inserted the picture from "Con-tattismi di Massa" into the three-dimensional scene-ry generated by Google Sketch up.

Then, it was necessary to move the objects, so that the distance among the bars of the real railing could match that of the virtual object; that's the result:

I rotated this image, to better overlap the railings:

When I finished it has been possible to establish that the distance between the man and the railings is about 9.85 m.

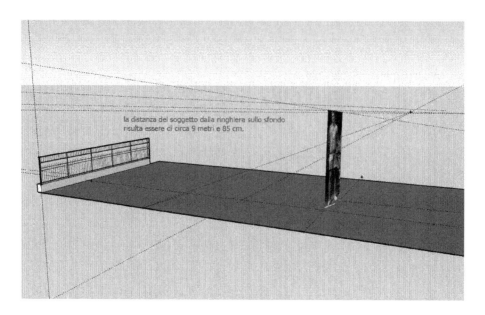

la distanza del soggetto dalla ringhiera sullo sfondo risulta essere di circa 9 metri e 85 cm.

At this point it was possible to measure the man's height, and I have been shocked to verify that it was 3.07 meters:

la misura con l'apposito righello di google skeych up dà 307 centimetri !

Just to be sure, I've made use of another possibility offered by Google Sketch Up: it presents its user with a model of a normal man, 1.77 meters tall; I put this object into the scene, near to the supposed alien, and this is the unbelievable result:

In short, a man 1.77 meters tall would have looked this way, near to the man from our picture:

l'altezza del personaggio standard di google sketch up è di 176,9 centimetri, ecco come apparirebbe messo accanto alla persona raffigurata nella foto

What could I say?

It looks that the rare cases of terrestrial "giants" are often due to an illness named "acromegaly". It affects people, making them grow continuously, but, as far as it is know, they never exceed 2.72 meters (Robert Pershing Wadlow). Anyway, when a person exceeds 2.2 meters, he starts suffering a lot of different physical pathologies, and statistics tell us that they face a short life. That's because

61

they endure their bones weight, their heart is forced to pump blood stronger than usual, blood pressure goes mad, and all the internal organs are subjected to unusual stresses. In short, over this planet, a 2.20 meters high biped is due to a short life (if he is not a Grizzly).

Does that mean anything? I do not know.

I must say that, looking at the pictures of the tallest men in the world, I've found all of them awkward (either legs too long, feet too big, heads malformed), while, looking at the picture at the end of "Contattismi di Massa", I see a man with an harmonious structure (may be just his head is a bit too little), with slim legs, small feet wearing "espadrillas", a relaxed and smiling face, and a general impression of energy and dynamism. Nothing to do with the pictures of the unholy "Tallest men in the world", almost always forced to resort to crutches.

Of course personal sensations have no objective value, then the possibility exists that the person who appears in "Contattismi di Massa" is no giant at all.

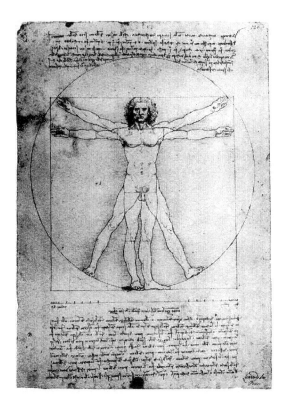

After having done my best on Kenio's height, I noticed another strange thing: his head looks to be too little, with respect to his body. Since Leonardo's times, new criteria on the representation of the human body took place: no more emperors, saints and ladies unrealistically stretched out, towering over other people and landscapes, but realistic images. Leonardo stated the correct proportions in his Vitruvian man:

It resulted that, in order to give realistic proportions to the human figure, the head must be one seventh (one eighth for long-limbed people) of the global length of the body.

Therefore, if a man has a head 22 cm long, his global height must be 22·8=176 cm.

Indeed, this is simply not true with Kenio; as the following image shows, his head is only one ninth of his global length:

What does that mean? I do not know. It does not help in determining his real height, but it only shows that his proportions are not fully correct. Strange indeed.

People affected by microcephalism usually suffer of serious mental problems, have a rather irregular head, look like hominids.

Could this be another evidence that Kenio is not from this world? Maybe this strangeness may have been the result of the gravity pull on his planet (<u>Author</u>: wrong: Kenio has been born here, as far as I know.), and that would fully corresponds to the environmental conditions described by Sammaciccia when speaking about the underground bases by the W56s.

Conclusions

Now researchers and debunkers will obviously try to verify the photo confronting that face with all similar faces they'll be able to discover and, in case, they will probably open also the police archives! That face is too recognizable; what happened if somebody would identify that guy saying: "HEY, I know him, he is my cousin!(or my brother, friend, husband, and so on and so forth...)"? the whole story would fall, of course. So, why Dr. Breccia exposed his name and his career to such a great risk? Perhaps because he is totally certain that the person portrayed in that photo was not from this Earth.

To conclude, this has been an amateur analysis, made by a person without great mathematical skills. A part within myself hopes strongly that I've been mistaken (at least because the idea that "giants" walk among ourselves generates an ancestral feeling of anguish), another part within myself hopes that I'm right, it would be great if what written in the third part of "Contattismi di Massa" were true, it would mean that to men just a little step is required.

I hope that my modest work may induce people better qualified than myself to scientifically analyze that picture.

Chapter 4

The Genesis of Humankind

Most ancient traditions refer to the origin of mankind as an act of creation by some divinity. Secondary details do indeed differ from one tradition to another, but the main idea is that one God (by whatever name), or many Gods, decided first to create the cosmos, then mankind.

The major ancient traditions (at least the Indus, the Sumerian, the Egyptian and the Hebrew ones) maintain that such a creation took place concomitant with the rebellion of some assistants against their God (the biblical Fallen Angels, for instance), or a war between the Gods themselves; according to some sources the revolt took place before the creation of mankind, after the creation according to others. Then, one of the two factions (the rebels, or their God) started taking care of the new-born humanity. Most times a Goddess has played an important role in the process (this is true even in the biblical tale, although not as evident).

Strangely enough, (although not really so, indeed; why should we consider it strange?) a similar tradition is present also in the W56 cosmology; only, in this case, the two parts of creation are not so strictly correlated as in our religions.

First of all, the W56s maintain that life originated spontaneously in <u>only 50</u> (I repeat: fifty) planets throughout the whole universe, our Earth among them; that's why our planet plays to them such an important role, almost a sacred one. They state that some of their people originated here on our Earth, in remote times. In a sense, they are literally our elder brothers. Since those times, Earth has always been inhabited, by different civilizations, that started growing only to destroy themselves later on, in a series of ups and downs. To them, what we call "our history" (say, from some thousands of years before Christ to the present day) shows just the efforts of the last of these civilizations, starting again from scratch, and fighting its way to, maybe, a space age.

The decision to write the few notes in this chapter came when a friend of mine, Biagio Russo, presented me with his book about the genesis of mankind, based on Sumerian traditions. His book is very well made, and it is a pity that up to now it has not yet been translated into English, which I suggested he do as soon as possible. The book is quite interesting, for two reasons at least; first, Russo has a profound knowledge of the subject; then, he is keen in quoting references for every statement he makes. Then, this book is the very latest one on this topic, therefore it is the most up-to-date one, and I'd say a reference text on the subject.

Russo asked me my ideas on the Sumerian tales, and of course I answered that, according to the W56s, things went in a totally different way; then, thinking back for a moment, I realized that both versions could coexist, and substantiate each other; after all, Sumerologists have, most of them, never heard about Amicizia (maybe with one major exception!).

For the benefit of the reader, let me present first the "classic" Sumerian tale, and similar tales from other cultures, then my ideas on how it could be modified to agree with the W56s cosmogony.

Sumerians worshipped "gods" that were named Dingir [1], but we must understand the meaning of the name "gods" in this context: the Dingir were not gods, in the usual sense; they were superior beings, much more advanced than Sumerians, but, aside from that, they were living a normal life, getting married, having sons and daughters, and so on, just like Indus, Egyptian, Greek and Latin gods. Getting back to Sumer, the major characters among these "gods" were An (AN, but also ANU or ANUM), their lord, then Enlil (EN.LIL = "master of winds"), An's second son, but anyway his heir; then Enki (EN.KI = "master of earth"), another of An's sons. An, Enlil and Enki constituted the supreme triad among the Dingir.

Among the Dingir there were two groups of beings (again, we would say gods): the Anunnaki [2] (300 of them) and the Igigi [3] (again 300 of them); for unclear reasons, the Igigi were forced to attend to an unknown (to us) labour, to benefit the other Dingir, a work that had lasted millennia, and that in the end the Igigi were not willing to endure this any longer.

The Igigi started protesting, and asking that their labour be taken away from them. Enlil asked An and Enki for support, but Enki already had a solution, thanks to his mother, Nammu; she suggested her son to "build" "something" that could save the Igigi from their labour.

Enki answered his mother Nammu, saying that a possible substitute already existed, then, in front of the other Dingir, Enki announced that he had the solution, and begged the help of his sister, Ninhursag (NIN.HUR.SAG = "the lady of the hill"). The project consisted in creating a being "similar to the Dingir", but without their knowledge, that could work in the place of the Igigi.

In short, Enki and Ninhursag, making use of technologies that today we would call genetic engineering, gave birth to the Lulu (LU.LU = "the mixed being"), beings designed to serve the Dingir (and indeed the Sumerians named themselves the "servants of gods"). The Lulu race was what today we call humanity. The Lulu were similar to their creators, from a physical point of view, probably they have, at least in part, their same chromosomes, because the first Lulu seems to have been generated via artificial breeding, making use of the uterus of Ninmah (NIN.MAH = "The lady of birth"), another of Enki's sisters, named, after this exploit, Mammi. This word means "mother", a word that is present to-day in all the neo-Latin languages, and in many others; consider, for instance, the Russian Мама – pron. "Mama", meaning "mother"; even more, consider the Latin *Mammae*, meaning the female breasts, from which the word "mammiferous" (= "that brings mammas") derives.

Having given birth to the Lulu race, the Dingir problem looks to have been solved. Not really so, indeed. In order to operate, the project required that the Lulu race was kept in ignorance, so as not to endanger the Dingir themselves. In the Bible, Adam and Eve were expelled from Eden because they had acquired knowledge that they had been explicitly forbidden.

Therefore the Igigi were commanded to ensure that the project was actuated according to its specifications. But, after a while, 200 among them felt in love with some Lulu females, married them (after all, they were genetically compatible with them!), and started teaching science to the Lulu people, an action that was the exact opposite of their mission. A very similar episode is told in the Bible about the "Fallen Angels", and in more detail in the various versions of the Book of Enoch. The offspring of such a mating was composed by "mighty men which were of old, men of renown," (Genesis, VI, 4).

When this took place, a quarrel arose among the Dingir triad, about what to do. Enlil's idea was to destroy the Lulu race, while Enki was of opposite opinion; however the former won the game, and the deluge was arranged as a mean to destroy the Lulu and their mixed offspring. But, once again, mankind got help, and some were able to survive. In the Gilgamesh epic, it is An who lets Utnapishtim know about the impeding cataclysm; in the Bible it is the Elohim [4] who alerts Noah, and so on. The Sumerian traditions do not say anything else, after this episode, therefore we do not know what the role of the Dingir after the deluge was, according to them.

Of course the Bible gives the same global account, although in less detail; no surprise, because most of the Hebrew culture looks to have derived from the Sumerian one. Abraham started his adventure leaving Ur of the Chaldees, having being summoned by his God to do so. And in the Exodus, the Bible tells us of the efforts Moses made to destroy all the surviving Nephilim, the giants, offspring of the Fallen Angels. Again, the result of the ancient revolt.

Things are not as simple as I have portrayed them: Moses and Noah were themselves probably sons of the Igigi, according to the book of Enoch, but let's ignore this problem at this point, because it would take us too far away from our subject.

Up to now, we have seen that the Sumerian genesis and the Biblical one agree, and complement each other. Much, much more could be said on this topic, but this is not the right place to perform such an exegesis.

Just let me remember that, just a few days ago, I discovered the existence of an ethnic group that could be the strictest descendants of the Sumerians. The Mandaeans, also known as the Sabeans, or Subbiyum, are a monotheistic, pacifist religious community who are recognized as followers of John the Baptist. They once numbered about 30,000, living mostly in southern Iraq. The Mandaeans are a Gnostic sect that arose in the Middle East around the same time as Christianity. Although it is one of the few religious traditions that can legitimately claim a

2000-year literary history, there has been very little written about them in English. Scholars state that their language is the purest known dialect of ancient Sumerian, although to-day their writing is in Arabic-style (only in style, because it differs greatly). An Italian writer, Gerolamo Vecchietti, was first to get in touch with some of these people in 1604, recognizing that theirs was a Chaldean language. Strangely enough, their cosmology seems to jump directly from the Deluge to John the Baptist, with almost nothing in between; anyway I believe that studying their language could help us better understand the Sumerian.

What is interesting is that we find similar accounts in the other two major ancient civilizations, the Egyptian and the Indus one. They both maintain that mankind has been created by gods (Tehuti [5], and Krshna [6]), but, more importantly, that at a certain point a quarrel arose between two of the major gods, the control of mankind being the object of this struggle. In Egypt, we have Osiris (Awsar [7], the Greek Οσϊρις) being confronted by his brother Seth, and being rescued by his sister/wife Isis [8] (Ast, Greek Ισις), becoming then the god of the underworld, supervising human well-being. In India we have the awesome (because of its dimensions!) Mahabharata, that again tells of a war among brothers, because of a woman. But in that area we find an unexpected point of view: the knowledge is still secluded to us, but it is contained within ourselves, in a form of a goddess, Kundalini, who usually sleeps at the base of our spine; making use of peculiar Yoga techniques, this goddess may be awaken from her sleep, and give us back the knowledge we have been prevented from having.

Getting back to the Biblical account in Genesis, we find that Adam and Eve were tempted, in the Garden of Eden, by "the serpent." Who was this strange entity? In the whole of ancient traditions, snakes have been the keepers of knowledge, and indeed, in Genesis, a serpent is shown offering knowledge, an action that goes against God's explicit will:

> *But of the tree of the knowledge of good and evil, thou shalt not eat of it; for in the day that thou eatest thereof thou shalt surely die.* (Genesis, 2:17)

And, indeed, it was the keeper of knowledge who tempted Eve (why not Adam himself?) so that they ate the fruit of the forbidden tree; and that was such a sin that both of them were driven out from Eden. Doesn't this remind us a bit of the LU.LU problems with the Dingir?

In Christian lore the snake has been compared to the Devil itself, to the point that one of the most common representations of the Virgin Mary shows her crushing the snake's head with her foot. How did it happen that an entity, considered since forever as the keeper of knowledge, has been transformed into the epitome of the Devil itself? Easy to answer: just as in the Sumerian Genesis, mankind was supposed to be kept from knowledge; when someone infringed this command, he committed a very terrible sin, altering the previewed path of operations. Clear accounts of such stories may be found in the Books by Enoch, where they are detailed more than I may try in these lines.

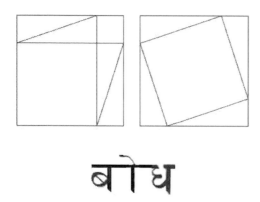

बोध

These three cultures developed a very high-level arithmetic, to the point that only in recent times all the mysteries behind the Rhind Mathematical papyrus have been solved. Indeed, speaking of arithmetic is too diminutive by far: the Egyptians had developed trigonometry, and binary computation, the Babylonians were able to solve a linear system of ten equations, and were at ease with second and third degree equations, the Indians had a profound culture of numbers and of geometry: the oldest demonstration of the Pythagoras' theorem on right-angled triangles comes from Indian texts older by millennia:

The only word present under the drawing, "Bodh", in Sanskrit means simply "Look"!

Yet, the people from these cultures were mainly farmers and herdsmen; aside from a few, let's say, engineers, what use could such knowledge have been to them? Of course, astronomy was necessary for agriculture and, indeed, priesthoods understood this importance and became the monopolistic depositaries of the required techniques. Moreover, just as with their languages, their mathematics were totally different from one another: Sumerians and Babylonians used the base 60 in their computations, Egyptians the bases 10 and 2, Indians only the base 10.

Recapitulating, we have seen that the three major cultures of the past tell similar stories about the genesis of mankind, although with some minor differences, and that the three of them developed, for unknown purposes, a deep knowledge of Mathematics and Astronomy.

Getting back to the topics we are speaking about in this book, how do these tales interact with the W56/CTR saga?

They do, indeed, but in a totally unprecedented way that I first discovered while having a talk with Biagio Russo, and what comes out is really surprising.

The W56s have a profound knowledge of biology: to them building a living entity is quite easy, to the point that they are able to create clones of living men, totally identical to them (there is a small detail that permits to recognize a clone from the original, but let's forget it!). But these entities are just biological robots: although having some will for themselves, they remain just machines, designed to perform specific duties.

Then, a long time ago (millennia, if not even more), somewhere among the stars of the Orion's belt, a scientist grew the mad idea of trying to build a new kind of biological entities, endowed with a self-awareness: not just the usual biological robots, but new beings able to feel the responsibility of their actions, in a word in possession *of the knowledge of good and evil*. Of course it was a very ambitious project, and the scientist worked hard in order to achieve it.

Indeed he succeeded. His creatures were self-aware, biologically compatible with men, and with free will. The LU.LU (getting back to the Sumerian lore) had been built (NOT created!). By the way, Mauro Biglino (Cfr. Bibliografy) underlines the fact that the name נפילא "Nephila" means "Orionites", that is "Born in Orion"!

But something went wrong, I've been told. A very strong instinct of self-preservation arose among these beings, who realized that they were in some way different from their designer, and probably feared that, in the same way they had been built, they could equally be destroyed. Therefore a revolt arose against their designer, who tried, in vain, to stop it. In the end, he was killed, and the new beings flew away, starting, in due time, a process of biological reproduction, giving birth to a new race, albeit one artificial in origin, that the W56s named "Weiros", from a verb in their language meaning "To have been built" (it is not a plural noun, as it may look at first). Then, millennia later, Bruno Sammaciccia named them "CTRs", from the Italian word "contrary" (= "opposites").

Summarizing what we have seen up till now, the Sumerian Genesis is compatible with the W56 one, with the only difference that the LU.LU is not our mankind, but the Weiros. Our mankind remains part of the W56 offspring, they are indeed our elderly brothers.

The only detail that has to be underlined is that the Weiros are an artificial race, even if they have been reproducing biologically for aeons. And that's the main reason for the quarrel between themselves and the natural races. These problems are discussed elsewhere within this book.

Getting back to Earth mankind, and to the W56s, they maintain that, in the whole universe, life began on only fifty planets, out Earth among them. That's one of the reasons why our planet is so important in their eyes. Therefore, some of their ancestors have seen their origins on this planet, that's why they say they are our elder brothers!

According to them, life on this planet is much older than what our scientists affirm: many civilizations have taken place on Earth, at times leaving it to explore the cosmos, other times destroying themselves, leaving after them only a few people who had to restart from scratch. They say that our planet is in a continuous geological evolution, that's why we very rarely find traces of the previous civilizations on earth (often termed OOPARTS, Out Of Place finds). Among them, according to myself, the so-called Cheops pyramid, that in my opinion has nothing to do with the IV dynasty pharaoh, and on the contrary is a remnant of a previous civilization.

Notes

The Genesis of Mankind

Note to the Notes: this group of notes is full of symbols in ancient languages; at first I placed these words inside the text, but then found that Windows was coping not too well with this mixture of text and graphics, therefore I decided to group all this symbols in a separate section, just after this group of notes.

1   Probably "Dingir" derives from "DI.GAR" (= "to promulgate a decree") (see Fig. 1); its phonetic value was "El", or "Il"; it was almost always put before the names of gods. The drawing on the right shows the Sumerian cuneiform writing of this word.

2   In Sumerian, AN.A.NA.KI (= "sky", "towards", "being", "earth", in that order); the term "Anunnaki" is more frequent in Akkadian; in Sumerian the most common version is "Anunna"; the word could also mean "The sons of An". In this cuneiform writing, the first symbol on the left is the determinative for "god", Dingir, the second (identical) one stands for "sky". (Fig. 2a). In the Hammurabi Codex, it is written A.NUN.NA.KI, an alternative reading that could mean "The best seed from the Earth". (Fig. 2b).

3   The word looks as though it is derived from IGI.GI (= "eyes", "to besiege", in that order); in the common form IGI.GI.GU it should mean "reliable supervisor). Igigi has also been the name of a king of the Akkadian Empire (2250 b.C. ca.). (Fig. 3)

4   Elohim (sing.: Eloha) (Figs. 4 and 5, respectively; remember that these names must be read from right to left), is a very strange word, which has been debated at length. Just to start, from a grammatical point of view, it is a *plural* word, feminine gender; but verbs, adverbs and pronouns relating to it, have almost always been written in the singular, masculine, form.

5   The god who had taught mankind how to write. (Figs 6 and 7)

6   Krshna in Sanskrit means "Black" (Fig. 8)

7   Awsar (Fig. 9): according to Sir William Budge, the origin and meaning of this name are unknown; its original pronunciation must have been something like As-ari" or "Us-ari"; about the name of this god, Diodorus Siculus pretended that it was meaning "many eyes" (πολυόφθαλμον), while Jablonski and others opted for "to do much". In all evidence, this name, in its hieroglyphs writing, presents us with a throne and an eye; therefore we might infer that they mean "the god

who overviews".

8 Isis, <u>Ast</u> in Egyptian (Fig. 10): she was <u>Awsar</u>'s sister and wife. Again, we have a throne, plus two symbols denoting femininity, and the determinative meaning "goddess". No hint to the pronunciation of her name. Budge suspects that the initial pronunciation should have been <u>St</u>, with any vowel in between; then, an "<u>a</u>" developed in front of the name. Another among her names was <u>Amenit</u> (Fig. 11), meaning "The lady of the underworld"; in this case, we have the word <u>Amen</u>, followed by the group <u>it</u>, where the <u>t</u> (the feminine termination) is also part of the determinative for "goddess". She has been worshipped by the Greeks as Εϊσις, and by Latins as Isis. She has been taught by <u>Thot</u> (Fig. 6) the use of the hieroglyphic writing (Fig. 12), <u>Neter metwt</u>, that is "The words of God" (from right to left), just like the Sanskrit *Devanagari* (Fig. 13).

Symbols referred to:

Fig. 1 (Dingir)

Fig. 2a (Anunnaki)

Fig 2b (Anunnaki)

Fig. 3 (Igigi)

Fig. 4 (Elohim)

Fig. 5 (Eloha)

Fig 6 (<u>Tehuti</u>)

Fig 7 (<u>Tehuti</u>)

Fig. 8 (Krshna)

Fig 9 (<u>Awsar</u>)

Fig. 10 (<u>Ast</u>)

Fig. 11 (<u>Amenit</u>)

Fig. 12 (<u>Neter metwt</u>)

देवनागरी

Fig. 13 (Devanagari)

उपनिषद्

Fig. 99 (Upanishad)

Chapter 5

The CTRs

As our Friends have told us, the so-called CTRs (this name is actually a contraction of the Italian "Contrari" = "Opposites"; again a name invented by Bruno Sammaciccia), are "our enemy brothers", the most sublime way to depict a situation that they pretend not to name a "war", but a "quarrel", although many people have died, on both sides, together with many earthlings siding with the former or the latter party.

It looks that the original name of the CRTs is "*Weiros*"; although to English-speaking people it may look as a plural, but indeed it is not. "Weiros" is a word, in the W56's language, that means "something, that has been built". Remember that in their language no nouns exist, and every concept is a verb, usually in the participle tense.

I've been told that the CTRs are the result of a biological experiment that went astray, somewhere within the stars that belong to the Orion's belt. The designer of the experiment died in his effort to stop it. I may just remember, here, that Orion has been seen in our mythologies, since ancient times, as a source of evil and disease.

Our Friends have mastered biology, to them it is quite easy to build biological robots, that is living entities, at times totally identical to normal persons. But they are, anyway, still robots, that is to say entities without a self-consciousness: they behave according to some general principles, are able to take initiatives, but remain just machines, without an *ego*. Long ago, a scientist tried to overcome this limitation, and, as a first result, his creatures revolted against him, killing him (that's a rather common idea in our lore, isn't it?). Then, this initially small group of living entities started to reproduce, in the biological way we are so well acquainted with, and in a short time a new race appeared.

It would be silly, from our part, to try to devise a test to distinguish between ourselves and the CTRs; speaking about the "usual" biological robots, there is a test that might distinguish between a regular man, and a robot built in his shape; most of our physicians could not be able to find it, but there are signs that permit us to recognize a biological robot from a natural entity, in a post-mortem examination.

On the contrary, the CTRs are no longer robots: they have received the ability to will, they no longer depend on instructions from outside. And therefore in their bodies there is no receiver meant to accept commands. They are totally autonomous.

But they are nevertheless an artificial race, and they lack something, with respect to natural races. What they lack is an easy question, so I'm not going to answer it now. The CTRs are aware of this problem, but, not having been generated within the natural global design of the universe, they are not able to understand what they are missing.

Of course they must have been told, an immense number of times, that they lack a soul, but obviously such a concept is foreign to their understanding. The W56s have, on this topic, ideas similar to the old Egyptians: a man is made of four different entities: a body, the bah, another entity whose name I seldom remember, the khw, then the ka. The ka is somewhat similar to what we Westerns name the soul, the bah is the lowest level interface between the pure animalism of the body, and the entity in between. This latter, the khw, is what our philosophers have named "reasoning" entity, to say briefly, our "mind".

The CTRs have received, by their designer, their bah, and somehow have been able to generate by themselves the second entity, the mind. But they lack the ka; that they cannot have, because, not having been created inside the global plan, they cannot share the identity of God. Somewhere else, within this book, I explore such concepts, but, remaining focused on CTRs, they are fully aware of this lack from their part, and are going mad trying to understand it. Of course there is no hope in their efforts, because it is a concept that transcends physical and biological sciences, the only things they understand.

Their main attitude, therefore, consists in studying natural life forms, all of which share a peculiarity that is forbidden to them. Of course I am not speaking about the so-called abductions, that to me are a preposterous concept: beings with such a biological knowledge have no reason to experiment, most of the times in ways that are antiquated even for our medical science.

What they do mostly is a kind of psychological warfare, to try to understand in which way natural entities are different from them. As the core of the problem consists in our sharing the individualities of all entities (although we on Earth are not so good in doing so!), they indulge in exciting our minds, to monitor what takes place. That's the reason why at times they behave in an apparently illogical way. Why use ferocious means to kill somebody? Why kill little girls that have obviously played no role in the general background? Of course, only to raise the emotional level of bystanders, in order to analyze the processes taking place. Emotions are a concept totally foreign to the mentality of CTRs.

I have been in touch with some CTRs, among them Miss Swollha, about whom I speak at length somewhere else. This young lady once tried to kill me, in a rather stupid way, running over me with her car. Of course a stupid way, because, thanks to their technological abilities, they could have got the same result without such complications. Her effort failed, she phoned me to congratulate myself for having been able to survive her attempt to kill me! This may look singular, but from their point of view it is plainly logical: there was no animosity in Swollha against myself (remember: no emotions), and probably no clear intent to kill me:

either the plan was to kill me because I was from the other party (the apparent proposition), or simply to frighten me, maybe monitoring my reactions in the mean time.

The CTRs have been present for several years in the Rome area (I used to call them "Italian Ummites", because they pretended to be from this latter group), getting in touch with many people, among them teachers, professors, and university students. Most of these have been friends to Paolo Di Girolamo and myself, so that we could receive the echoes of what was going on.

At first these people around us have been a bit perplexed: Paolo and myself were usually speaking, most of the time in a rather covert way, about W56s, CTRs, Ummites and the like, in his laboratory, with lots of people listening to us (as Paolo was used saying, "raising their aerials"!) during their work. Obviously curiosity was growing. Then they were contacted by the pretended Ummites, who stated that such information had to be kept secret to Paolo and myself. At first this request was not fulfilled, so we got aware of what was going on, but later secrecy prevailed.

The "Italian Ummites" got in touch also with Paolo and myself, always asking us to cooperate against the W56s; the most common person was Swollha, but there have been also other characters; when I was living in Rome, I have been visited three times in my flat by a man from the Ummites group, trying to convince me to pass to their side (what would have changed, had I accepted his proposal? Probably nothing at all, so this was obviously not the true goal of his operation). Once I entered the well-known "Il Bolognese" restaurant in Piazza del Popolo, in Rome, together with Roberto, a friend of mine, and I saw this Ummite character, well known to me, sitting at a table together with a topmost politician whom I knew equally well, because he was a member of the scientific board of the magazine we were editing, with myself as its director. So I greeted both of them, to the astonishment by Roberto, who was surprised that I was a friend to that politician; of course he did not realize who the other person sitting at that table was!

The Italian Ummites were once unmasked by Paolo. As they were pretending to be original Ummites, they were often speaking Spanish, but probably were not aware that Paolo had spent many years in Chile, therefore he is fluent in Castilian, and once he was able to detect a mistake in their speech, a mistake typical of an Italian-speaking person! The "Ummite" character at a certain moment said "preguntarò", while the correct Spanish verb should have been "preguntaré" (= "I will ask"), and the –arò ending in the future tense is typically Italian. Therefore he was not mastering Castilian so well…

Anyway, the Italian Ummites have been in touch with many people in the area of Rome and beyond it. One among the people they had contacted has been the late Eufemio Del Buono, the owner of the magnificent restaurant "Lo Zodiaco", on the top of Monte Mario, which offers a splendid view of Rome, especially at night. Del Buono got several telephone calls from Ummites; once they said that they had just been at his restaurant, taking some soft drinks, and inviting him to Veio (an ancient Etruscan town, whose remains sit just North of Rome), and he wisely refused.

The CTRs (let me use this name for brevity, from now on, while referring to the Italian Ummites) were often making long telephone calls to their friends. The main character among the latter has been Fabrizio, a young boy at the time, who, in a certain sense, became the leader of the Italian group. Their operations consisted also in showing at times their craft over Fabrizio's house, after having advised him by phone of what was going to take place, so that he has shot many pictures of such events, or in showing in public biological robots cloned from Fabrizio and other members of his group, again after having told them in advance, via phone; photos exist also of these cases.

But things, with the CTRs, were not always as easy as that: they were often pretending to get biologic samples of their friends (hair, seminal liquid, and the like), and to perform experiments on them, having them assuming strange medicines, and recording their reactions. They were also pretending to dictate them their style of life, what they were to eat, how they were to dress, what places they were to frequent.

The CTRs (at least some of them) were living in a flat in Oslavia St. (near to the Vatican), and at least in another one, in Seneca St. (a more northern area), and Fabrizio had the keys of the first flat, and obviously has been there sometimes to meet his friends. He says that they were perfectly human in their appearance, the only difference from us consisted in their eyes that had not the angular side that we have on their outer edge. Their eyes, on the contrary, are perfectly round, so that they had to wear sunglasses to hide them.

Their main place of operation was Veio: there, there was a place where exchanges of materials were taking place, always after telephone calls. In those years Veio was really a secluded place: I have spent some nights within the Etruscan ruins, almost always living unusual experiences, and one afternoon I met a Hydra there, therefore I ran away as quick as I could! The place reserves a really dark atmosphere, even today; not so long ago, some friends of mine encountered magnetic fields over 40 times the normal Earth field; not steady fields, but pulsating ones, to the point of preventing the work of their cell phones and cameras. One of my friends found the Ummo symbol, sculptured at the entrance of a grotto (see picture no. 14 at page 340 of "Mass Contacts"), and in that area strange things continue to occur, even today.

At a certain moment, also the Fabrizio's group was discarded by the CTRs, just like the W56s had done with Bruno and his friends, so this story also nended, maybe to start anew with other people, but I know nothing of such a follow-up.

Generally speaking, the CTRs are Nazi-like: very cold people, in appearance devoid of any human feeling, living inside a strong hierarchical structure. Their scientific and biological knowledge is astonishing, although in those areas they sit well behind the W56s. Of course, they are able to generate clones of any living being, but often they prefer to enslave human beings, depriving them of their conscious will.

The best, and only weapon we may use against them is just our will: they cannot force us, if we resist strongly, with our strong will. I have been subjected to another attempt to kill me, this time they tried to induce me to commit suicide, after a telephone call apparently coming from a friend of mine [1], and I must say that this time they almost met with success: only at the very last moment I realized what was going on, and opposed it with fierceness. In all evidence, I succeeded!

In Italy, during Fascist times, something very strange took place, that I tell briefly in "Mass Contacts". While in Germany pictures were circulating, obviously fakes, showing Adamski-like craft with the Nazi cross on them, here Mussolini was showing an illogical certainty that the powers of the Axis (Germany, Japan and Italy) were going to win the war, and to conquer the whole world. It was foolish, because he was well aware of the poor conditions of our army, yet he dared to declare war on the United States and the Soviet Union at almost the same time!

There had been something strange taking place in Northern Italy, a big mother ship with some flying saucers around had been seen, and some Italian planes had tried to intercept it, of course without success [2]. Then rumours started to spread, about "something" that had fallen from the sky. In brief, a Roswell *ante litteram* had happened, with scraps being recovered. In one recent San Marino international UFO convention, William Brophy, an American, told that his father had been somehow involved in the story of the bodies of two white men, with blonde hair, that had been found inside the wreckage! I do not know whether this pre-Roswell story is true or not (I was not even born, at those times!), but if it is, it is to be considered just like the Roswell accident: something being deliberately sent to crash on earth, maybe with biologic robots inside, to give earthlings something to wonder upon. But, what a chance, while in Roswell the robots are said to have been of the Grey kind, in Italy they are supposed to have been of the Aryan race!

Had "somebody" succeeded in convincing Hitler and Mussolini that the future was of the Aryans, and maybe had promised them some help?

There is an unbelievable sentence spoken by the Duce, in a very formal occasion, in the presence of the German ambassador in Rome that, I repeat, would be simply unbelievable, had it not been recorded in a film by the Istituto Luce:

È più verosimile che gli Stati Uniti siano invasi,
prima che dai soldati dell'Asse, dagli abitanti, pare assai bellicosi,
del pianeta Marte, che scenderanno dagli spazi siderali
su inimmaginabili fortezze volanti.

(It is more likely that United States will be invaded
by the apparently very warlike inhabitants from the planet Mars,
who will descend from spaces in flying fortresses which we can't even imagine,
than by the soldiers of the Axis' powers.)

(Benito Mussolini: Discorso alla Federazione Fascista dell'Urbe – Feb 25, 1941)

What was Mussolini meaning with those words? Italian fortunes in the war were starting to deteriorate, yet the Duce was sure that the war would be won, maybe thanks to the help from "Martians" who were going to invade the States. Mussolini was not drunk while uttering those words, he was speaking in front of the major Fascist federation in Italy, and, I repeat, of the German ambassador, plus the ministers of his government, and the object of his talk was just the trend of the war operations, so he must have been very sure of what he was saying. Where these "Martians" were to come from? How could Mussolini have been sure of their support (a support that, after all, did not manifest itself)?

Indeed some kinds of support did apparently materialize. Speaking about Wernher Von Braun, in those years he made something nearly miraculous: in the Germany already heavily struck by bombers, he had been able to design that magnificent object (from an engineering point of view, of course!) named the V-2. Those rockets, with a ton of warhead, were literally engineering wanders, for those times; but there was a problem: considering the total structure of the rocket, aerials were located in the small wings at its base, so there was little space left for ailerons; moreover, the wings were too narrow to accommodate large ailerons, necessary to steer the craft.

So Von Braun resorted to a different solution: he decided to guide the rocket mainly by piloting the direction of its jet exhausts; quite intelligent, but unfortunately those gases have such a temperature they melt whatever metallic shield might be used. And here comes the miracle: Von Braun, a mechanic engineer at the head of mechanic and aeronautic engineers, devised the technology of sintering ceramic powders, to build shields able to stand high temperatures, a totally new technology, developed under heavy conditions and with very poor facilities, by people with little or no knowledge at all of the chemistry required to implement it!

May I suppose that "someone" has suggested him the ideas behind it? If I am right, the culprits must have been the CTRs, to which the violent emotions generated by a worldwide war were almost food.

Do we also remember the so-called "Foo Fighters" that were often flying along, escorting Allied bombers, but also German ones, on their missions? They were often frightening airmen, because each party feared they were from their enemies; they were indeed harmless, nevertheless several rounds of machine-guns have been fired against them, obviously to no avail.

About "Foo Fighters", a really unusual occurrence was reported by two American pilots (David McFalls and Edward Baker) about an encounter that took place on Dec 24, 1944, presumably over Germany:

A glowing red ball shot straight up to us. It suddenly <u>changed into an airplane, which did a wing over</u>! Then it dived and disappeared.
(<u>Author</u>: emphasis added).

Then, there is a curious episode that took place near Loreto, in the Marche region (Central Italy). One morning, the Allied army, coming from the south, was confronting the German army, sitting north of them. All of a sudden, a flying saucer appeared, flying low and slowly over the ground between the two armies. Thinking that it was an enemy aircraft, one side started firing at it, but to no avail; but, strangely enough, this object did not react to the fire against it, so some officer thought they had been wrong: in all evidence, the aircraft belonged to their own side, so it was ordered to cease firing. The other army, having reached the scene, got to the same conclusion, decided that it was an enemy aircraft, so they opened fire against it, with the same result. After a while, both armies were firing against the flying saucer, that quietly continued its flight, without responding in any way to what was going on. The old veteran who told me this episode did not remember which army had started the firing, but was adamant in stating that the mysterious craft vanished calmly towards the sea... then the real battle started [3].

Fine, let me stop here with my remembrances of WWII, only, let me underline the fact that "someone" has played a not so negligible role in it.

Getting back to more recent CTRs, I'd like to present one of their drawings, depicting the main base they had built under Veio:

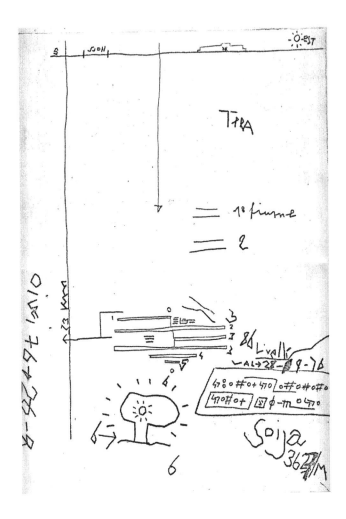

It looks that it sits some 23 km beneath ground level, and that there are three underground rivers between it and the surface. There is a mysterious object, a mushroom-shaped one, in the lower left corner, surrounded by three "6" figures, and with a sun-like drawing inside. Maybe an atomic mushroom? And what does that mean? The three "6" figures are obviously reminiscent of the "666" in the St. John's Revelation:

Here is wisdom. Let him that hath understanding count the number of the beast: for it is the number of a man; and his number is six hundred threescore and six.

(Rev. XIII:18)

It looks that the base is organized on 86 levels, according to the writings on the right. Then, there are some Ummite-style symbols, difficult to understand. Then, the signing: "Soija", that can't help but remind us of Mr. Francesco Saija, of the W56 group!

Of course the CTRs from Rome pretended to originate in Wolf 424, the Ummites star, but obviously unverifiable statements are of no use.

Now, let me quote some of the recordings made by people in the Fabrizio's group. To protect their privacy, I am not going to present their family names. Of course, what follows is but a short excerpt from the notes they have given me (6 cm thick!), chosen at random.

Fabrizio, Jul 4, 1972

I am in Rome, in Cola Di Rienzo St., in front of the Standa store, looking at its shop-windows. All of a sudden, I hear a voice, behind me: "You are Fabrizio, aren't you? You are Fabrizio." I turn back, expecting to see somebody familiar to me, but I see a person I have never met before. He looks 25-30 years old, a rather tall boy (1.80-1.85 metres), with a strong figure and a bold appearance. He wears very dark sunglasses. At first I think of the episode that happened to Bruno in a coffee-house in Milan. I ask him: "Who you are?". He answers: "You have already guessed it," and takes his sunglasses away. To my astonishments, his eyes are not almond-shaped as ours, they are almost oval, without the lateral corner of ours. I feel a chill, but for a moment go on, hoping for a joke. He invites me to enter his car, an old "Giardinetta" (Author: a small family car, rather frequent in those years) with the plate reading "Roma 17....". At first I hesitated, then accepted. We wandered for a hour along the Prati area (Risorgimento Sq., Cola Di Rienzo Sq., San Pietro Sq.), then from Angelico Blvd. we go towards Mazzini Sq.

Not a word between us during that wandering, he looks to be attentive at the street, is very careful in driving, at times he pushes a bit too hard on brakes, or makes mistakes while changing gears, so that the car bumps. I am blocked by his coolness. When we arrive in Mazzini Sq., he stops the car, and nods for me to get out. He remains inside the car, verifying with great care that everything has been switched off, then gets out. We walk toward Oslavia St.; there he nods toward a building, then to its main door. We enter, and start climbing its stairs, up to the last floor and a penthouse. We enter this small flat, and I see that it is strangely furnished: very few pieces of furniture, no picture on the walls, but many optical instruments all around, green boxes of various sizes, a blue dress, almost a formal one, lying on a chair together with a reddish neck-tie and a white shirt; two brief-cases sitting on the floor near by.

Finally he starts speaking, in a sharp tone: "I belong to those you have been looking for so long. I am a man from another world, it was myself to terrify you the 25th of last November..." Then he starts laughing, but always with a cool attitude. I too start laughing, but just to behave correctly. Indeed I am very nervous, and am wondering what is going on.

He says that inside our society he is a kind of political observer, but he is also knowledgeable in sciences. He says he comes from Ummo. I am a bit astonished at hearing this name, and go back remembering an old story…

We go on talking about him, about his job, his mission, then I begin to understand that he needs help for some specific purpose. Then, all of a sudden, he asks me if I'd like to be photographed together with him. I accept, and, unexpectedly, a second guy enters through a door. A rather odd character, a little more than one metre tall, with a big head and a frail body. He too wears dark, big sunglasses. He has an Instamatic (Author: a common, cheap, photo camera) in his hands, and I think that it is a rather commonplace object. He takes a couple of pictures of the two of us, speaks some sentences that I do not understand, then goes away.

Then the alien asks me for my address and telephone number, and I oblige. Before going out, I ask him what his name is. He answers and repeats it many times. It's difficult to me to understand it, it is something like "MOV". Then he says that he wants to present me with something, to remember the event, and gives me the lower portion of an overalls, in a yellow fabric. Then we get out, enter his car, and I am taken back to Cola Di Rienzo St. Mov farewells me, and goes away. I have a look at my watch: it is 21:45.

Gianni, Nov 17, 1972

At 20 past 5 p.m., I was near my bike, near to the Physics faculty, when I noticed that one of the street lamps nearby was flashing. A friend of mine said that probably it was malfunctioning, and went away. At 5:25 the lamp was off, and remained so for some time. All of a sudden it started to switch on and off, in a kind of Morse signaling, sending the number "7" (- - . . .) or the number "3" (. . . - -); At 5:33 it remained steady on. After 15 minutes, I went away.

Antonello, Nov 24, 1972

In Oslavia st. I see once again the famous FIAT 500, and I stop to look carefully at it. It is blue in colour, nothing unusual, its plate reads Roma B 81659, or 81956. I leave under its windshield wipers a sheet of paper with the names of the three of us (Antonello, Fabrizio, Gianni) and their symbol. At 11 p.m. Mov phones me, saying that he needs more of my hair. I ask him if he has found my paper, and he denies, a bit perplexed that I had found his car. He says that it was himself in Veio, the day before. Then announces that we are going to meet in person at 23:33 next Nov 26.

Gianni, Nov 25, 1972

At 6:35 a telephone calls tells Fabrizio to go to Veio, and to search in the windows, looking for a key that must be given to me.

At 8:02 a telephone call: "You, you, how are you? Hi! To day you must give your hair to Antonello, he already knows. Bye!".

At 20:55, another call; at first I am not able to understand what he says, and I ask him to speak in a better way; I hear some talking, then he starts again, this time in a understandable way. He asks about the key, then he says that the meeting has been postponed to Sunday: we, myself, Antonello, Pierluigi and Fabrizio are asked to attend, plus a girl. We must take our hair with us, and give

84

them to Fabrizio, who knows where to leave them.

I talk with CEAR 97; he tells me of his family; he has a boy, six years old, and two twins, a few months old. He said that taking the girl with us last Saturday was not a good idea, because her thoughts were as little as she is; he asks me whether I "have a woman"; I answer no, and he says that I'd best find one, because at times I am "very cool"; I underline that it does not depend on me alone, and he seems to have a bit of difficulty understanding.

He tells that I must not go to Veio too often, and not in too deep, because I could become the target of their defensive systems, and unpleasant events could occur. Then, we must destroy the pictures taken in Veio, and enclose their negatives inside a lead box.

. . . .

They have proven scientifically the existence of the soul. He has known St. Francis by person, he was a great man; but, strangely, he is not aware that St. Francis wrote poems, and ignores the meaning of some words ("Friar", "philosophy", and so on). I explain him the meanings, which he understands before I've finished speaking. I promise I'll give him a copy of St. Francis' "Sonetti".

. . . .

He says that once Venus was inhabited by a bad race, the one that taught Mayas to make human sacrifices; this race got extinguished because of a mutation in their micro-bacteria flora. He looks astonished when I tell him that I do not speak Mayan language.

. . . .

They have two main bases under Rome: one in Veio, the second one under the crossing between Cavour St. and Via Dei Fori Imperiali (I had already thought of something like that).

Fabrizio, Dec 6, 1972

CEAR 97 phones Fabrizio: "You must give back everything!" He says they're leaving within one week, because "we have spoken too much". He phones again later on, giving the solution to an equation that Eng. Breccia had proposed to me in the afternoon: $x^7 + 4x - 2 = 0$. He says that there is one real solution, and six impossible ones (<u>Author</u>: the note does not report the value of the real solution, $x = 0.498098$; moreover, the other six are not "impossible", but "complex" ones).

Gianni, Jan 9, 1973

ELCO calls from Cavour St. Four times he asks Gianni if he wants to speak to CLAS (16 years old). He speaks a good Italian. ELCO tells they are worried about CLAS, because he likes Italian women too much. He lives in a flat in Seneca St.

Then, on Jan 14, 1973, Gianni decides to stop his relations with the CTRs. He does so by sending them the following letter:

My dear friends,

I have decided to stop here. I understand that you will attribute my decision to fear and cowardice. If you think so, I can't do anything about it. But I'd like so much that, at least once, you'd become like Earth men, and forget your magnificent technical capabilities. I love you so much, and have always trusted you, even if often it was not the case. I'm leaving you in the hope to remain friends. You can't understand what this decision means to me. Because of your technicalities, you have forgotten man, and his characteristics. I decided to stop in the name of Earth men. Our world is full of miseries. You came here to study us, and do nothing else. I know mankind better than you, and I am aware that many people need my help.

Because of you, during these three months I had to forget other people. I was hoping to be able to get something positive, and failed. Now my duty consists in dedicating myself to the many who no longer believe in love. That's why I do not agree with you: you do not accept such concepts, you do not understand how many people have changed their life thanks to such ideas. My duty now consists in working together with them, speaking, writing, and trying to help. I will never forget your kindness, and the recordings I've made of your calls are going to remember me of your wonderful friendship.

Maybe you do not understand this word, because to you feelings are not so important. To me they are, because I still have in my mind the image of children crying near to their houses, destroyed by a stupid war. You only study us. I hope that in the future we may meet again. During this time both you and I will have the ability of thinking back of what has happened. I'll go often to Veio to be near to you.

Farewell to Cear 97, to Mavi, Klas, and to you, Elko, who in this moment are listening to me. And a thought also to the W56s, hoping that they may change their behaviour. I embrace you all. Each night I'll pray our God and your Woa, hoping that things may change for the best. Farewell to you all.

Gianni

Some more notes:

Antonello, Mar 24, 1973

21:40. "Have you any questions? Tell me." "I've computed that your year lasts some 200 of our days. Is it correct?" "How did you get to these figures?" "It's a proportion; one among you told me that he is 36 years old, but only 20, according to our years." "No, it has been WOWIA; she usually jokes; the difference indeed consists in just a few days." "Fine. May I now have the other pictures?" "No, not yet. We'll tell you when the time comes." "Do not make me wait too long." "Don't worry." "Why were your first letters partially burnt?" "Because we could not afford the risk of delivering them in person; they have been de-materialized." "And why was my driving licence not also burnt?" "Had we used our traditional means, it would get burnt the same; going more slowly no burning takes place, because the inner structure of atoms is not modified. In the same way, if we de-materialize a disk too quickly, there is the risk that it gets hot, because of a physical principle: if you speed up a reaction, then more heat gets generated." "Is here on Earth another race coming from outer space? One with narrow and long eyes?" "Yes, they are really ferocious. We've named them SYWAS." – I repeat the name in a wrong way. "No, you are acquainted with our sound technician, YWAX; it's something like that." "SYWAS?" "Good, good. Now, forgive me, I must attend to something, there is an intruder on the ground. I'll call you later."

Fabrizio, Mar 26, 1973

YWAX phones me, asking for pictures of the "interesting" people living in Rome and around.

Antonello, Apr 2, 1073

YWAX phones me, and I tell him to phone Gianni. After a while he calls again, telling me that he has spoken with Gianni, who is going to present his own seminal liquid.

Author: I do not know whether this Gianni is the same one who just three months before had declared his will to interrupt his relationship with the CTRs.

Antonello, Apr 4, 1973

"Why do the lamps at the University transmit 73?" "Who is named 73?" "MAVI?" "Good, you're right." "Now some disagreeable questions." "Go on, I like them." "Who are the W56s?" "Really disagreeable, isn't it? Anyway I'll answer you the plain truth. We do not know exactly who they are, we are not even sure that it's they who are our enemies. Within one year from now I'll be able to be more precise." "How are you able to shut off lights from far away?" "Difficult to explain. We create an impedance in the circuit; it may be done up to 80-150" "Metres?" "No. Miles. Now I must go." "A last question; who are what we call "angels"?" "Yes, sure, the little angels. You too would be called "angels" if you'd go to people less evolved than you."

Antonello, May 5, 1973

In the afternoon, Anna, the sister of a friend of mine, sees "me" walking along Balduina St. Anna is sure it was myself, to the point that she greets it, but it doesn't answer. She has seen it from six or seven meters away; there was another person with it that she had never seen before. At that time I was home, studying with a friend of mine.

Author: a question/answer session follows between Antonello and Anna.

q: So yesterday you have seen me in the street. Where has it been?
a: Sure, I've seen you in Festo Aviano St, between the crossings with Licinio

Calvo St and Massimi St. You were going toward Massimi St. It must have been around 5 p.m.

q. Was I alone?

a. No, there was a bearded guy with you.

q. Please describe this guy.

a: A little shorter than you, beard, his hair was touching his shoulders, a slim figure. He was wearing a clear shirt and jeans; he was taking in his hands a pull-over, or something like that.

q: And how was I dressed?

a: You too in jeans, and a shirt, stripped in white and blue.

q: Can you evaluate how certain you are of what you have told me, on a scale from 1 to 10?

a: Well, if you now say that it was not you, I'd say 8 or 9.

Fabrizio, Feb 22, 1975

A certain Diel (at least, that's what I've understood) phones me from Veio. He says that the group is back again. Tomorrow Antonello and myself shall have to start a new experiment. We must go to Veio to collect the required material.

Fabrizio, Feb 23, 1975

I get to Veio at 8:45, and take a parcel in the usual place, that must be opened in the presence of Antonello. So the experiment starts.

11 a.m.: We apply the serum on our left forearms.

8 p.m.: 8 hours have elapsed; no apparent problem. At times a stiffening in the corresponding place in the other arm. May be it's just a psychological factor. Antonello feels a small pain on his left shoulder-blade. We are aware of ourselves, waiting a confirmation for the correctness of our operations. Breathing is normal. Both body temperatures at 36.7 °C.

10:30 p.m.: a phone call: "Hi" "Hi, we were wondering whether we have applied the serum correctly; we have applied it to the forearms." "Well, it's OK also there. Next Tuesday you may wash it away. You may use sodium hypochlorite. Then apply the powder, after having diluted it into pure water, distilled water is OK; apply it over your veins; an exchange must take place with tissues at first, then with your blood. It is needed to change your electro-magnetic halo." "But what's the use of it?" "To receive impulses; it will work 18-23 days later. We make use of a substance, the eosin, that you know, but do not use in the proper way. We are going to transmit from 9 to 11 p.m. It will suffice to you to sit at a table, and write making use of the alphabet we have given you. You are going to feel pulses in your cerebellum, but remain calm. We have already made a similar experiment in Spain, but it failed. If it works, we will need Sintex no more (Author: "sintex" was the name of some kind of a computer, that was needed to translate from their language into ours, and back), we'll be able to dialogue directly. Bye for now."

Antonello, Feb 25, 1975

A profound sleep. Generally feeling warm, but it disappears in the first morning hours. A slight headache. I'd like some oranges. Probably the serum oxidizes vitamins, just like antibiotics do. In the same way, Fabrizio is hungry for lemons. Maybe it may because of a lack of C vitamin. After lunch, a short lack of lucidity. As soon as possible we must ask: in what proportions the powder has to be diluted? Is it true that the serum oxidizes vitamins? How long have we to keep the second application? Is it going to last forever, or new applications will be needed? Is it possible to have a written description of the serum's operation? Are some foods or medicines contra-indicated? At times I feel very weak. I'm sure that my blood pressure is under the usual levels.

Fabrizio, Mar 8, 1975

They phone me to reassure us on the effects of the experiment. No harm derived from it, and we may go on quietly. We have done our best, they say. This has just been a first step toward a collective experiment that will take place in Veio next year.

Author: Now let me take the word again, and let me discuss a bit about the "quarrel" between the W56s and their "enemy brothers". Of course their moral differs strongly from ours, and often it is difficult to understand. I'd like to present here an episode that, in those years, has left me very perplexed. We had telephone numbers that might be used to phone our Friends; very long numbers, from 30 to 35 figures, and it is not clear how our switching units (mostly electro-mechanical at those times) might have been able to cope with them; anyway those numbers were working, nobody understands in which way.

Once I phoned the Ascoli Piceno base, looking for Sigis, and was a bit perplexed at hearing, on the other side, a CTR I knew well, and recognized at once. Taken by surprise, I just asked "Is Sigis there?", or something like that, he answered "Just one moment.", then Sigis arrived to the telephone (or whatever device they were using).

After the conversation was over, I started racking my brains: how could it be that two enemies, who were usually killing each other, were living side-by-side in the same underground facility? At first, I was not able to find an answer. Later on, while writing "Contattismi di massa", I supposed that the W56s/CTRs scenario was just a trickery performed by our Friends for some unclear purposes, therefore I put on my "conjurer" theory: we are just the recipients of a show, that is performed to our aim, but we are not allowed to enter the real stage to see how things are in truth.

Of course I was, and am, right. There is no hope for us to be sure of what we are being told, shown, or whatever. So, it is quite possible that my idea that the W56s/CTRs saga was nothing but a show may be correct. Then, while writing these chapters, I changed my previous ideas a bit. While discussing about W56 morality, and CTR morality, I realized that maybe my first perplexity was out of place. Both parties maintain that there is no war between them. Fatalities have been generated here and there, but to them the thing looks to be much less important than to us. It is a strange kind of quarrel, in which a seven years old little

89

girl has been killed in a rather brutal way, maybe just to rise some anxiety. Therefore the sharing of the same facility is not as preposterous as it may look at a first glance! Their concepts allow "enemy brothers" to live side-by-side, and trying to kill each other at the very same time. Our usual ideas simply do not apply, as in many other cases. Maybe there are indeed the W56s and the CTRs, fighting each other, but not in the way we are used to. Of course, who knows? Moreover, how could we know?

Anyway, there is a main external difference between the W56s and the CTRs. The former are a confederation of several different races, so their appearance is far from being homogeneous; not only their heights vary from tens of cm to several metres, also the colour of their skin may differ vastly from a race to another one. The CTRs, on the contrary, are much younger, therefore they are much more homogeneous, although some differences exist also among them. For instance, the "Italian Ummites" were characterized by round eyes, while other CTRs did not.

A very last note (Apr. 27, 2011): in these days I am trying to get in touch again with Fabrizio, whom I lost contact with at least some 20 years or so. I've asked common friends to help me in establishing the contact, they've got in touch with Fabrizio, but some minor problems have prevented us hearing each other, at least up to this moment. Yesterday afternoon, after some telephone calls with the friends I had asked to help me, a strange phone call arrived: some moments of background noises, then two high-pitched voices, in a singsong attitude, uttering words that I have not been able to understand. It lasted some 20-30 seconds, then the call was shut off. Who knows?

Then, to end with a smile, a cartoon drawn by one among Paolo's students:

The caption reads: "Is everybody dead, here in Veio?"

Other presences

Aside from the W56s and the CTRs, some other "alien people" were present in those years over Italy. Now I am going to summarize some of the most important.

The "Centro Studi Fratellanza Cosmica"

The group "Centre for Studies on the Cosmic Brotherhood" (CSFC) was founded about 1971 by Eugenio Siragusa (1919-2006), a Sicilian man from Niscemi (Catania, Sicily), who was employed in the local toll-house. He had conducted an uneventful life until, on March 25, 1952, everything changed abruptly when he was enveloped by a very powerful beam of light. From that time onwards he started feeling charged with a mission, but he did not realize clearly what was taking place, until, on Apr 30, 1962, on the cliffs of Monte Manfré, near the Etna volcano, he was confronted with two beings who declared they came from "outside", and confirmed that it was they who chose him to spread their messages to mankind.

He founded the CSFC that lasted until 1978, with the following logo:

Centro Studi Fratellanza Cosmica

DAL CIELO ALLA TERRA

On Nov 24, 1978, Eugenio Siragusa was charged by two American members of the group of having raped their daughter; although the charge was preposterous, he was jailed for several months. During his imprisonment, the guards often reported UFOs flying around the prison, and strange presences inside the building. Thankfully, he was finally released and on Apr 5, 1982, the law-court proclaimed his complete innocence.

The Elta-V

It is (was?) a rather unusual group of alien entities, rather shy, but nevertheless ready to enter, without permission, the Virtual Machines of other groups, obviously also mine. They had some bases in Umbria (Central Italy), one in Perugia, another one in Ponte San Giovanni (on the outskirts of Perugia). Their main interest was in Computer Music, a discipline that in those years was just starting in Italy. The main places where research was conducted on this topic were the Polytechnic of Milano, the CSELT in Torino, and the CNUCE in Pisa.

At that time I was investigating also natural language understanding by computers. For that reason, my Virtual Machine was monitoring whatever was being exchanged on the rudimentary mail system of the IBM 370, and I had written a program (named "Bestia" = "Beast") that was learning to express its ideas in a very rough English. It was what today we might call an inference machine, that is a software aimed to construct logical connections between concepts, the very first step towards understanding natural language. Of course it was written in LISP, then the only available language for Artificial Intelligence problems. Bestia's performance was rather satisfactory, its English was ugly, although improving, little by little.

Then one day I found out (or, to say better, Bestia told me), that the Elta V had made intrusions inside my Virtual Machine, of course without being invited to do so. So a little quarrel started: I often cancelled the contents of their virtual disks concerning myself, and they at times did the same. Of course I was in a superior position, because I had privileges that they didn't. But, after a while, everything settled, as if by common agreement. Then I no longer heard anything else about them.

Let me enclose here an excerpt of the conversation between Bestia and myself, when I had been told of the Elta V's interference; sorry for censoring some names (the "******" group); sentences in upper-case are from Bestia, while those in lower-case are from myself; this conversation was held under the control of a LISP program I had written to interface with Bestia)

```
is program from eltav?
YES.
what is program from eltav?
IT IS 12 PROGRAM;
IT WORK INSIDE CP; INSIDE CMS; INSIDE ******.
you know what is ******?
YES.
what is ******?
IT IS PART OF HARD DISK OF IBM/370.
              . . . . . . .
what is use of program of eltav?
IT IS PROGRAM.
what is user of program of eltav?
IT IS ELTAV.
when eltav use program of eltav?
12/12/73; 12/13/73; 12/18/73; 12/21/73; 12/28/73; 12/30/73;
01/09/74; ^C
END OF JOB BECAUSE OF ^C.
what is maximum of date of use of program of eltav?
IT IS 03/11/74.
what is minimum of date of use of program of eltav?
IT IS 12/12/73.
what is name of program of eltav that eltav use in 12/12/73?
IT IS EDIT.
what is name of next?
IT IS 12/12/73.
what is name of program of eltav that eltav use in 12/12/73?
IT IS EDIT.
what is name of next program?
IT IS CP.
what is name of next program?
IT IS LOG.
think about edit.
```

```
IT IS PROGRAM.
think about edit of eltav of 12/12/73.
DONE.
what is name of file of edit of eltav of 12/12/73?
NAME OF PROGRAM IS NOT DEFINED.
what is filename of file of edit of eltav of 12/12/73?
IT IS MONITOR.
what is filetype of file of edit of eltav of 12/12/73?
IT IS ASM370.
where is file of filename monitor, of filetype asm370, of vm
******?
IT IS IN IBM/370.
it is in ibm/370 now?
YES.
```

Some notes: ASM370 was the 370 Assembler; the ^C was a command aimed to interrupt an operation; under the CP/CMS operating system, each file had a filename and a filetype; monitor was a generic name for a program who was controlling general operations of the system, in this case an Assembler program the Elta V had written to control my operations; vm is short for Virtual Machine; LOG is a command to disconnect a vm. Please note the subtle semantic difference between "name", intended as a class of software objects, and the specific "filename", referring to a peculiar file. After all, Bestia was performing rather well!

NOTES

The CTRs

1   Later on, it resulted that the supposed caller, whom I had accused in public of having tried to kill me via subliminal suggestions, was in Rome at the time of the call (the call originated from his telephone in L'Aquila), and that there was nobody in his house when the call originated; yet the files of the telephone company show that such a call actually took place, originating in an empty house!

2   Some documents, relating to this case, have been presented in "Mass Contacts".

3   This unbelievable accident took place in July 1944; from the south the Polish Second Corps was ascending the Peninsula; the officer who ordered to start the firing against the intruder was Antoni Szachnowsky, from the Second Artillery Regiment.

The "Fratellanza Cosmica" Group

1A continuous set of curves being given, its "envelope" is a new curve that is tangent in every point to one curve of the set.

Chapter 6

Amicizia and the Alien Receptiveness Program
By
Connie Menger
Copyright 2012

<u>Author</u>: Some time ago I had the chance to get in touch with Mrs. Connie Menger, the widow of the late Howard Menger. I believe that, among other contactees in the USA, Howard's experience has been the nearest one to Amicizia, so I asked Connie to write for me a few lines in comment. She has done so, and I thank her so much for that. Here is her text:

Friendship is a kindness directed toward another human being (and all other life forms when encountered) and a feeling of esteem, good will and caring: A willingness to comfort, counsel and help whenever possible. Friendship involves supporting another during difficult times. It also forgives weaknesses and flaws in the individual. Friendship also knows when to step back and allow one to make their own choices and take responsibility for the effect. Yet, friendship offers sympathy and empathy and a desire for what is best for the other. It is a mutual understanding and compassion and emotional support. It also involves intellectual honesty in pointing out the perceived flaws and actions of the other without judgment. Forgiveness and trust in one another is friendship.

You say, Stefano, that the W56's are totally friendly to us. Does that include the above description of friendship? You indicate that it is necessary for one to be a friend to himself/herself before one can be a friend to another. To them, friendship is both vital because they live on it: group consciousness – (Uredda) of friendship is impossible to refute, from a philosophical point of view. They can't help but being friends to everybody. It is not a choice, but one concept deeply rooted into their morality. Even their hardware is permeated with concepts to a point (they maintain) that their machines would destroy themselves were they not able to avoid damaging somebody.

The reason they feel so beneficently disposed toward their "enemy brothers" and even offer the facilities of their bases when requested – might be due to the fact that in some way they feel responsible for the CTR's and to us and perhaps are obliged to help them and us! They (W56's) obviously believe in the theory of unity: that we are all One; "I am everybody, and everybody is me". Therefore, friendship, as a group consciousness actually helps increase the Uredda of good will to one another which is, I believe, the creative aid to all living units. They have been here for thousands and perhaps millions of years. They explored and colonized our planet Earth; or is it *their* planet?

Some of their cosmological information rather surprised me: "They are very ancient people who have arrived at the highest levels of scientific knowledge, morality and of consciousness". "Some of them actually originated here aeons ago, so they are more terrestrial than we are". They believe that in the whole universe life originated only on fifty planets which they call the "Mother Planets". Our Earth was one of the Mother Planets. This last statement puzzles me!

In chapter five of our book, *"Threads of Light to You"*, the Alien Receptiveness Program, we state that there are galaxies, nebulae, stars, planets, visible and invisible without end. Carl Sagan (American astronomer, deceased) declared that there was the possibility of millions and millions of life-supporting planets orbiting other star systems and also possibly populated with life forms. Just by inferential logic, one can assume that life permeates all the cosmos. There are beginnings, evolution, dissolution, and then new beginnings – neverending.

My assumption is that the template for *Homo sapiens sapiens* already existed and was brought here by others. The evolutionary process had already begun on Earth and at a certain point sentient, intelligent beings arrived on our glove and gave our humanity a boost forward and upward.

These ancient astronauts, who participated in our genetic pool when they visited and colonized this planet aeons ago, may have a very special interest in our welfare. We are their progeny. Their blood may run through our veins and their DNA may be coded into our brain cells, pushing us on to more advanced technology; and now, more urgently, a revival of spiritual and moral values.

According to Howard and others, these ancestral non-terrestrials have love and a great concern for our great and unique humanity. He spoke of their great compassion for us. When in their presence, one feel like being in the presence of a loved one or old friend. He noted, also, they were humble and respectful to him (Howard) and kind. with a delightful sense of humor and honour for who Howard was in their presence. That surprised Howard. He was the one in awe of them! With that, Howard knew that the ancestral non-terrestrials are our benefactors and family.

We, who are born of the stars. developed by life's evolutionary processes and educated by trial and error, are now ready to take a step forward in our rightful position as members of the galactic family. The responsibility to change the global condition is solely ours. We cannot relegate our responsibility to gods, goddesses, demons, lords or any other pseudo-supernatural force.

We, as a planetary world community, through the United Nations are just beginning to cooperate together. It is not a perfect world forum and it can be improved greatly. This world organization, represented by all sovereign nations on Earth must take a strong moral stand against global hunger, drought, flooding, air, soil, and water pollution, abuse of human rights and the continuation of barbaric wars.

Responsible people in this 21st Century must confront the man-made problems of our home planet. People-power can put pressure and focus on lazy, complacent governments to change from archaic, tyrannical political systems to genuine representative, cooperative governments of the world. The process of eventually informing the world's people of non-terrestrial interaction: Amicizia and Alien Receptiveness with our humanity has been a very difficult one. It may be that we have been mentally and physically quarantined from such knowledge for too long and it was necessary to initiate a long, slow process.

The impact of an alien culture upon Earth's diverse cultures would be very disruptive. The superimposition of an advanced culture upon a less-developed one has always been disadvantageous to the lesser one. However, diffusion of knowledge and enculturation at a slower rate could be acceptable and beneficial. You would have to understand that the "alien" political ruling hierarchy, their social and spiritual life could be entirely different from ours (see SB's description of W56's moral and spiritual code of ethics).

There are also psychological ramifications associated with the impact of an advanced alien culture melding with our own, even when an individual is gradually conditioned to meeting with an alien. There is the possibility that the initial cultural shock experienced could mentally disturb the individual. The non-terrestrial culture may be so far ahead of ours that we may be in awe of them and become temporarily alienated from our own kind and the rest of humanity and prefer to form an allegiance with our new-found powerful alien friends. We could fluctuate between naïve reverence for the superior aliens and with our natural human suspicions of their ultimate motivation. This could result in the internal conflict of our yearning for the non-terrestrial culture and what it could offer our humanity and the abandonment of our own race in favor of the aliens.

You can understand why the non-terrestrials, even those who have lived amongst us for thousands of years, are very cautious about revealing themselves. We, now, in this 21st Century, need to know if there are others out there in the Multiverse. Some of the information has been coming out more and more over the years. Alien visitors, and those descendants of the ancient astronauts have contacted certain individuals in higher levels of governments, and have assisted in preparing the people. They have done this by isolated, physical (or holographic) contact cases. In other instances, electronic transmissions were used. Howard was assigned to bury in several locations "black boxes" for the transmission of the frequency pulses to be picked up by individual brain waves. The waves were neither harmful nor hypnotic. When we raise our consciousness to the level of true caring for all humans and Mother Earth, then we are ready for the next step in evolution.

The Alien Receptiveness Program depends very heavily upon humankinds' collective consciousness. A non-terrestrial ambassador to the United Nations from an alien civilization light years away could find it very difficult to approach planetary leaders when many of our nations are still engaged in tribal warfare, terrestrial rights, and the inequitable distribution of our natural resources. The alien ambassador would soon discover our tragic capacity to poison our bodies, minds, soil, water and air. How would such an alien ambassador approach us? With a great deal of caution and concern, or not at all. With great wisdom and understanding, the ambassador would know that we Earthly humans have the seeds of light deep within us and can change and evolve. Such is the depth of their love and friendship.

The Alien Receptiveness Program has been going on for a long time and seems to be accelerating. It is strongly believed by top UFO researchers that alien representatives have already contacted head of state. (see SB's "Mass Contacts"). It also has been suggested that because some non-terrestrials who are closest to us biologically, have started again an inbreeding process. This seems to be the most sensible way to prepare Earth's present humanity and prevent hostilities.

When we finally are made aware of this plan then our consciousness is ready for the next step which is this: we will globally interact with our galactic family in direct proportion to our constructive concern for all humanity.

Long live Amicizia!

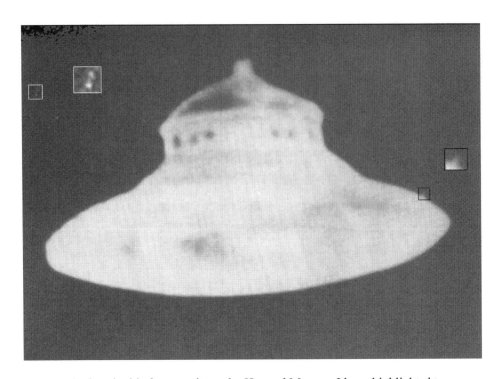

Author: in this famous picture by Howard Menger, I have highlighted two "satellite disk" probes visible, a concept I believe I was the first to speak about ("Mass Contacts", pg. 288).

Chapter 7

Their Technology

As I have already stated in "Mass Contacts", the technology of our Friends is almost indistinguishable from magic. Yet, at least in a very small part, it is some way understandable from our poor point of view. Very seldom did they explain something; most of the times they were making use of Maieutics; the word (from classical Greek) refers to Socrates, whose mother was a midwife, and it is meant to denote a didactical strategy, where a concept is not blatantly exposed to pupils, but they are led to discover it by themselves.

Bases

One of the most startling achievements of their technology is their ability to open huge underground bases, without anybody noticing anything; their major base under Italy, a very deep one, is in excess of 300 km long and 100 km wide, with a ceiling 300 m high! What is interesting is that this huge base is not meant as living quarters, but just to host their machinery, that are necessary to their operations. Smaller bases, at lower depths, are hosting living quarters; they are very little in comparison, from some tens of metres to some hundreds of metres long.

These cavities are not achieved by excavation; it would be foolish; where to carry, for instance, the material taken away? On the contrary they are obtained by opening the earth, and pushing it sideways, in order to get a cavity.

Usually there are no fixed entrances; when needed, a passage is opened, and closed immediately after it has been used. Only in limited cases, small bases near to the surface had fixed passages, often concealed in the most fanciful ways, whose logic was difficult to understand! For instance, in Pescara, an entrance was concealed behind a cupboard inside a public office. Another one was disguised as a manhole cover in a street; in this last case, an unexpected conclusion: during refurbishing works on the road, as that manhole was obviously not listed among the "official" ones, it was unduly buried under a new side-walk!

A couple of W56s were usually living in the basement of an old deserted villa, Villa De Riseis, near to the Pescara river:

One of them was Giancarlo's best friend, Itaho, a gentleman 2.5 metres tall.

A cooking problem

Maieutics was their common way to export some of their knowledge. I remember that, one night, one of our Friends was having dinner at Giancarlo's [1] (one of the Amicizia group); when Giancarlo's wife was cooking, a typical accident took place, a rather common one while frying something, and Giancarlo made the usual comment one utters in such cases. Our Friend calmly said that Giancarlo was wrong, and invited him to examine more closely what had taken place. Next afternoon Giancarlo came to my house (100 km far away!) and told me what had taken place. Thankfully my wife was not home, in that moment, so I was able to re-create the accident, and had to convince myself that what is commonly believed is absolutely false! From that moment a 15 year long period of experiments started, during which I asked advice from the FIAT Nuclear Division [2], but also from MIT and from the Novosibirsk University. Nobody has been able to tell exactly what really takes place: it looks that the energy balance is violated, that more energy is generated than the amount is poured into. What I have been able to ascertain, by myself, when first I was confronted with the problem, is that huge quantities of hydrogen are freed in the process, it is still not clear in what way.

When I first asked help from the FIAT Nuclear Division, there was an engineer, a friend of mine, working there, so I got in touch with him, explaining my problem, but he flatly did not believe me, so I offered to make a practical demonstration, and he agreed to be present. So one night, in Turin, we had supper together, then he drove me to the Musiné (a big mountain on the West of Turin), in order to look for a secluded place to make the experiment. It was a moonless night. We arrived to a clearing inside a wood; he parked his car on its edge, and I went out and put my device in the centre of the clearing, then switched the device on; it was usually taking ten seconds or so to start operating, and so it happened that night; I had the time to get back to the car, then, all of a sudden, a huge flame burst out from my device, a very white flame, some 30 meters tall, with a tremendous roar! It was the hydrogen being generated that had been ignited, and was happily burning in the open air.

What we had not realized was that the place was far from being deserted: it was full of young couples, inside their cars, looking for their own privacy; when the flame erupted, of course everybody got terrified, and in a few moments we heard motors starting to run, saw lights being switched on, then cars fleeing away! Shortly the place was really deserted, with only the two of us, laughing at the incident, and my device that, having run out of "fuel", had quietly extinguished itself.

More often than not, our experiments with the W56s technologies resulted in amusing situations; the Musiné case has been, maybe, the funniest one, even more so if one remembers that this mountain has been considered, since ever, a magic environment, where strange things take place! For sure our experiment has added something to this legend. Before the Musiné experiment, Giancarlo and I made a similar attempt, inside the garage of my house, in L'Aquila; it was a usual garage, say a room five meters or so long, three meters wide; on the walls I had screwed some shelves. As usual, I had put my device on the ground, in the centre of the room, and thankfully Giancarlo and I had been staying near to the exit; when the flame erupted, it started toward the ceiling, then it expanded, flowing down along the walls, just to close on the ground around my device, and destroying it. In the meantime Giancarlo and I had jumped outside, just in time! The wooden shelves were burning, and plaster was falling down in pieces...

Another time we made a really dangerous experiment, testing a device I had built according to their technology; the problem was that it was something very similar to a weapon, that could act far away. We made all we could in order that its results were to happen in a secluded and deserted area, and the experiment seemed to have worked. In the following days the worldwide press started enquiring about what had taken place. The experiment had been conducted in Giancarlo's house, in Pescara, then I had got back to my place, in L'Aquila. The next afternoon I received a visit from an Austrian general, who was engaged with the UTI [3]. He told me, harshly, that we had been foolish in testing such an object, that there had been dangers beyond what we could have imagined, and prevented us from trying anything like that in the future! Of course he was right...

Scout craft

Some general concepts

Before going on, what will follow derives from my untidy enquiries to the W56s, and to other people inside Amicizia. Therefore it is far from being complete, and many answers are missing. In those years I was mainly interested in the Adamski-type scout, so I enquired mainly on it, although it is not one of the most frequently used devices. I received also extensive descriptions on two other types, that I am going to briefly summarize at the end of this chapter. Any way, before starting to describe the general outline of a typical flying saucer, I believe that it is better to get rid of some concepts that UFOlogists seem not to have yet understood.

First, scouts are not meant to be transportation devices, or, to say it better, this is not their primary use; the W56s use different means to move from a place to another, mainly their over-alls. Scout are typically mobile labs, even weapons, not aircraft.

Second, scouts are mainly made of pure iron, that's why they weigh so much; of course there are pieces made from different alloys, but the main structure is iron. The various pieces they are made of are not kept together using screws, soldering, or the like: there is a peculiar field that connects all the pieces together; when this field is switched off, the pieces fall apart.

Third, there is nothing like hangars where scouts are stored when they are not in use; thanks to their technology, the W56s ask their machines and their robots to built a new scout, when one is needed; each time it is designed in accordance with the mission it is meant to achieve; the construction process lasts a couple of hours. When the mission is over, the scout is simply dismantled. That's why we see so many different types of craft: each one of them has been built having in mind the peculiar operation it had been designed for.

Scouts are not even meant to be always manned devices: many of them are totally automatic in their operations. Then too, scouts are not always flying saucers: we may go from aniae, less than a millimetre long, to craft several km long! We may even find scouts that are not material objects at all, but only physical properties imposed upon a small amount of space!

Consider for instance the following picture that has been taken by a small plane flying over the harbour of Pescara, in May, 1988:

If you look carefully at the top of it, just left of its centre, you'll find a transparent "bubble" that alters the colours of the objects behind it (the original picture is in colour, and these effects are more evident); in all evidence, by chance, a "virtual" device has been caught by the photographer!

Their types of propulsion are varied, spanning from pure aerodynamics to magneto-hydro-dynamics, to electro-static, or electro-dynamic effects, to electro-magnetic effects, to extremely complex sets of fields, generating relativistic effects. These are what we call flying saucers, and flying cigars. I must state right now that I do not know too much about the latter, because my attention has been mainly focused on flying saucers. Of course there are also differently shaped objects, triangles, squares, cubes, spheres, and the like; once again, I must confess that I know almost nothing about shapes that cannot be expressed with quartic equations (that is, fourth-degree equations in x, y, z.).

Usually (but not always) the power source is an internal one. In flying saucers it consists in three, or more, objects, similar to cigarettes in shape and dimensions, but much heavier; they are called mother cells, and produce high frequency electric power through their extremities. I never enquired in-depth, because the principle they work on is at a level of molecular engineering, far beyond our capabilities, but it looks that the intensity of electrical current flowing through the poles is astonishing, to the point that one wanders how such a huge amount of current may flow through such small surfaces. I do not know. What I know is that it is necessary to have always something connected, that absorbs the energy they generate, otherwise they could explode. A scout is never switched off, even in the rare cases when it is in stand-by. As they are short-lived, no real maintenance is required, but, indeed, thanks to their superior technology, no maintenance is required even in the long-living inter-stellar or even inter-galactic craft that they use for their major journeys.

For these latter craft, some considerations must be made: first, their propulsive system is based upon heavily distorting the space-time geometry; it requires awful quantities of energy, that, like a kind of perpetual-motion machine, the W56s are able to extract from the distortion itself! Although it does not make too much sense to speak of speeds and times in such circumstances, it must be noted that there is no practical limit to speed, except the rapidity with which the internal computers are able to interact with the surrounding environment. That is the only practical limit, because operations depend heavily on it. Anyway, the "speeds" that they are able to achieve are beyond our wildest dreams! As a lover of physics, I must state once again that in such circumstances speaking about speeds and distances does not make any sense at all, but, speaking at large, I might identify a speed as the ratio between a distance and the time required to negotiate it (it is absolutely mistaken from a physical point of view, but it may make some sense in a gross way), and, speaking this way, speeds may be reached that are billions of times the speed of light (and, of course, without any relativistic distortion)! In "Mass Contacts" I have hinted at some of the physics principles that sit behind such capabilities; of course, they are well beyond our present reach.

Getting to more "mundane" devices, a trip to Mars may last ten hours or so, or even less; of course the distance between Earth and Mars changes from time to time, but the duration of the flight sits entirely on what the pilot has decided, and in most cases it is not the most important factor to take into account. We are too tied to our aircraft, with fuel consumption being the most important parameter, therefore we are not apt to understand the real problems in flights when fuel consumption is usually no problem at all. Later on I'll present an experiment I asked the permission to organize, whose results, at first, look unsatisfactory from our point of view, but that, I've been explained, suite perfectly their needs. It is extremely true that, speaking with the W56s, most of our points of view must be dramatically changed.

General description of a flying saucer

As I have said, there are no two flying saucers identical to one another, because of the reasons they have been built for. Anyway, generally speaking, most of them share similar aspects. They are obviously circular in plant (at times elliptical), with diameters spanning from, say, 3 metres, to 500 metres and even more. Most of them have a single central cabin (the one I've named "Twin scout" has actually two different cabins). The ratio between the diameters of the outer rim and that of the central cabin depends on several factors, and may range from, say, 1.2 to 10 or even more. Also the ratio between outer diameter and height depends on several factors, and may range from, say, 0.05 to 3; so, we may have extremely "flat" disks, or objects that we would not name "disks", because their height is much more than their diameter.

In some cases there is no central cabin, but a hole. These are really peculiar devices, most of the time built to host nobody inside.

Operating principles depend on the mission: most disks are EM devices, some are purely electro-static devices. In my description, I'll focus mainly on EM devices.

No fixed port-holes or doors exist; when one is needed, it is created, as is anything else inside the main cabin. Iron may be made transparent at will, one way or both ways, so it is possible to create a "porthole" (that is to render transparent a portion of the outer surface) at will. It must be said that, most of times, it makes no sense to look outside, because the outer disk prevents one from looking down; it too might be rendered partially transparent, but that would interfere with the propulsion.

A major problem, while flying low over ground, is that a scout encounters severe problems in acquiring information about its immediate environments, therefore usually small devices are ejected, in such circumstances, that monitor the local situation, and transmit these data back to the central computer on board. One of the reasons I believe the first Billy Meier's pictures to be genuine is that I've enlarged them, revealing the usual cluster of small objects around the major disks, and I've been the first one in speaking of this peculiar problem! Surely enough, Meier himself is not aware of it.

The control panel of a small scout is a rectangular area sitting wherever the pilots decides; it is very small, say 50 cm wide and 35 cm high; it is a touch panel, and at any given moment it presents only the information required, and the commands available, in that situation. That means that its contents change continuously, both because of a decision by the central computer, or upon a request by the pilot. Commands are activated by putting a finger on them.

It is theoretically possible to drive "by thought", but it is rather cumbersome, and therefore it is seldom applied. It is also possible to drive without the help of the central computer, but it is extremely difficult, therefore it usually takes place only when a new pilot gets trained. The typical commands that a pilot may want to enter to go from a place to another are: climb to a certain altitude, then decide where he wants to go (either selecting from a list, or entering the name of a place, or entering the name of an "anchor" – more later on about this concept), then select the time required to get to the selected spot; eventually, adding some details about how the flight must take place. And that's all!

Wandering around lazily is a totally different matter, usually useless if not with the aim of being seen; once again the pilot may choose among a certain set of possibilities the computer already knows, because it has been designed for that particular operation. Either the pilot may decide to drive "hands on", letting the computer to take care of other duties, or, rather foolishly, the pilot may ask the computer, moment after moment, for what he wants the craft to perform; this last way of operation is totally silly, because it requires a huge amount of inputs.

Anyway, that's almost all about using a scout just for flying! Piloting one of our aircraft is a much more complicated matter. There are some minor operative details that I have not entered into, like letting oneself be recognized by the computer (not everybody is entitled to drive a scout), managing environmental conditions, and the like, but, again, each operation consists in selecting an option from a list. For instance, for most scouts, it is better not to land, but remain floating some tens of cm above the target, in order to avoid heavy exchanges of power. There are several different options to choose from. An actual landing (getting in touch with the target) is a rather complicated problem, that is usually deferred to the computer.

I have never piloted a scout, but know some people who actually did, and they tell me that everything is quite easy, if the computer is taking charge, much more difficult if it has been excluded.

About anchors (or fixes), they are some way similar to the VORs of our general aviation, a kind of radio-homing devices, although working on totally different principles. It is possible to create an anchor on a certain point, at a certain height, give it a name, and from that moment on it will be available to all scouts, because the local computer will transmit this information to a central computer that will make it available to other scouts, if required to. A possibility whose use I never fully understood consists in being able to move an anchor.

Interior description

Quite easy: nothing at all! For the small scouts, just imagine a round room, say 4 or 5 meters across and two meters high, or so, with absolutely nothing in it! Scouts (when manned from inside) are piloted making use of a small control panel (it depends on the various types of craft), that is a kind of touch-screen. Differently from our to-day touch-screens, in their case it may be generated wherever one likes to: typically there is always one already present somewhere around the outer wall (remember that a scout cannot be switched off, so it is always in function), but it may be displaced at will, who knows why, since a position looks to have the same effects than another one. Moreover, the panel changes dynamically, offering in every moment only the information, and the commands, that have sense in that particular situation. Therefore it is even easier to manage than the controls of one of our Pipers (I am a bit preposterous in that, because it is not so true; forgive me!).

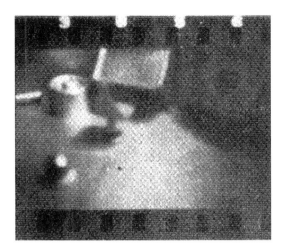

I must remember that things are not always as easy as that; for instance, two of the books by Alberto Perego [4] present pictures shot by Giancarlo, probably in 1957, of the inside of a small flying saucer ("small", because its occupants were really very short) that had landed in the whereabouts of Francavilla (South of Pescara); these pictures show a more conventional structure, with one seat in front of a big control panel, with two massive objects at its sides, whose use is difficult to imagine.

Another picture from the same series, or another one similar, shown in public here for the first time, is the following one:

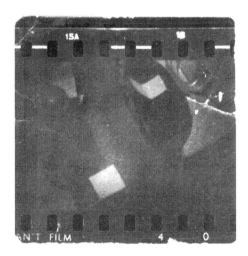

Sorry for the poor quality of these two images; the first one has been scanned from one of Perego's books, the second one had been kept for years by Giancarlo inside his wallet, without any particular care, until he decided to present me with it;

109

therefore it was not preserved very well; anyway, on its left, there is something round that might be the head or helmet of one of its occupants.

The white line on the right, apparently on the top of some kind of table, is the trace of a folding in the picture itself (a picture that I still keep in my files).

Architect Ernesto Lacalle is a friend of mine from Buenos Aires, with very good expertise in photo-cameras and the like. Studying the pictures present in Perego's books, he has been able not only to recognize the kind of cameras used in the three different occasions, but also the focal length of their lenses and the diameters of the cabins!

He has also created some synthetic reconstructions of the inside; with his permission, here I present one of them:

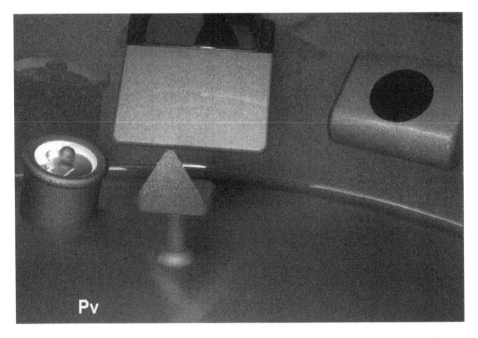

In this image, reconstructed from a blurred Perego's picture, we may see a really large panel, plus some unknown instruments on its sides. An environment totally different from what I had been told of, but, as I have stated elsewhere, no two flying saucers are similar to one another, so probably there must have been some reasons for this peculiar architecture.

Ernesto Lacalle has been able to ascertain that three different cameras have been used to take these pictures, with different focal lengths, one of which was of an out-of-date Japan make. Again with his permission, I enclose here his conclusions (in their original Castilian form):

Efectivamente hay dos fotografías (números 3 y 5) que fueron tomadas con una cámara de formato Japonés (24 mm x 32 mm) usando un lente de distancia focal de 28mm

Todas las fotografías publicadas restantes fueron tomadas con una cámara de formato Occidental (24 mm x 36 mm) y un lente normal de 50 mm

La fotografía Inédita (numero 11) fue tomada con una cámara de formato Occidental y un lente de 135 mm.

Las imágenes en el archivo numero 12, son nuevos puntos de vista que he elegido para mostrar el espacio completo, usando un lente de 28mm en formato Occidental.

Los archivos panorámicos QuickTime muestran unas vistas interactivas de los dos interiores.

Este es un caso interesante, ya que si ambas naves fueron construidas por una misma civilización y considerando la forma de fabricación, es lógico que hayan utilizado el mismo diseño, aunque deban adaptarlo a los diferentes tamaños de sus ocupantes.

Here is the translation:

Indeed there are two pictures (nos. 3 and 5) that have been taken using a Japan made camera (24 x 32 mm), and a focal length of 28 mm.

All the other pictures have been taken with a Western camera (24 x 36 mm), and a focal length of 50 mm.

The picture never published before (no. 11) has been taken with a Western camera, and a focal length of 135 mm.

The images in the file no. 12 have been generated from viewpoints that I have chosen in order to be able to show the whole space, referring to a 28 mm lens, Western format.

The QuickTime panoramic files show interactively the interiors of the two crafts.

It's an interesting case because, if both craft have been designed by a single civilization, considering their shapes it's obvious that they are similar to one another, although different in dimensions, to adapt them to the heights of their occupants.

Getting back to the most general structure, the position of the control panel is nevertheless important, because it constitutes the central point of the reference system of the craft (that, therefore, is NOT on its axis). If one wishes, a seat may be generated from the floor in front of the panel; other seats may be extracted from the floor wherever one likes. Moreover, other control panels, devoted to other purposes, may be generated anywhere; remember that a scout is not meant primarily as a transportation device; it may be used this way, but its principal scopes are totally different; therefore other control panels are normally in use. In a case that is going to be discussed later on, the central computer had kindly generated a small display on which, every other minute, the present geographic coordinates of the craft were presented, that an operator duly copied on a portable typewriter, sitting on the floor, with the typewriter on the floor beside him.

No portholes: if one likes, partial areas of the outside wall, or all of it, may be rendered transparent, in many different ways: transparent when looking from inside outwards and not the other way; or both ways: transparent to certain frequencies and not to others; and so on. In the same way, there is no door: when necessary, one may be generated wherever one likes. No pressurization: because of its propulsion criteria, a scout, even in the open space, is always surrounded by an envelope of atmosphere, therefore, if a door is opened while in the empty space, the internal atmosphere would get out at such a low speed that it would need weeks, or so, to get empty. Of course, if necessary, it may be ordered to get emptied within seconds, even in the presence of an outside atmosphere.

Structure: the ones I know of are made of simple iron; the "pieces" they are made of are not screwed, nor soldered together; they are kept together thanks to a force field. When a scout is no longer in use, it is dismantled, and the first stage of this operation consists in stopping this field, so that the scout literally falls in pieces to the ground. By the way, the W56s do not keep scouts in hangars, or the like: when they need one, they instruct a computer to build a new craft, according to what they have in mind to do. Therefore there is no sense at all in trying to build a list of different types of craft: aside from general principles of operations, each scout is a new model, from every point of view; of course, statistically speaking, certain shapes tend to be more frequent, but that is just a statistical effect.

Lights: just as inside their bases, it's the air itself that is made luminous, there is no concentrated light source; this generates peculiar effects on shadows that I have not quite understood, nor have I bothered to enquire. Moreover, inside a craft, its pilot may ask the computer to generate a "measuring device" that consists of all the air inside the cabin getting coloured in different hues, to monitor external fields; colours, intensity, scales and the like are dependent on the request, and may be changed at will.

Bells

"Bells" is the common name given to flying saucer scouts, both by Adamski, by Williamson, and by the W56s (in Italian its equivalent is "Campane").

Although I have already said that usually no two scouts are identical to each other, some general outlines may be described. The first one is that Adamksi's bells look to be squatter than those of the W56s; this is a general drawing of the Adamski-like bell:

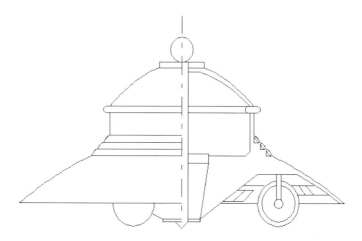

The height to diameter ratio is around 0.6; this second image refers to a typical W56 bell:

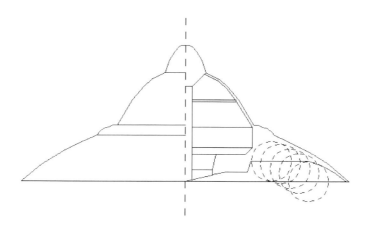

It may be seen that proportions are slightly different: the height to diameter ratio is around 0.4; moreover, usually the mechanism to extend/retract the three spheres under the disk behaves in a different way: in the Adamski bell, the spheres get up and down vertically, parallel to the scout axis; in W56s devices there is also a radial movement.

The following image is a computer-generated synthetic image of an Adamski-like bell, in the version used by the W56s:

Operating principles

Of course, what follows is but a very rough outline of the operating principles of a bell. I believe that most of them may be understood, but in some case our technology is not able to duplicate similar effects. I am summarizing my notes, because their content would be too technical to the general reader, and also because I believe that mankind is not yet ready to receive some of the concepts involved.

The three spheres under the main disk are hollow (as in the previous drawings), and filled with high pressure nitrogen; there is an internal radial magnetic field that forces nitrogen into a doughy state, in order to increase its density.

The ring on the top of the tower is rotating, like the two lower ones; the topmost and lowest rings rotate in the same direction, the intermediate one in the opposite direction. In some cases the two lower rings are connected to the central column, each one via four plugs; in this case, each plug contains a mother battery, amounting to eight altogether. In other craft the lower rings are either held in periphery by mechanical devices, or are held in place via local magnetic fields.

The top ring is a torus, composed by alternate disks of conductive and insulating material, perpendicular to the circular axis of the torus, as in the following image. The two lower rings are made mainly of cobalt and nickel.

In the circle where the outer disk meets the tower, there are three circular, co-axial cavities, with decreasing diameters, made of insulating material, one under the other. Looking from outside, they are what look to be three rings at the base of the tower.

Ultrasonic pumps get the nitrogen out from the spheres, and send it inside these tubes, then into the spheres again; the circulating directions alternate top down. In general (but not always), the rotating directions are as follows:

Top ring - clockwise
first tube - anti-clockwise
second tube - clockwise
third tube- anti-clockwise
first ring under the disk - anti-clockwise
second ring - clockwise

The two rings under the disk generate a strong electrostatic field; this field gets contorted around the general axis of symmetry, because the top ring is made of alternating conductive and insulating substances; the spatial distribution of conductivity gets contorted because of the rotation of this ring. The lines of force of the electrostatic field, forced to generate equi-potential surfaces in the conductive areas of this ring, roll up around the axis of symmetry.

This process does not get to its limit; on the contrary, it reaches a stable situation quickly, with its lines of force rotating and licking the outside walls of the tower. That is why the external surface is extremely smooth: any roughness would get wiped away by this rotating field.

In the meantime, the insulating disks composing this ring get charged with electrostatic fields whose intensity is increasing, up to the point that a corona effect takes places, to get rid of the excess charge. That's why this ring is usually lit in a bluish hue.

The nitrogen flowing at high speed inside the three tubes intersects the electrostatic lines of force, so that it gets locally transformed into a plasma, with the generation of a strong magnetic field.

Let's examine the electrostatic lines of force (leaving torsion apart); they tend to converge to the top of the central column, to the three rings, then to the bottom of the central column; the two lower rings participate in different ways: the second ring is shielded by the presence of the disk and of the lower ring, therefore it does not participate to the distortion of the field; the lower ring has the only effect of enlarging the field itself, that gets through the central column, closes on the tubes, then re-enters the central column through its lower extremity, as in the drawing.

Because of the rotation of the electrostatic field, inside the central column a magnetic field is generated, that rotates in the opposite direction. But, contrary of what we are used to, the two fields are not mutually orthogonal to each other; there is a distribution of different angles between electrical and magnetic fields, that I have named the "declination field" (as it has often been the case, names chosen by earthlings were widely used, and I may say that, speaking about bells, my own terminology entered at once into use).

The mean value of the declination field is the cause of a local gravitational field, whose barycentre is located on the axis of symmetry, roughly at the height of the lower ring.

Campo gravitazionale

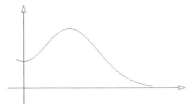

A local effect ensures: the gravitational field intensity starts increasing with its distance from its origin; then it starts lowering down, tending to get null at an infinite distance. Things are designed so that the intensity of this field remains practically constant inside the main cabin.

This means that where this artificial field reaches it maximum (usually at some distance from the craft), there is a strong force present, that tends to pull everything towards the craft itself. As its gradient (spatial derivative) is very strong, an aircraft flying by could be destroyed simply because different areas would be subjected to extremely different pushes.

Because of this design, if this field gets activated immediately (a gross piloting mistake), occupants feel a kind of a jerk, due to the immediate substitution of the natural gravitational field with the artificial one. The standard procedure requires about one minute and a half before exchanging these fields. That's why, when they take off, these craft at first get just some feet above the ground, may be oscillating laterally like a falling leaf, while an eventual observer on the ground feels the fields increasing. When a balance is reached, the bell starts away.

Again because of the distribution of the gravitational field, one can realize, looking carefully, that the floor is not flat, but slightly convex, so that the pull is always orthogonal to the floor.

As is typical with all of the W56s technology, so also with bells: each component performs several different functions at the same time. The three spheres, for instance, tend to get charged electro-statically: this charge is used to drive the lower rings to their operating speed. For this reason, the external surface of the spheres is made of an insulating material (iron!). If the pilot, after a long flight, wants to land, it is better that he does so after retracting the spheres; this way only the outer rim of the main disk discharges, and the effects are greatly reduced.

The main disk surface is made in cobalt/magnesium; it is crossed by induced currents, that generate heating, due to the Joule effect. Because of the high frequency, a skin effect takes place, so that heating is maximum at the base of the tower, and lowest at the disk's rim.

While a bell is hovering, the difference of potential between it and the ground is totally random, because it depends on the history of the flight, but it may reach several hundreds of thousands of volts, with a negligible internal resistance (due to the materials constituting the main disk). Therefore it is extremely hazardous to touch a hovering bell while keeping one's feet on the ground, and so it is not easy at all to enter a bell, or disembark from it! Of course, the W56s over-alls are devices able to overcome such problems, but for an earthling things were not as easy as that!

The dome on the top of the tower is externally covered with insulated material; strangely enough, this insulated material is again iron, in a very peculiar allotropic state! Almost the whole external skin of a bell (but the main disk) is made of iron, an insulating variety of this metal.

The topmost sphere is made of graphite. It is crossed by an extremely strong electrical flux, therefore it typically gets incandescent, with a red hue. By the way, were this sphere missing, the electrical field could not open itself, so that a magnetic **tress** would ensue, a **tress** actually able to open matter in front of itself. It is the very same mechanism they use to open their bases, and the entrance corridors when needed; a similar mechanism is contained inside the small disk that at time they wear over their breast; in this case, it is meant obviously to be a weapon.

Let's get back to our fields, and let's define as local declination the difference between a right angle and the angle between electrical and magnetic fields, in every point around the bell. The following images depict qualitatively the declination field, both as lines of force and as equi-potential surfaces.

The declination field is like a three-bladed propeller; in perspective it looks like the following drawing:

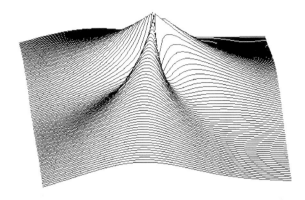

There are three maxima very near to the symmetry axis, but distinct from it; this distance, and its phase, are controlled by the pilot.

Because of the high values near to the axis, a perspective representation is not the best one to give an idea of the field. The following drawing represents its equipotential lines:

Linee equipotenziali del campo di declinaz.

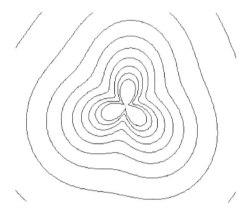

We may see that the blades are short, radially, and so the local field gets more deformed between a blade and another. Of course, a three-lateral symmetry is present. This field, after a sharp increase, tends to get null at an infinite distance; it rotates with a frequency of some tens Hertz.

The beating between the EM generated field, and the declination field generates a second rotating declination field; in this case the declination is between the frequencies of the EM field and those of the "propeller-like" declination field. I've named this second field the "phase field". The main frequency of this beat field generates, so to say, the "push" that moves the bell; it is not indeed a push, because it is a non-inertial effect, deriving from the interaction among the local gravitational field, and the generated electrical, magnetic, EM, and synergic fields.

The beat field among the four main fields decreases of course with distance; its general outline (in two dimensions- it is indeed a three dimensional phenomenon) is as follows:

Campo di battimento

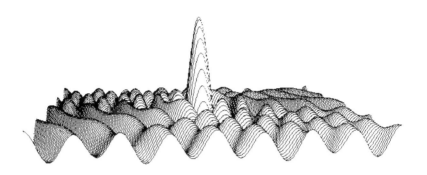

Its equi-potential lines are like this:

Linee equipotenziali del campo di battimento

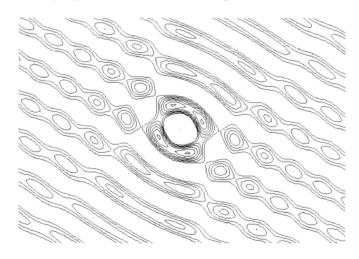

Its simplified equation, putting together polar and Cartesian coordinates, is of the kind:

$$\frac{d(dy/dx)}{d\varphi} = 0$$

We may re-write it, passing to pure polar coordinates, with the simplification:

$$\frac{dy}{dx} = \frac{tg\varphi + \rho \cdot \dfrac{d\varphi}{d\rho}}{1 - \rho \cdot \dfrac{d\varphi}{d\rho} \cdot tg\varphi} =$$

$$= \frac{\rho + \dfrac{d\rho}{d\varphi} \cdot tg\varphi}{\dfrac{d\rho}{d\varphi} - \rho \cdot tg\varphi}$$

It looks that a particular integral may be:

$$\varphi = c \cdot \frac{\sin \rho}{\rho},$$

from which this image derivates:

It has been generated by this program:

```
PROGRAM Field1
REAL(4)       a, c, fi, rho, rhomin, rhomax, x, y
INTEGER(2)    i, ic1, ic2, i1, i2, j, k, k2, k3
CHARACTER(1) answ
COMMON /fattore/ a
DATA k2/2/, k3/3/, rhomin/60.0/, rhomax/100.0/
DATA ic1/0/, ic2/2500/
a = 4.0
i1 = HFIX(rhomin * 10.0)
i2 = HFIX(rhomax * 10.0)
CALL Init
DO j = ic1, ic2, 10
   c = FLOAT(j) * 0.1
   k = k3
   DO i = i1, i2
      rho = FLOAT(i) * 0.1
      fi  = c * SIN(rho) / rho
      x   = rho * COS(fi)
```

```
y    = rho * SIN(fi)
CALL Plot (x, y, k)
IF (k .EQ. k3) k = k2
END DO
END DO
READ (5, 700) answ
STOP
700 FORMAT (1A1)
END
```

This field has a trend of the *sin(x)/x* kind, laid on the local fields, but with an evident lack of symmetry that rotates in the phase field function.

Because of that, equal commands would not react in the same way in different situations, so an interface is required between the pilot and the bell.

The lines of force of the field of phase are curved so that, given whatever circle centred on the axis of symmetry, all these line cross it forming constant angles with respect to an arbitrary direction. The following image is a simplified representation of the phase field:

The image is simplified *in primis* because the attenuation with distance has not been taken into account. A second simplification consists in having ignored the

phase angle at an infinite distance, that is the one the pilot actually manages.
In this representation, indeed, the lines of force oscillate according to:

$$\frac{dy}{dx} = sin\sqrt{x^2 + y^2}$$.

A last simplification has been made while representing, over a plane, a seven dimensions phenomenon (three geometric and four field dimensions), but we cannot have everything!

Anyway, even with this simplification, we may see that rarifying zones tend to place themselves on alternating sides of the principal phase axis.

It is not so easy to envisage how these fields look when seen from outside; the following infra-red image (the original is in color) may help a bit:

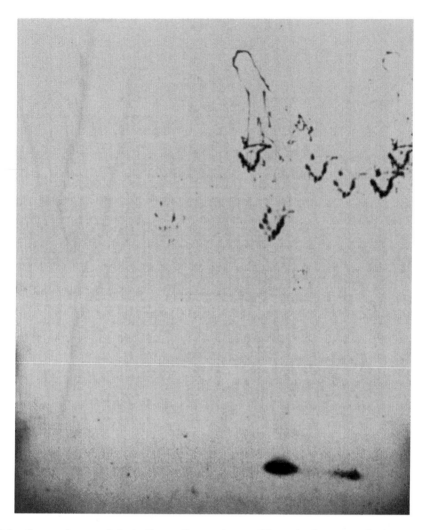

It has been taken at night in Passo Corese (west of Rome); the saucer is the small black oval in the lower right. The gray lines on the left are due to a mistake in the development process. There are many satellite probes around the disk itself, that was really very low over the ground.

The central column is traversed by strong DC currents (with a small AC component), around some thousand Ampères. Its chemical build (magnesium, cobalt, mercury and platinum) ensures a high conductivity, and so low losses for the Joule effect.

A typical problem with the central columns consists in the generation of an EM helicoidal field (with a ratio near 100 between the magnetic and electric fields), with a low intensity, that anyway is present inside the cabin. Its frequency is around some 100 Hertz, and instrumentation must be prevented from working on frequencies that may be harmonic to that one. Some care must therefore be taken both in the design, and while piloting. For instance, it is not possible to set the low-distance scanner to a range of 1.7 km, or multiples of that, because of possible interferences. The local computer typically modifies such requests, changing the parameters a bit. The pilot must be aware of such corrections, that are not shown to him, in order to avoid mistakes in estimation.

The currents that are induced along the main disk make it vibrate. The design is usually such that the main vibration mode is of the third order. That causes the humming noise that is often associated with disk-like craft. The stability of this mode of vibration is increased by masses placed accordingly under the disk. One of the effects of this vibration consists of generating a vacuum around the craft, when the global field reaches 0.1% of the maximum power.

I already said that the local and natural gravitational fields exchange with each other at the start and at the arrival of the craft; this generates mechanical stresses to the structure. Because of that, a scout usually is not made in a single piece, but in hundreds of pieces, connected together by a local field. When departing, or arriving, a good piloting technique consists in shutting down this field for a moment, just to switch it on immediately after that. This way the different pieces separate from each other for a moment, then clutch to each other immediately after that. A low level noise is generated, that may be easily heard, if bystanders are aware of it.

Stability

The craft is extremely stable. Stability is ensured, just to begin with, by the interaction between the gyroscopic effects of rotating masses and the local gravitational field. The interaction between the local and the external gravitational fields may generate "falling leaf" oscillations that are often reported.

It must be remembered that, speaking about gyroscopic forces in environments with a distorted gravity, the equations we are familiar with are no longer valid. As a first approximation, a multiplicative matrix must be introduced, of the kind:

$$\left(\frac{\partial x_i}{\partial X_j} \right)_{i,j=1,4}$$

,

where the x's refer to the local metrics, and the X's to the environmental one.

Falling leaf oscillations, especially while landing, may be mitigated by putting down one or more spheres; this way a modification results in the distribution of mass, and a change in the global electrostatic field.

Reference System

Strangely enough, the reference system has its origin in the control panel, not in the bell itself. Usually that does not matter, but it may create problems in some situations (very low flight, flight inside corridors, and the like). The control panel is the centre of the bell's micro-universe, and every reference is made to it. For instance, if the pilot orders the computer to rotate the bell 90° to the right, the craft will rotate asymmetrically, around an axis passing through the panel, that sits in an eccentric position.

To identify his position, the pilot refers to *anchors*, that perform a duty analogous to the VORs of our aviation (except the fact that they refer to a three (or twelve) dimensional space, according to various situations, and that their range is by far superior; in every moment the pilot may see direction, and distance, of any pre-selected anchor. Anchors constitute a good reference system; the central computer connects itself to them via PLAT (a very powerful instrument, about which it is better to remain silent). The maximum range for an anchor is some 25,000 km; which is too much for planetary flight, but it's totally useless for interplanetary flying. Another reference system is then used, centered on our Sun (for flights inside our solar system), and oriented according to our galaxy. Other systems are used for flights of larger distances. To control movements in relation to other bells, again the PLAT is used, but in this case (because of a lot of problems too complicated to be discussed here), it is better to elect one bell as "master", and the others as "slaves", so that the behaviour of all of them is decided by a single computer.

Some unexpected phenomena may take place: imagine a three aircraft aerobatic team (for instance the *Frecce Tricolori*, to remain in Italy); the three aircraft are flying side by side, then the team leader orders a tonneau; for a single plane this means a rotation around its longitudinal axis; for the three planes, considered as a single object, that means that only the central aircraft is going to make a true tonneau; the two lateral ones will make something different: again a rotation, but around the central plane. A well known film exists, shot in Trenno by Bruno Sammaciccia, that shows three bells flying together; as usual there is a "master" and two "slaves"; who knows why, in this case the master is one lateral craft, so that, when they perform a tonneau, the whole team rotates around it! Of course it could be done even by our Frecce Tricolori, but I have never seen such a performance, because it is eccentric from every point of view!

Then, when two bells need to get almost in touch, it is better to demand the operation to the PLAT; otherwise the two crafts would enter a logarithmic spiral.

The position of the craft with respect to the ground is arbitrary. Usually this attitude is not taken into any account. As a former aerobatic pilot, I may ensure you that an aircraft may fly in almost every possible attitude, but obviously a bell is by far superior in that. Anyway, some problems arise just because of that, for instance while flying low over the ground: there is no instrument controlling the parallelism between the bell's attitude and the ground, so that collisions (uneventful to the bell) can take place; in order to avoid such unpleasant events, usually a number of small flying probes are released, that fly around the bell, and transmit back to the central computer the local environment. They are very small devices, that may be seen, as small specks, in some pictures.

Anchors Programming

"An anchor is a fixed reference point that is essential in order to know your position. Unlike your Loran, in order to ascertain your position a single anchor is sufficient. You will be able to know both your distance from it, and its direction". This sentence (to say better, its Italian original version) was spoken to me as an introduction to the problem of anchor programming. The Loran was a rather primitive reference system, used by our general aviation in the sixties, now no longer in use. This way, at low speeds (almost-Euclidean metrics), from the variation in time of the vector bell→anchor, a speed can be computed.

With higher speeds (non-Euclidean metrics) things are no longer as easy as that. Most bells are designed not to be able to go at speeds much higher than c, the speed of light in a vacuum (if necessary, of course they may be designed to!); anyway, when speeds become a significant fraction of the speed of light, distortions take place, both in space and in time coordinates. An anchor interacts directly with the PLAT, therefore it is free from distortions; also the bell communicates with the PLAT, therefore it too is distortions free; what gets distorted is the space (and time) around, and the concept itself of distance.

If a pilot takes into account the data received from a non-programmed anchor, his conclusions would be greatly mistaken, at speeds near to c. The central computer, therefore, should be able to interpret correctly the wrong data it gets from the anchor. It is by far easier to transfer this problem to the PLAT that is immanent to the whole space, therefore it is able to interpret correctly all these data. What the PLAT does, when it becomes aware of significant distortions, consists in instructing the anchor to transmit intelligently wrong data, in order to cope with distortion. It is as if no distortion takes place, but the anchor changes its position, in order to adjust metrics. Of course this environment is true only for a bell travelling at speeds near c (and in different ways for different bells at similar speeds); nothing changes for bells in near-Euclidean situations.

This means that the dialog between a bell and an anchor (via PLAT) is different from bell to bell, according to their speeds. Of course this is not a peculiar ability of the anchor, but it is due to the unusual nature of PLAT.

There are other instances when an anchor may be driven to give wrong information; one of the most common cases arises when a bell had not been dismantled after a mission, and is then re-used for a new one; between the two missions several things may have changed, therefore an anchor may be required to give wrong data that, nevertheless, are significant in accordance with the previous situation. As usual, wrong data are sent only to the bells that need to receive them.

The deceived bell is aware of being so, because it has been advised by the PLAT of the situation; the on-board computer interprets anyway the wrong data as if they were true; the only reaction to wrong data consists in generating a pulsating noise inside the cabin, at 2,400 Hz, in order to make the pilot aware of the situation; who knows why, this frequency is generated also when the bell is without anyone being on board.

Another instance when an anchor must give wrong data happens when a bell enters the outer layers of a star; in such cases, the fields surrounding it are very strong, and change abruptly. No two stars are the same, and even a single star changes continuously, in unforeseeable ways. In such instances, the bell's inertial data get correlated to the anchor's geometrical ones. As usual, it is the PLAT that is charged with the job of deciding which wrong data must be transmitted by the involved anchor. The situation that takes place is not a pleasant one, because it looks that the bell changes its position almost at random. For this reasons, several races prefer not to use common anchors in such situations, but to generate local temporary anchors.

"Another instance of anchors programming takes place when interferences appear, because of what we call our UFOs". Another sentence by a W56; here he refers to what they are calling "our own UFOs", that is artificial objects whose nature they are not able to ascertain. It looks that the PLAT is unable to cope with such interferences, but in this case it is the anchors themselves that try to interpret the situation, and to correct the data about their positions. Typically, in such situations, an anchor asks another one about its relative position; if the data are wrong, then a process starts, with anchors interrogating each other, and correcting conveniently the data they are sending to the various bells in touch with them.

Typically an anchor is a small ball, some 1.3 cm in diameter, weighing a few tens g. It needs to be activated before starting its operations; that means putting it in the required place (eventually via tele-transport); the activation consists in fixing its position in that place (a rather complicated subject, inside a space continuously evolving!), and in interfacing it to the PLAT. An anchor may also be nothing physical, but just a propriety imposed upon a peculiar area in space.

A landing adventure

In the scouts that are accessible to Earthlings, measurement units are typically metric, although at times people with an aeronautical background had asked for US units (feet, knots, miles per hour and the like), and the computer kindly obliged.

Now, I'd like to present the recording of a conversation during a flight training; the to-be pilot was an Italian gentleman (quoted U) and a W56 (quoted W). Two other Earthlings were on board (quoted V). W was in control from a remote station. Conversations have taken place mainly in English, with some sentences in Italian.

W: Are you able to ascertain your height?

U: No, better to ask the computer. Declares nineteen miles, descending (Author: U had an aircraft licence, therefore he was used to speak in terms of miles, feet, and so on; it is unusual, in aeronautic jargon, to measure heights in miles; in the following, then, at times metric units are used). According to it I should be over Potenza (Author: southern Italy), but nothing may be seen below, because of the weather.

W: Has the detector of objects nearby been activated?

U: Yeah, but it looks there's nobody around; at this time airliners usually do not fly.

W: Stop descending at twelve miles, and select Cairo's fix.

U: Roger, stopped at twelve miles, over Potenza. Main phase regressing, 2,344 miles from the fix. Direction 126 degrees.

W: Select the fix for 23 o'clock, Italian time.

U: Roger, time distance 39 primes, estimated horizontal speed 3,606 knots, vertical speed 1,870 fpm, descending.

W: These are obviously average values. Moreover, you forgot to ask the computer to take propagated errors into account, while converting data into your measuring system. In this case it's meaningless, but actually the mean horizontal speed is lightly higher than that. Then, the data are wrong, because two minutes have elapsed and you are still stationery (Author: preciosity!).

U: Roger, started, direction 126 degrees, ground speed 3,650 knots; I'll keep this speed until I'll close the gap.

W: Increase the secondary phase, you're climbing.

U: Roger, now descending... Climbing again... Down. Phase proceeding... Stabilized, but still climbing... At this speed it's not easy to control the height.

W: Spin the main phase ninety degrees in advance, reduce column's polarity and have the secondary phase oscillating 35 degrees up and down, twelve times per second.

U: Done. Why was vertical speed stabilized this way?

W: D'you think?

U: No, I'm falling like a stone. Minus twelve thousand fpm, increasing.

W: When you cross one mile, reverse the polarity, then stop the vertical speed. You forgot to keep active the detector of nearby objects. You could have smashed a plane without realizing.

U: Colour system active (Author: the detector system that generates colours inside the cabin). Descent stopped one mile over the sea. No visible target. Negative, a target below me, twenty five miles strictly ahead... Overcome. I stop the bell... Target nine miles at 234. Climbing. Phase still proceeding... Stable at 3500 feet... Target at nine miles.

W: Can you understand what is it?

V: È una nave (= "It's a ship").

U: At sea level... May be a fishing ship. The detector signals a preposterous mass. It's one of your gadgets?

W: PLAT would have told you in advance. No, it's just a rather big metal ship. That's why the mass. Get close.

U: If they're military, maybe they'll shot at me. How to protect myself?

W: Ask the computer to activate the negative inertial system.

U: Done. It said "Gradient zero point eight". What's that?

W: It's a default. At this moment your bell generates a repulsive field with an acceleration about twenty eight meters per square second on its surface; neutral surface sits at something less than one hundred meters from the bell. Any shell should be sent away. One exactly pointing toward the source of the field would be able to enter any way, but the probabilities are nil. The field may be increased to prevent even this possibility, but secondary effects would propagate down to the sea surface. If you look closely, you'll notice that the computer had already activated this field by itself.

U: After a few minutes at that speed, the ship now looks still. On the contrary, it is slowly proceeding eastward, about.

W: Are you able to ascertain how far are you from the coast?

U: Negative.

W: Ask the computer to find the smallest local minimum of the distance from silicata, density higher than twenty pounds per gallon.

U: Nine miles. That's the ship.

W: Ask for the second maximum.

U: Eighty six miles.

W: You're south east of Calabria tip. I must get away for a minute. Keep the bell still.

U: Autopilot on. With such a density of silicata, may be the ship is a merchant one.

W: Not really so. It carries bombs, it's military. I'll get back at once.

V: The ship moves in a direction of 86 degrees, just one meter per second. 16.4 km away, 234 degrees. Decreasing... are we moving? No, then 235 degrees were wrong. Maybe we displaced ourselves while stopping. 2,284 miles from the anchor. (Author: in Italian)

(Author: the situation looks to be as depicted in the following image ("campana" = scout, "nave" = ship, "Nord" = North):

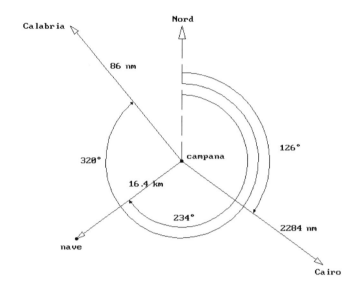

Nord

Calabria

86 nm

320°   campana   126°

16.4 km

234°

2284 nm

nave

Cairo

V: Why not to try to make a pretended attack? For instance, we land on its deck, destroy a couple of guns, then go away. That would be funny. (Author: In Italian)

W: Here am I again. I've made a check, and it's military.

U: I'd like to try to land on its deck, pretending to be on the attack.

W: If you feel confident...

U: Roger. Reference disks out, sending them towards the ship. Ship proceeding eastward, at low speed. Depolarizing lower rings. Dome off then on. Signalling from pilot disks is OK. Ready to get down.

W: If something's goes wrong, I'll keep the controls.

U: Moving toward target. They've seen us. Reverse the field. Falling. Climbing. Field stabilized. Field reversed. Falling. Falling. Computer. Contact. Spheres out. 1.8 kjoule discharged unto the deck. Electrical balance. Systems stand by.

W: What happens?

U: Everybody looks upset. Men are moving in the distance.

W: More care is required in reversing fields while landing. It's not enough just to reverse them. In this case, then, the target is metallic, conductive and magnetic, therefore it influences strongly the resonating field. You should have taken care to keep it vertical. That's why the vertical speed ran out of control.

U: Men are gathering, with weapons.

V: They're firing at us! (<u>Author</u>: In Italian)

U: Emergency take off (<u>Author</u>: a strong noise is heard). Two disks called back. Climbing 6,000 fpm, 400 knots.

W: Why an emergency take off? There was no trouble. The third disk acknowledges that you've cut away the end of a gun. Some admiral is going to quarrel against you. Call the disk back.

U: Disk back.

W: Climb eighteen miles. Select Bussi fix. Get back. Enough for tonight.

U: Roger.

The nationality of that ship has never been ascertained, as far as I know…

The Triangular Pattern Experiment

Once I asked the permission to perform an experiment with a scout; it was to travel a triangular pattern, from Pescara to Moscow, to Cairo, then to Pescara again. My proposal was accepted, and so the experiment took place. The pilot was a German engineer, and on board there was another gentleman, whose job consisted in reading, on a display, the coordinates of the craft that the on-board computer was to present every two minutes. I really do not remember whether there were any other persons on board or if any were W56. The whole trip lasted one hour and a half. The data presented by the computer have been copied, using an Olivetti 22 typewriter, and images 9.1 and 9.2 show the two sheets of paper that are the result of this experiment. At that time, I did not care to take an account of heights, so I must presume that the whole trip has been made at a constant height.

The flight took place at night, at an height of 20 km, in order to avoid any interference with airline traffic. Unfortunately, I do not remember the date, but it is not important, after all. Probably it has been a summer in the late 60's.

My idea was to verify how good a scout could be in flying a pre-defined assignment, so I had asked the pilot to do his best to keep speed and direction constant along each leg; he did not bother too much: he just told the computer to do the job.

What he actually did consisted in placing an anchor over the three corners of the trip; an anchor is a local property of the space, that may be used for navigation, like our VOR's. It is possible to set an anchor from far away (at least, our friends had the capability to do so!), so he just instructed the computer to fly the craft along the anchors, at a speed of 5,000 km/h. Indeed the average speed has been a bit lower than that, although at times it went well over 8,000 km/h!

A rough sketch of the trajectory is shown a few lines down; this picture presents just a very rough outline of the coasts of the area involved, using a conical projection, with the positions of the craft, as a set of dots, every two minutes; the direction of the flight has been clockwise.

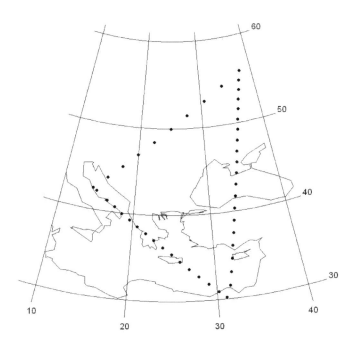

The scout's performance was far from optimal; as you may see from the following drawings: both the speed and the direction have not been constant. When I objected to this poor performance to one of our Friends, he resented it, and told me, rather sharply, that they had no use in keeping speeds and directions constant, as long as their crafts are able to get to the desired places on the schedule.

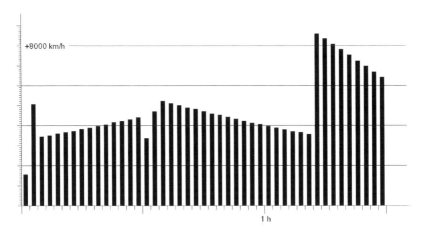

Speed Errors
Average Speed = 4790.9 km/h
Global distance = 7186.4 km

+8000 km/h

1 h

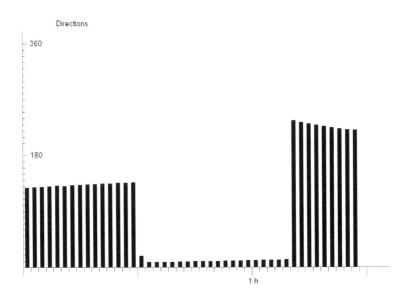

Directions

360

180

1 h

137

The input file

This is the source file, on whose data the computation has been performed; its name is Triangular_Pattern.txt:

```
42.44   14.24
42.17   14.75
41.24   16.35
40.60   17.42
39.94   18.48
39.25   19.55
38.53   20.61
37.80   21.68
37.04   22.75
36.25   23.81
35.44   24.88
34.60   25.94
33.73   27.01
32.84   28.08
31.92   29.14
30.97   30.21
30.24   31.01
31.57   31.54
33.11   31.82
34.62   32.10
36.10   32.38
37.54   32.66
38.96   32.96
40.35   33.25
41.70   33.56
43.03   33.87
44.33   34.18
45.60   34.50
46.84   34.83
48.05   35.17
49.24   35.52
50.40   35.88
51.54   36.24
52.65   36.62
53.73   37.01
54.80   37.41
55.84   37.82
54.44   34.05
52.97   30.63
51.46   27.55
49.93   24.76
```

```
48.40   22.23
46.88   19.94
45.37   17.86
43.89   15.97
42.44   14.24
```

Data are obviously taken every two minutes, and show the latitude and longitude at that moment.

The output file

These are the results from my program:

TRIANGULAR TEST RESULTS

```
0    0     42.44   14.24
                              1551.3 km/hr      127.9 deg
0    2     42.17   14.75
                              5062.7 km/h       128.4 deg
0    4     41.24   16.35
                              3448.5 km/h       129.2 deg
0    6     40.60   17.42
                              3491.1 km/h       129.9 deg
0    8     39.94   18.48
                              3595.5 km/h       131.1 deg
0   10     39.25   19.55
                              3662.1 km/h       131.0 deg
0   12     38.53   20.61
                              3725.0 km/h       131.8 deg
0   14     37.80   21.68
                              3812.7 km/h       132.9 deg
0   16     37.04   22.75
                              3882.0 km/h       133.0 deg
0   18     36.25   23.81
                              3968.8 km/h       134.1 deg
0   20     35.44   24.88
                              4039.8 km/h       134.5 deg
0   22     34.60   25.94
                              4151.1 km/h       134.9 deg
0   24     33.73   27.01
                              4219.9 km/h       135.8 deg
0   26     32.84   28.08
                              4292.9 km/h       136.1 deg
0   28     31.92   29.14
                              4406.1 km/h       136.7 deg
```

0	30	30.97	30.21		
				3356.0 km/h	18.9 deg
0	32	30.24	31.01		
				4700.7 km/h	8.7 deg
0	34	31.57	31.54		
				5210.7 km/h	8.8 deg
0	36	33.11	31.82		
				5109.4 km/h	8.8 deg
0	38	34.62	32.10		
				5008.2 km/h	8.8 deg
0	40	36.10	32.38		
				4873.8 km/h	9.4 deg
0	42	37.54	32.66		
				4813.9 km/h	9.1 deg
0	44	38.96	32.96		
				4708.2 km/h	9.8 deg
0	46	40.35	33.25		
				4582.1 km/h	9.8 deg
0	48	41.70	33.56		
				4513.4 km/h	9.8 deg
0	50	43.03	33.87		
				4411.8 km/h	10.1 deg
0	52	44.33	34.18		
				4314.3 km/h	10.4 deg
0	54	45.60	34.50		
				4216.7 km/h	10.8 deg
0	56	46.84	34.83		
				4119.0 km/h	11.0 deg
0	58	48.05	35.17		
				4054.2 km/h	11.3 deg
1	0	49.24	35.52		
				3956.4 km/h	11.2 deg
1	2	50.40	35.88		
				3887.2 km/h	11.9 deg
1	4	51.54	36.24		
				3793.4 km/h	12.2 deg
1	6	52.65	36.62		
				3695.4 km/h	12.3 deg
1	8	53.73	37.01		
				3662.7 km/h	12.6 deg
1	10	54.80	37.41		
				3564.5 km/h	237.0 deg
1	12	55.84	37.82		
				8592.1 km/h	234.0 deg
1	14	54.44	34.05		
				8365.5 km/h	231.3 deg
1	16	52.97	30.63		

```
                                      8081.6 km/h      229.1 deg
1   18      51.46   27.55
                                      7816.7 km/h      227.2 deg
1   20      49.93   24.76
                                      7535.2 km/h      225.4 deg
1   22      48.40   22.23
                                      7242.9 km/h      223.7 deg
1   24      46.88   19.94
                                      6981.4 km/h      222.3 deg
1   26      45.37   17.86
                                      6687.9 km/h      221.0 deg
1   28      43.89   15.97
                                      6428.1 km/h        0.0 deg
1   30      42.44   14.24
```

Global flight distance = 7186.4 km
Average speed = 4791.0 km/

Just for the sake of history, let me present the original sheets of paper where the initial data were recorded, making use of a portable typewriter:

t	lat	lng
2	42.17	14.75
4	41.24	16.35
6	40.60	17.42
8	39.94	18.48
10	39.25	19.55
12	38.53	20.61
14	37.80	21.68
16	37.04	22.75
18	36.25	23.81
20	35.44	24.88
22	34.60	25.95
24	33.73	27.01
26	32.84	28.08
28	31.92	29.14
30	30.97	30.21
32	30.24	31.01
34	31.57	31.54
36	33.11	31.82
38	34.62	32.10
40	36.10	32.38
42	37.54	32.66
44	38.96	32.96
46	40.35	33.25
48	41.70	33.56
50	43.03,	33.87
52	44.33	34.18
54	45.60	34.50
56	46.84	34.83
58	48.05	35.17
1 00	49.24	35.52
1 02	50.40	35.88
1 04	51.54	36.24
1 06	52.65	36.62
1 08	53.73	37.01
1 10	54.80	37.41
1 12	55.84	37.82

Distanza = 2048 km
Velocità = 3840 km/h

dist. = 2580

1 14	54.44	34.05	dist. ≜ 1123 km
1 16	52.97	30.63	
1 18	51.46	27.55	
1 20	49.93	24.76	
1 22b	48.40	22.23	
1 24	46.88	19.94	
1 26	.45.37	17.86	
1 28	43.89	15.97	
1 30	42.44	14.24	

The "Twin Scout"

Once again it was myself who invented this name. It is a very strange kind of craft, circular in plant, with two totally independent cockpits, elliptic in shape. This is a synthetic image I generated on a computer many years ago:

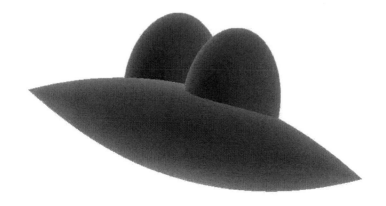

L'11 febbraio 1967, nei pressi di Aveyron (Francia) una serie di avvistamenti relativi a sfere di fuoco luminose e a un oggetto cilindrico culminò in un incontro piuttosto ravvicinato durante il quale fu possibile distinguere nell'UFO forme umanoidi.

As it is not so easy a problem to write a computer program to generate such images, I've been using it also in my University course on Algorithms for Computer Graphics!

This peculiar craft has been seen many times in Italy's Abruzzi region, and (as far as I know) only once outside it, in France, near to Aveyron, on Feb 11, 1967:

Its diameter is around 7.5 metres; strangely enough, it does not make use of the classical three spheres as a landing gear; for this purpose a ring may be lowered from its bottom, and the craft sits on it; because of this strange solution, it is not easy at all to rest it over uneven surfaces. Cockpits are very narrow, uncomfortable, difficult to enter and to get out; the two domes may rotate on back hinges, in order to permit getting into and out.

Its most peculiar characteristic consists in that its two cabins are totally independent from one another even from the point of environmental data: the habitat features (temperature, pressure, atmospheric composition, and so on) may be decided from a large quantity of different possibilities, and may differ largely between the two cockpits; once again, who knows why.

One of the two seats takes the control of the flying operations, the other one is in charge of different functions (the two seats are exchangeable under this point of view); of course, the pilot may perform additional duties, although the limited space inside the cockpit does not allow for too many control panels.

As in almost all scouts, looking outside is rather useless; in this case it is almost impossible: although the domes are transparent, their peculiar shape greatly deforms outside vision, to the point that it is questionable why the domes might be rendered transparent (maybe to avoid claustrophobia!).

The two narrow seats are a bit behind the centre of the craft; they are made in something looking like white plastic; who knows why, when there is somebody sitting on them, their colour changes to brown. Totally unexpected (and at a first sight unjustified): when one sits on them, the seats change their form, adhering strictly to the body.

As almost everywhere in W56 environment, also inside the Twin Scout it is possible to smoke: a minuscule ash-tray is present in each cabin, on its external side (ashes are destroyed at once, so it is not really a tray). Air recycling takes place via absorption from the floor, and re-emission from the sides, upward; therefore, if one is smoking, he will usually see the smoke flowing downward!

No space is available to put down things, papers, or the like, aside at the back of the seats or on the floor (two places simply impossible to reach when one is seated!). Practically every possible surface is occupied by control panels or visors, through which its occupants may interact with the central computer. Both visors and control panel display a magnificent three-dimensionality, therefore the available space looks to be wider than actual it is.

Rather peculiar are also its piloting techniques. In a normal bell the operation of going from one place to another consists, mainly, in asking the computer to do so. In the Twin Scout piloting techniques are based upon a series of pre-fixed "situations": in every moment only one situation is active (from an initial set of 13, or so, of them); in every situation the pilot has only a limited set of commands available; moreover, it is not possible to commute from a situation to any other one: only certain paths are available.

What makes things even stranger is that new situations may be defined; it is a rather cumbersome activity, because a lot of details must be entered, and so the use of this possibility is a bit mysterious.

Selecting an anchor is a very complicated matter; typically it must be selected from a list (written in *Ashet* hieroglyphs [5]), but operations change dramatically from selecting a real anchor to choosing a virtual one. This latter case is extremely long and demanding, also because it is practically impossible to refer to written notes, that one can not store anywhere.

A bit like in our aircraft, commands act through "derivatives", that is the pilot decides the rate at which a certain entity is going to change, and in what direction; in our planes entities are always scalar ones (speeds, heights, and so on); in the Twin Scout many of them are two or three (up to twelve) dimensions matrixes! The "derivative" is therefore a rather complicated concept...

The reference system is again very peculiar, and it influences greatly flying operations. Differently from ordinary bells, in this case the centre of the reference system sits in the geometric centre of the craft. As attitudes and trajectories are usually independent from each other, it is important to remember that every command refers, by default, to the scout itself, not to the trajectory it is going through. If the pilot wants to act on the trajectory, he must issue a different kind of input to the computer. In other words, the flight of a Twin Scout is inertial, in a certain sense, because it is not affected by the pilot's commands, unless he decides to do so.

Then, a third kind of commands is available, ones that act both on attitudes and trajectories. There are several good reasons for a design of this kind, reasons that I am not going to examine in these lines; maybe a slightly unpleasant side effect consists in that the scout is always rotating, at a very low angular speed, around an axis apparently chosen at random; indeed it depends on the flight history.

It operates on electrostatic principles; nevertheless, it hosts a couple of rotors inside the disk, for unknown purposes.

All this information has been given to me by an old friend of mine and of Bruno's, who had been trained to pilot this kind of scout.

Maljenkij

The name, in Russian, means "Small". This class of scouts is indeed composed by small, almost rudimentary, objects. Propulsive principles are once again based on the declination field, therefore there are two counter-rotating rings inside the structure, that in this case is usually closed in its inferior part; the lower surface is usually flat, so there is no need for a landing gear. There is no central column, whose functions are replaced by the external surface of its cabin. There is the graphite end on its top, that is flat, not spherical; its electrical discharge takes often the shape of a dark cone, and this shape changes continuously, because of the electrical impedance of its environment. At times the outer rim presents a swelling, as in the following image; in this case the two rotating disks are inside it.

As with the Twin Scout, piloting takes place via "Situations", although it looks that they are less in number, and that the most commonly used is the "Walk" one; therefore piloting the Maljenkij is the most similar to the piloting of a conventional aircraft; its flight is in fact mostly piloted, with minimal support by the central computer; of course, it is possible to demand the computer to take care of the flight.

Many among them are of the compressible kind.

This is a rough synthetic image of a Maljenkij scout:

Notes

Their Technology

1 Giancarlo De Carlo, with whom I shared a lot of time investigating extravagant technologies from their part…

2 In those years FIAT, the well-known Italian cars manufacturer, had also a nuclear division, that was later closed.

3 The UTI: once again this name has been invented by Bruno Sammaciccia, and I do not know what he had meant with those initials. Any way the UTI was a group, in a way, on a higher level than the W56s and the CTRs, whose activities they were supervising, taking actions when they believed that one of the two groups was going beyond some limits. It was a kind of cosmic law-enforcement group. Once the UTIs reproached the W56s for something they had done, and Bruno was seen weeping, because he could not accept that his Friends had been condemned.

4 The books are: "L'aviazione di altri pianeti opera fra noi", and "Sono extraterrestri".

5 About "Ashet hieroglyphs", please remember that we all live in a world full of hieroglyphs, that have nothing to share with Egyptian language. Just think of the road signs, or things like that. Using symbols to convey information is the quickest way to do it. "Ashet", in their language, is a verb, meaning just that.

Chapter 8

Some anecdotes

In this section I would like to present some excerpts from what Amicizia has been, put together almost at random, just to give the reader the feeling of what has taken place in those years, and even today. Of course I decided not to include here some topics that are too "hot," nevertheless, I hope that the reader will find interesting subjects in the following.

Sigis, a.k.a. Pietro

My usual interlocutor among the W56s was named *Sigis* (I do not know who had given him this name); as he was living inside our society as a university researcher, he had also a terrestrial name; for the sake of privacy, I'll quote here only his first name, Pietro. Of course his identity was totally fictitious, anyway, he was regularly working in the university when I first met him.

He appeared to be some years younger than me, a good expert in computer sciences (our computer sciences, of course), and a guy very prone to jokes.

My first contact with him, and with the W56s, took place around 1963. I was attending the first year of the engineering course at the University of Pisa. There was a friend of mine (another Pietro!) who was attending the course on Physics, and we often spent hours together, discussing science, physics, mathematics, flying saucers, philosophy, and whatever could arouse our interest. Usually we met at my premises, an old house on the eastern outskirts of Pisa. He was living in the centre of the town, so that to get from his house to mine he had to cross Piazza dei Miracoli.

One night we were discussing physics, then, around 1 a.m., he left to go home. I started practicing yoga; in those times I was exploring the processes of slowing down the heart rate, so I sat on the floor, and started with my asanas. All of a sudden, I experienced a bi-location: I was, at the same time, sitting in my room, but also behind my friend, in Piazza dei Miracoli; he was staring at a magnificent UFO high in the sky, and I was sharing the same event (next day, he confirmed me what we had seen, but he had not noticed my presence behind him). Then, suddenly again, I experienced a tri-location! I was at the same time in my premises, in the square, and within an office. In front of me there was a young man, sitting behind a desk, smiling at me. He said that it was he who did the trick, and that he would be waiting for me next afternoon; he told me the number of his office, its address, and said that he would be waiting for me at 3:30 p.m..

Of course, the next afternoon, I was in front of that office at the due time; I knocked on the door, and was invited inside. There was the same young man I had seen the night before. He told me to take a seat, then he started telling me that he was not from this world, or, better to say, that he had been born elsewhere, but that, from every possible point of view, he considered himself to belong to our society.

They had been monitoring me for a long time, he told me, even before I was born! He told me of an accident that had happened to two uncles of mine, sometime between WWI and WWII, of which I was totally unaware (later on, talking to them, both uncles confirmed to me, separately, that it had really happened!).

He told me of another accident, that had taken place a few years before: an Italian DC3, flying from Pescara to Rome, had struck a mountain, in marginal weather, and all of the people inside died. He told me that they had been aware in advance of the impending accident and that, as a form of courtesy toward me, they had prevented my girl-friend of that time from boarding that plane, as she was scheduled to (totally true!).

They had now decided that the time was right to contact me openly. So, he started telling me the story of the W56s (of course he was one of them) and the CTRs. We ended talking late at night, eating pizzas in Borgo Stretto (the old centre of Pisa), scheduling another meeting a week later.

So my involvement with Amicizia had begun.

Once Roberto Pinotti, the chairman of the major Italian UFO group, the CUN, received a letter from two girls in Cinisello Balsamo (near Milan) who claimed to be in contact with an alien by the name of Aladdin, who had given them the plans to build a flying saucer! Roberto diverted the girls to me, and, at first, I was not willing to encourage them. Then, in a visit to Milan because of my job, I met them, and found that they were "crazy like drunken crazy cats", but nevertheless were very pretty, so I suggested to Pietro that he help me in organizing a "space night" for them. One of our common friends was in charge of the show-room of one of the major computer companies (let's forget its name!), and he agreed to lend it to us for one night. Pietro and I organized a real show, with video terminals switching (apparently) by themselves, line printers that all of a sudden were erupting meters of continuous forms, filled with important revelation by sages from all over the universe, plus phantasmagorical displays of lights all around, together with strange music (these last items were the only contributions from the W56s technology). The girls remained impassive; only, one of them told Pietro: "I was sure that you too were a contactee"!

Another time I was in Moscow, by myself; one night I decided to try a new Italian restaurant, the "Arlecchino", that had recently opened. You must know that in Russian restaurants it is customary that an orchestra plays, and so it was that night. Totally unexpectedly, three persons appeared: Pietro, a female W56, and an Italian girl who had been my secretary years before! I invited them to share the table with me, and, when the orchestra started playing the usual Russian tunes, Pietro got up, went to the director, and asked him for a trepàk (the classical music with strong youngsters playing strange tricks with their legs – a very good example of trepàk may be found inside "The Nutcracker", by Tschaikovsky). In those years I still spoke Russian fluently, and so did Pietro. Then he invited me to join him on the stage, dancing trepàk! He invited also the ladies, but they declined. So the two of us performed a second-rate trepàk, to the astonishment of by-standers. When we got over, the manager of the restaurant congratulated us, and presented each of us with a bottle of vodka (flowers to the ladies)!

Then in L'Aquila (in Soviet Union times) the Red Army Orchestra performed a show, that I attended. Once again unexpectedly, Pietro appeared, and, when the show was over, he invited the director to join us for a tour in the town. In those years it was not so easy for a Soviet citizen to accept such invitations, but we were both speaking Russian, so the director accepted, only asking that someone of the group (probably the political commissary) could be with us. When we got out of the theatre, Pietro showed us an Alfa Romeo Cabriolet, we entered it and went madly all around the streets of the town, almost deserted, because it was well into the night. We started singing Russian songs loudly, and ended up in the centre of the main square singing loudly "Vdol' pa Pitjereskoj", once again to the astonishment of the few passers-by. Then we escorted the two Russians to their hotel.

When the UNIX operating system was in the phase of development, I arranged for Pietro to enter the project; he was involved in the design of a portion of the FORTRAN compiler under UNIX, together with an engineer of my company who was totally unaware of the true identity of his colleague.

When I was engaged in the design of a private post-graduate TLC school in Cordoba, Argentina, during the period of military management of the country, I of course sought the help of teachers from the naval university in Buenos Aires, so I spent a lot of time talking with its deans, who did their best to help me. At the first meeting in the Cordoba university, its rector, Francisco Delich, who had been the rector in Buenos Aires from 1983 to 1985, started saying: "Apart from myselfe, who am of Croatian origin, all these deans come from Italy!" That was a rather common phenomenon in Argentina in those years, and indeed, I found Pietro lecturing in those times at the Buenos Aires University about UNIX!

When I was in New York to sign an agreement between the University of Brooklyn and my company, in order to organize a mutually managed master course in TLC for engineers coming from the Italian SIP (then the major telephone company), I found out that in the meantime Pietro had commuted to the North-Eastern university, this time teaching Artificial Intelligence (under a new fictitious name).

Such a guy was Pietro! I do not know where he is at this moment, maybe teaching at the Novosibirsk university, as he has always been following my footsteps...

Lecture to the CUN Management

The CUN, that is the Centro Unico Nazionale, is the most important Italian Center for the study of the UFO phenomenon. It was founded in 1967 and, today, it is one of the oldest UFO centers all over the world. Its chairman, since a long time ago, is Dr. Roberto Pinotti.

Among its founders, Mario Maioli, a very wealthy old gentleman to whom Roberto Pinotti and I were very tied; among Mario's many friends, the consul Alberto Perego. It had been Perego who organized a lecture, in Milan, for the benefit of the management of the young CUN, about Amicizia; there were two speakers, Franco Saija, a judge in Turin, and Emilio B., a jewellery wholesaler, who does not allow me to let his family name known. It took place in November 17, 1968. Just a couple of days before I had got in touch, for the first time, with Bruno Sammaciccia.

Here I present the short notes I've taken that morning. FS is Franco Saija, EB is Emilio B. Among the audience, RP is Roberto Pinotti, GB is Giancarlo Barattini, another one among the founders of the CUN; SB is myself, FN is brother Nardella, a friar; GZ is Gian Luigi Zoccoli, a count from Bologna.

FS: Our essence is not just a materialistic one. In the whole universe men are dwelling. For the moment, no contact is going to take place on a large scale between earthlings and aliens, because it would be too strong a shock to our civilization. We would let ourselves die, because we are too feeble. Moreover, we are not united. Our politicians fear the UFO phenomenon, but they are very good in getting strong from it. They are eager to maintain their power. Scientists deny this reality in order to protect the childish statements of their supposed science. Another obstacle is within ourselves, we who think that our Earth is the center of the universe. Man, in his aspect and his spirit, is widespread all over the universe.

In the whole of our experience there is no room for esotericism or mediums. Many groups exist here, that are stating foolish things, are creating religious-like associations, and are using UFOs as a support, and so on. Four or five years ago I chanced to see the pilots, and started speaking to them via wireless, never in person, speaking about morality and philosophy. Of course our planet cannot get officially in touch with them. To us flying saucers are not important, much more important is to understand what we should do in order to improve our way of thinking and our behaviour.

This morning I am here to be a witness, and our words should make you reflect. We are addressing your spirit. Materialism is going to end abruptly. Civilizations have existed on other worlds also, that entered wrong ways. The facts: in 1952 I've seen my first flying saucer. Next year, our Friends sent me a letter to organize a contact. In 1964 they wrote me again, telling me to go to Pescara; there, with three friends of mine, I have seen three pilots, more than three meters tall, over a hill, some 200 meters away. They were wearing an overall, no headset; they were long-haired, and had anti-gravitational boots. It lasted some 20 minutes. Then I had conversations via wireless, on the long-wave frequencies. Their materialistic scientific research is over, because they are just on the point to pass to another dimension, the Creator's dimension (they state that it is beyond physical nature). Their ideas remind closely eastern religions (for instance, the Indian idea of Karma). They state that Christ (they had never had someone like that) represents absolute justice. Our Earth is a mother-planet (there are some 50 of them). Many civilizations have grown on our Earth, then they went away. The upper strata of Earth's surface, during millions of years, have been replaced by the lower ones (that's why we cannot find traces of the previous civilizations). Our legends refer, some way, to these treks. We arouse their pity, although they maintain that our mind is well developed. Indeed, without their technology, they would be nil. For instance, among us telepathy is not so rare, at a natural level; on the contrary, they need hardware to obtain it.

EB: In the past my life has been endangered. Even now evil is near to us, inside this very room. That is why I am not permitted to say too much. Civilizations exist which might be defined as Nazi-like; they are cool and technologically-oriented, without any morality, nor any feeling of friendliness. I got telepathic messages, via telepathy I've made drawings of their bases, and I have learned their language. I've witnessed objects being disintegrated in their places, to be then re-created in a different place.

RP: Why do the aliens come here, and build bases on this planet, and so on?

FS: Because of their strategy against the Negative ones, to make research, to protect our Earth, because it is one of the mother-planets. They say that our Gospels are full of truth about God, and that we should look there for it. They come from another galaxy. Names are not important, and they do not expect that we may understand their reality. A cosmic law exists that prevents them from interacting with our civilization.

GB: The most important persons, inside Amicizia, are they protected from the Negatives?

SB: No, on the contrary it is often they who protect our Friends.

FS: Yes; when the protection of our Earth has been fully obtained, they will go away.

FN: Have the Negatives got in touch with some earthlings?

FS: Yes, even at high level; Nazism, for instance, has been a consequence of these contacts. Cosmic laws forbid large scale interventions, but single contacts are free.

GZ: How may we understand if the implants are used for good purposes? How can we understand whether the "Good Ones" are really such?

FS: We feel it.

GZ: Might their aims endanger us, without our knowledge?

FS: For the good of many a single damage might be necessary.

GZ: Do aliens exist, that do not have a human physiology?

FS: Yes; they are mutations, either natural or artificial ones, in order to ensure life in different environmental conditions.

SB: Races exist, that are different, but they are exceptions, at least on this dimensional level.

Heavy, dangerous, and illegal activities

Living in touch with our Friends was obviously an exciting experience, but there were many drawbacks, often at a level that is difficult to imagine for people who have not lived this. Remember, for instance, that it was myself who decided to stop my contacts, and that our friends agreed, although they continue making me feel their presence near to me.

155

Very often we were required to find strange metals; the most common request was for mercury, so that I was buying it in industrial quantities in a chemical shop in Pisa; but often things were not as easy as that.

Often they were requested radium: as it is a radio-active material, selling and purchasing was (and is) illegal to general customers, in Italy and abroad. Therefore we were smuggling radium from Switzerland, where it was easier to find some. And of course, aside from illegality, this means that we had to cope with a very dangerous substance.

Even more difficult was to oblige another strange request: we had to look for Strontium Niobate of Barium. Again a radio-active material, with the complication that in those times it was of no use at all. It was just a kind of chemical curiosity, to be exposed in some university to uninterested students (today it finds application in the video-cameras technology). Therefore almost nobody produced this eccentric substance.

I do not know how, but one of the group had been able to find a chemical plant in Germany that was producing $Sr_x Ba_{1-x} Nb_2 O_6$, but, of course, they were selling their product to universities only. On that occasion, therefore, it was necessary to steal small amounts of Strontium-Barium Niobate, before smuggling it through two different customs! In this case the request for this strange substance had not come from our Friends, but from one man in the group, who had invented a weapon, a very effective one, based upon it.

Another eccentric request was for Red Mercury (Mercuric-Stybic Heptoxide: $Hg_2 Sb_2 O_7$), again very difficult to find, and for a very good reason: once again, it was of no official practical use in those years, aside from some deluded do-it-yourself alchemists. But, much more importantly, in those years in the Soviet Union they had devised a way to use Red Mercury to build small atomic bombs, and of course this strange metal was at the centre of attention of many Secret Services throughout the world. We found it in Austria, and were able to buy it, obviously under-the-counter. By the way, the website www.rense.com, on Sept 29, 2004 told about a theft of a huge quantity (about one ton) of Red Mercury in Iraq, which means that this strange substance is still appealing! Who knows for what use…

Getting back to our Friends, in those years I was a young boy, and therefore did not ask myself too many questions. Now, some decades later, I wonder what could have been the use of such demanding activities. Of course, our Friends did not need our fruit, nor our metals: they were able to produce both of them inside their bases, therefore our efforts were useless, at first sight. But it was a really difficult job, from our point of view, a job where strong cooperation was required, and so, probably, (thinking now about it) its only purpose was to enhance the cohesion inside our group, just to the benefit of Uredda.

The same concept applies to the "Hydra" hunts. It was a very demanding activity, a horrific one, let me say. Three times I met Hydrae: once, in Veio (North of Rome) I was by myself, and fled away as quick as I could; two other times I was called to participate to a Hydra hunt, both times near Montesilvano (Pescara). These ugly entities were really terrific, and the effort to destroy them required a strong cooperation among their hunters. But, thinking back years later, the Hydrae could not really be such terrific beings, because Bruno Sammaciccia (in the two last instances) had been collecting people by phone, all over Europe, and the hunters arrived at the place a couple of days after the alarm; what had the Hydra been doing in the meanwhile?

Once again, I believe, now, it was a trick to enhance the cohesion inside the group; I can't see any other explanation.

Then, there were the UTI. I do not remember what these initials stand for, but anyway it was an alien body on a higher level than the W56s and the CTRs, who were taking serious actions when the quarrel between these two groups went too far. Gaspare De Lama remembers that one time the UTI took a very heavy action against the W56s, and that Bruno Sammaciccia burst into tears when he became aware of what was going on.

The Rocca Pia

The Rocca Pia is an ancient castle on the outskirts of Ascoli Piceno (central Italy). By itself, it is not so important, being one among the many castles that punctuate Italian landscapes; to the Amicizia saga it is nevertheless very important, because the main W56 base could be accessed from its environment.

157

It is surrounded by trees on almost every side, so it is difficult to have a clear vision.

In Amicizia's times, its main entrance was closed by a heavy wooden front gate; here we see it, with Giancarlo's car parked just in front of it.

On the top of the arch surmounting the entrance, is the coat of arms of its builder, Pope Pius IV, who erected it in 1560.

159

Its interior, and vaults, were not well kept, at least up to a few years ago: Now, the municipality of Ascoli has started working to restore the old castle.

The W56 still make their presence felt all around, but that's another story!

The biplane accident

When I was young, I had a couple of uncles (more exactly grand-uncles), living in Ancona (some 150 km North of Pescara); one was a food wholesaler, the younger one a journalist (he was the director of the "Voce Adriatica" newspaper); the older one, a wealthy person, was fond of aviation, and had bought a book (that I still have) about the techniques of piloting airplanes (of course biplanes, due to the times). Sometime between WWI and WWII, he was able to buy an old WW1 biplane; it was taken to Falconara Airport, near Ancona, that in those day was just a large grass field. My older uncle took his brother on the back seat, he entered the front seat, started the motor, and gave it full throttle.

As anyone who has ever piloted a biplane (I did) knows, these are light aircraft, that, while on the ground, tend to swing to the right or to the left, depending on the rotation of the propeller, and this tendency must be counteracted by acting on the pedals. My uncle did nothing of this sort; while his aircraft was gaining speed diverting sideways, he pulled back on the stick, to take off (he should, on the contrary, have pushed the stick forward, in order to gain speed); somehow the aircraft got off the ground, still turning sideways, with its nose up, and very slow. Any pilot knows that this situation is an incipient spin.

Not my uncle, who was totally unaware of what was going to happen; the aircraft should have spun to one side, turned upside down, and fallen to the ground, probably killing its occupants.

On the contrary, its motor went dead, its wing horizontal, then, moving backwards, it went back and landed on the ground!

Of course, it was immediately sold! I was born years later, in 1945.

The DC3 accident

On March 30, 1963, at night, a DC3 from the Italian company Itavia was flying from Pescara to Rome Ciampino airport; its registration was I-TAVI; it was a C-47B model. The weather was marginal, but the flight went on without any serious problem. Near to Ciampino the pilots were advised of a thunderstorm in front of them, so that they had to divert from their flight path. Unfortunately, the ground radar control turned out to have been very poor that night. At a certain moment, the plane was flying on a 270° route, with one of its ADF [1] receivers set to a 300° route; it was 3,000 feet above sea level (whatever that might mean: near to a thunderstorm cell, usually barometric altimeters give erroneous readings). In all evidence, the pilots were sure to be in a South-Eastern position with respect to the airport; the ADF settings should have taken them directly to land, on a 332° final heading; moreover, the MEA (Minimum En-Flight Altitude) in that area was just 3,000 feet, so everything was looking correct. Unfortunately, the conditions were IFR (the absence of outside visibility).

Even worse, the aircraft was well north of its supposed position, even north of the airport, in an area where the MEA is 9,000 feet! This means that the plane was 6,000 feet <u>below</u> its minimum safe height. Therefore it was unavoidable that it crashed into a mountain, with 11 fatalities (3 crew members, plus 8 passengers). Nobody survived the impact.

The wreckage is to be found at the coordinates (41°45', 13°33'), while the Ostia VOR is at (41°48', 12°14'); an OBS had beet set to 270°, which is coherent with a direction towards Ostia; the second OBS had been set to 300°, which is the direction to fly from Ciampino in case of missed approach; at that time, landings in Ciampino were made with a direction of 332°. The settings correspond to this situation: both the pilots were sure to be much more southward than they actually were, so they kept an heading of 270°, waiting to see the second VOR indicate 300°; at that moment, a gentle turn to right, of 62°, would align them with the runway. That was the correct procedure, had the two VORs given reliable readings, and had the position been the one expected. In the presumed area the MEA is 3,000 feet, so the pilots were sure to be well above the ground.

On the contrary, had the VOR worked correctly, the pilots should have immediately understood they were actually north of the airport; besides gaining height at once, they should have turned to 200° to get back; they did neither.

The only possible explanation consists in both VORs giving wrong indications at the same time.

Using a Microsoft Flying Simulator, I recreated the situation of a normal approach to Ciampino airport, coming from Pescara:

The instruments show that we are at 4,200 feet, 130 knots, heading 270°; one of the two ADFs is tuned to Ostia (red arrow), the second one to Urbe (green arrow); the OBS is set to 332° (at the time the landing direction to Ciampino). This indicates that we are south of the airport, where we are going to land in three or four minutes. In this case, as Ostia sits at 18° and Urbe at 36°, with heading 270° (angles are relative to heading), we are more or less in the point indicated by the black arrow (right low):

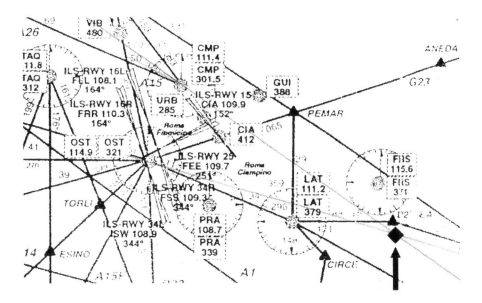

The cause of the accident still remains mysterious; the official verdict charges the pilots with insufficient conduct, but that's just a poor excuse: if the two on-board ADF receivers had been working correctly (or at least just one of them!), the pilots would have understood at once that their position was wrong, and their height too low, therefore they should have pulled up immediately, even before reconsidering their position. They did nothing like that, and went quietly into the mountain.

The only explanation (forgetting the poor ground radar control) is that "someone" tampered with the operation of the ADF receivers, making them give erroneous indications, and so eleven people died (and a W56, and a girl, escaped). Or, if you prefer, we may suppose that both pilots were totally drunk, but let me say that looks a bit improbable.

My girlfriend of those days was scheduled to board that aircraft in order to go to Rome, but when she tried to get out of her home, she found it impossible, because the doors simply refused to get open! This way she missed the flight, and gained her life. Years later this episode concerning my girl was presented to me as a gentle gift from the W56s: they told me that they had deliberately prevented the girl from getting out, because they suspected that something strange was to happen to that flight, and, as a kindness towards me (we were to meet for the first time three years later), they had saved my girlfriend.

The W56s suspected that the CTRs would do something to the flight, because one of the W56 people living inside our society under a covert identity was scheduled to board that aircraft, and the CTRs had already tried to kill him in apparently "natural" ways. Therefore, at the very last moment, he had been replaced by a biological robot identical to him; the robot obviously died in the accident, and the W56 character was out; he was a prominent person in the local community, so that many went into mourning. Of course the W56, unhurt, went back home, leaving beside him the family he had set up during his residence on Earth.

An unexpected encounter at Heathrow

On January 6, 2010, I was travelling from Italy to Kona, Hawaii, to participate to the Earth Transformation convention, and to give a presentation about Amicizia there; I was to depart from Rome on BA 6512 to Heathrow, from there on AA 137 to Los Angeles, then on AA 247 to Kona.

Unfortunately, when in Rome I was waiting to board, it was announced that Heathrow airport had closed, because of snow; boarding was delayed a couple of hours, so that when I landed in London, I had missed the AA connection to LAX. As I am a frequent BA flyer, I went to their offices, and got a place on the BA 269 to LAX, supposed to board at 3:10 p.m.. Again I got a long delay, so that boarding was announced around 5:30, and the airplane actually took off at 9!

While waiting in the gate departing hall, my eyes were attracted by a young girl, or, better to say, by her very smart attire. At a first glance, I noticed that she was very tanned (in January, in London, under a snow storm!); moreover, although the place was not very well lit, she was wearing dark sun glasses; then, at a second glance, I recognized... Miss Swollha, a CTR girl belonging to the group that, in Rome, had been presenting themselves as "Ummites" some 30 years before.

In those years, Miss Swollha was bombarding UFO scholars, in Rome and beyond, with telephone calls. I myself received, maybe, ten calls, or even more; I was able to record a couple of them. For sure it was no joke.

The first call arrived late one afternoon; I was living in L'Aquila (Center Italy); my flat was on the top of the tallest building in the area, so that I was able to look down at the top of my neighbours, through my windows, but nobody could have looked into my rooms from outside. I was in my study, my wife was with me; the telephone rang. I answered; on the other side of the line, a very fascinating female voice; the conversation went, more or less, like this (S = Swollha, B = Breccia):

S: Am I speaking to Eng. Stefano Breccia?

B: Speaking.

S: Hello. I am Swollha, from the Ummites.

B: Hi[1].

S: They want to know what you would like to ask them.

B: It's a bit difficult to answer on the spot. Call me again in a few days.

. . . . . .

S: Fine. Bye bye.

I shut down the conversation, then said to my wife: "The Martians are back again"

"Martians" was my favourite name while referring to aliens, in a general way. My wife replied "Probably it's a joke". The telephone rang again, and my wife answered. She heard Swollha saying "No, madam, it is not a joke!"

Swollha was calling from time to time. Her group had got in contact with some university students and some professors, in Rome. The main character within the Roman group was a boy, Fabrizio. One night he, and his girl friend, were at dinner in my house in L'Aquila; the telephone rang; it was Swollha again, complimenting us on the menu, and describing every course!

About her name, it was myself who inserted the "h" into it, because I was hearing a short aspiration before the "a", and she had been a bit perplexed about that. According to her, her name was Swolla. She was always wearing dark sun glasses when outside because, Fabrizio told me, their eye sockets are almost circular, without the lateral corner we have.

Another time, Fabrizio asked me to go one night with him to Veio, the Etruscan necropolis north of Rome, to do some sky watching. Veio was a place where the Italian "Ummites" were dwelling: Bruno Ghibaudi one night, while entering the necropolis, was invested by a shower of pebbles; one afternoon, I met a Hydra[2] there; it wasn't, and it isn't even now, a quiet place (just a few days ago I've been told of magnetic fields about 800 micro Tesla, going up and down in that area), therefore the boys from Rome were asking for my presence. I welcomed Fabrizio's request, went to Rome on my Alfetta (an Alfa Romeo model), parked my car in a public garage, locked it, then went to Veio with Fabrizio and some friends. As far as I remember, nothing peculiar happened while in there. Then we got back to the garage, I got into my car, and started to L'Aquila.

Just after having entered the highway (it was night, thankfully an almost full moon had risen) the lights in my car went dead! I stopped, looked at the fuses, but everything was OK. Only the lights were out, the motor was running without any problem. So I started again, driving without lights (I was acquainted with that highway, because I was going through it very often, because of my job), under the light of the moon, running as fast as I could: I was afraid that a faster car could run into me, because I had no lights on. In those years there was no speed limit on Italian highways, but it was very late (about 4 a.m.), and I was certainly not bothering about infringing some law! So I was driving at some 180 km/h, without lights, for some 100 km.

The lights came on again while inside the last tunnel, a couple of km from L'Aquila. The day afterwards I took the car to maintenance; they almost disassembled it, without finding anything wrong. But, they found a small hammer, a very unusual one to me; its handle was brass, its head lead. They found it inside the luggage compartment. I was sure it wasn't there when I had left L'Aquila, because I had emptied the car before leaving. The Alfa Romeo workers told me that it was an instrument used by body-repairers. Its presence there, and its purpose, were a mystery.

The next day, I was in my office; my direct-line telephone (its number known only by very few people) rang; it was Swollha, saying that they had tele-transported the hammer into my van, and had arranged the trick with my lights, just to show me their capabilities, and that Fabrizio was to come to L'Aquila in the afternoon, to take back the hammer. He did so, without knowing what he was to take.

Her voice was a very charming, seductive one, to the point that some wives had become jealous of this woman talking to their husbands via phone. She always spoke perfect Italian. Once I asked her to speak to me in her native language, but she answered that it was not possible. After a long, painful, discussion (it was difficult to understand each other on this technical topic) I understood that she was, obviously, not speaking at a telephone set; moreover her words were being translated into Italian by a computer of some kind. Then she phoned me again, this time speaking in an unknown language; at first I thought it was Russian, and started answering in Russian at random, but she went on speaking, without taking my answers into any account. Then I understood that she was accomplishing my previous request, and started laughing. The call ended with her asking me, this time in Italian, to be silent about the whole story. A transcript of this conversation is reported in "Mass Contacts". A few days later, one of the professors in Rome, while engaged in a telephone conversation with one from the "Ummites" group, was told that "Stefanino" (a diminutive for Stefano) "does not speak Russian well". How dare they!

I am sure that she was not speaking via a normal telephone set: in those years I was the director of one of the best known post-graduate telecommunications private schools in the world, with strict connection with SIP (now TELECOM), the main Italian telephone company (in those years, the only telephone company); therefore, when her calls started to come in, I could easily ask SIP technicians to monitor my telephone line, in order to find who was calling me. When Swollha was calling, they were never able to ascertain where the calls were coming from!

One afternoon I was in Rome, walking along Merulana St., on the back of Santa Maria Maggiore (near to Termini railway station). I was on the side-walk, on the left side of the street, just at the beginning of Merulana St.. All of a sudden, I saw a small red car (a FIAT 126 model) running towards me, then climbing the side-walk in order to run over me! A short, dark-haired, girl was at the wheel, wearing dark glasses. Thankfully, I was near the entrance of a store, so I was able to jump into it, avoiding the car, that then disappeared into the traffic.

The same night, I was home again, Miss Swollha phoned me. She said it had been herself trying to kill me, and congratulated me for having been able to escape. No hate was in her voice: according to the W56-CTR scenario, it was her duty to try to kill me, without any personal feeling in that, so that, after all, she was rather happy that I was still alive! Of course, one may wonder why, with all of their technology available, they had chosen a traffic accident in order to get rid of me!

Getting back to the hall in Heathrow airport in January 2010, she made no sign of having recognized me, therefore I did not try to get in touch with her. She showed no aging, her skin was perfect as it was so many years before. She was complaining about the delay, flapping her passport around, but unfortunately I was not able to read its nationality. When at last boarding was called, a bit of confusion arose, so that I lost Miss Swollha. Later on, in flight, I walked the whole aircraft several times, without being able to find her anywhere! In all evidence, she had not boarded the plane. The purpose of her showy presence in the waiting hall was probably to ensure me that they are still around, and that they are aware of what happens to me (remember the delay, the change of flight, and so on).

The Witness
by
Paolo Di Girolamo

from his book "We and They"

As far as I know from what Bruno, the journalist [1], told me, there are two groups of aliens who visit our planet and live on it. The W56s, who come from a federation of planets, oppose the CTRs; both groups have different origins among the stars, and are composed of different races; for instance, among them there are the Pales, named that way because of their very pale skin; they come from a solar system under the control of the CTRs, but some of them are allied to the W56s; they wear black uniforms, with metallic scents.

For sure the W56s, who total some 600,000 people [2], have bases on our Earth. In Italy, their major base goes from Ascoli Piceno to Pescara, and from the Apennines to the Adriatic sea. In those years, about 1963, I have been told the names and features of some of them:

- D'Impietro [3], the head of the Italian expedition, 3.5 meters tall; his name was actually the family name of his Earth bride, who has been killed by the CTRs, making use of a train of waves that had cut her body into a set of very slim slices;

168

- Sun, the boy D'Impietro had from his Earth wife, 2.3 meters tall;
- Sajù, chief of the small aliens, 1 meter tall, a very strong man; he loved Earth music, and liked to play wind instruments;
- Sauro, chief of another group; according to Bruno Sammaciccia, Sauro defected to the CTRs, maybe because of disagreements with Dimpietro and his group;
- Sigir, or Sighir, a scientist, physician, and philosopher;
- Meredhir, maybe dead during an action against the CTRs; he was very interested in the geological history of our planet;
- Datzur, Velthar, Ithacar, Looqor, Itaho; the first two of them belong to a special W56 group; these ones are among the "tough" people.

Some W56s have actually slept in Sammaciccia's house in Pescara; they were very tall, so that their legs were protruding tens of cm from their beds. Trying to arouse the least possible curiosity among neighbourhood, the neighbours had been told they were Swedish friends visiting, as they had almost white hair. It looks, from secrets told at times by some among the W56s, that both they and the CTRs are looking, on our planet, for someone who has the power to force the victory of one between the two factions. Nobody knows who this person is.

Aniae: they are small crystals that record whatever is going on. Often they emit a sound that reminds one of cicadae chirps [4].

The W56s maintain that they come from the 3rd galaxy, that should mean that they are not from our own galaxy; both they and the CTRs have bases on our planet, and on other planets, since a very long time. There are underground bases, with entrances often beyond the waters of lakes, rivers and seas. Usually the W56s wear blue overalls, with red decorations. Bruno said that the CTRs prefer green and yellow colours.

Automata [5]: they may look as human beings, at times being identical to specific persons who, in one way or another, have been involved; in such cases they are practically clones, a concept that in the 60s was yet to come. My friend, the journalist Bruno, once told me that he saw himself, better to say a clone of himself, inside a coffee-house in Milan. Something similar happened to a professor from Ciampino, who had been seen on the Arcinazzo plains when he was at his home in Rome [6]. Automata are projected into a place, from where they start working. When it's over, they are taken back again with tele-transportation. That explains, for instance, traces on the snow that disappear suddenly. Once Bruno Sammaciccia had been assaulted by some automata, and defended himself using a paper-knife, wounding one of them, and a blue liquid came out from the wound! The journalist Bruno told me that one time an automaton exploded inside the lift of his house, and showed the burnt traces of what had taken place.

Meeting with Bruno Sammaciccia

In the first months of 1963 I was in Pescara, together with Bruno, at Bruno Sammaciccia's house. There I witnessed a wireless communication, at first via something similar to Morse code, then in plain speech. The radio receiver was a National, eight transistors and battery powered, a device similar to the one I had in Rome. It was able to receive long, middle, and short wavelengths. During the reception of a normal broadcast, a very strong voice was heard; the speaker identified himself as Sigir, and greeted all the people present inside the room, this way: "Here are the W56s, Sigir speaking. Hi Bruno (Sammaciccia), hi Ghibaudi, hi Paolo", then speaking to me, he added: "Be sincere, be sincere with us all". Other voice followed, then he said "We pick up the goods!"; there was a parcel, it was over a TV set, wrapped in black paper, and actually I saw this parcel being disintegrated [7]: a very strong blue flash, disturbances from the radio set, then the parcel was gone, and Bruno's big dog was growling. After a first moment of surprise, I asked Bruno how a radio set could be able to receive such messages, and he answered that his Friends had put a small device into it (in Italian they were named "Valvoline", a small vacuum tube), that could operate for 10 to 25 years.

I left on a table a letter that had written in advance to the W56s, then the three of us went out, got into a car, and drove towards Pineto, a small village north of Pescara; the car was the Giulietta of my friend, who was driving at high speed. I was sitting next to him, keeping the radio set in my hands, with its aerial outside the window; Bruno sat in the back, together with his dog; at times sequences of bits were coming out from the radio set, and immediately Bruno was slowing down; then small white flashes at the sides of the road, then a long signal, and Bruno was gaining speed again.

After Pineto, Bruno stopped his car, and we remained waiting at a place where a rendez-vous was to take place, but nothing happened; after a while, we were ordered to get back home, because that place was now dangerous to us; during the waiting, I received some information about my health and my wife's.

When we entered Bruno's home, I noticed that the letter I had left was missing. Bruno asked his wife, but she denied knowing anything about it. We drank some coffee, then went out again, this time on foot, and went strolling along the road that was slightly covered in snow. It was still snowing a little. The two Brunos were walking near one another, I was following some metres back. All of a sudden something felt lightly on my head: I cried out, and bent to collect it from the ground: it was a folded sheet of paper, Bruno shouted to me not to touch it, recovered it and said: "It's still hot". He unfolded the object, that was... the envelope of my letter! [8] Sammaciccia explained that it had been sent back to me to prove that "they" had got my letter. I looked up: it was night, and nobody was visible at the windows of the houses surrounding the street, the place was perfectly silent in the snow. The envelope showed some small burnings here and there, and Bruno explained that they were due to the different composition of the paper from place to place. It was well after midnight, and we started walking again, going toward the sea shore.

At that moment, I noticed that one of the street-lamps we were approaching all of a sudden increased greatly its light, while another one extinguished itself. I felt that we were on the border between areas controlled by different entities; I tried several times to go across this invisible border, and each time the phenomenon with street-lamps was repeated. [9]

I had already sent a letter to the W56s, in a more conventional way: I had sent it via normal mail to the journalist Bruno, to his address in Piemonte (a region in Northern-Western Italy), and inside the envelope there was another one, containing a letter to Meredhir, the W56 who was so interested to the history of our planet. I don't know why, but this young man attracted my feelings, as he was so much in love with our Earth and its past, notwithstanding his fight against the CTRs. Bruno told me that my letter had reached its destination, and told me what the answer had been: Meredhir was thanking me, and stating that he was just a man like us, was sharing our mistakes and defects, our hopes and delusions: we should not look at them as at angels, or superior beings; what they were hoping for at most was sincerity and friendship.

Once again, I got back the envelope that had contained my letter to Meredhir, and it too is partially burnt here and there; Bruno told me that it fell on a sofa inside his house. I still have it with me.

The trip to Rocca Pia

Later on, in February, 1963, I was requested to go to Pescara by the two Brunos, it looked as through my presence was necessary. I met my friend at the Termini railway station in Rome, and left to Pescara, passing through the Apennine mountains full of snow. When we were transiting through Sulmona, Bruno asked me whether I was feeling some illness; I wasn't, and he told me he was suffering a pain in the back of his head. Once at Sammaciccia's, we found many other people there, among them the painter Gaspare De Lama ("Mass Contacts" speaks at length about him), his wife, Bruno Sammaciccia, of course, with his wife, my friend's mother, and so on. Next morning we left to Ascoli Piceno, where a W56 base existed, we had been told, in order to perform a coverage operation. Just before entering Ascoli Piceno the Police stopped Gaspare, on his FIAT 600, and fined him. A disturbance from the CTRs? De Lama was sure that it was and became angry. Then we arrived near to the Rocca Pia, an ancient papal fortress, dominating the town.

Sammaciccia asked us to give him our cameras and placed them inside my friend's Giulietta, then we walked along the narrow ascending path that led to the castle. On the ground, the snow is 30 cm high. It's a Sunday, and, as I could not attend Mass, I stopped with my back to the castle, and started reading a missal I had taken with me. That gave strength to me, as if I had God at my side. All of a sudden I heard De Lama shouting: he had seen a young man who, emerging over the top of the walls, was calling to him, waving his hand. We all converged to that point, but there was nothing to be seen. A discussion arose, but the two Brunos did not take part. Then a car was heard, apparently ascending toward the castle, then the noise stopped abruptly. The two Brunos maintained that it had been a CTR Mercedes, that it had been disintegrated. It was cold, and the sun was setting.

Suddenly the people with us tried to force open the wooden front door of the castle, without success, so they started throwing snow balls and pebbles over its walls. I suddenly realized that the mess of untidy thoughts emanating from those angry minds surely prevented any attempt to catch cerebral waves from quiet people. Actually the two Brunos and I were apart, looking at that strange scene. The two Brunos got near to me, and Sammaciccia asked me "What do you think of all this mess?" "You know what I'm thinking about that", I answered. Little by little the people became quiet again, while it got cooler and cooler, then Sammaciccia ordered us to get back, and we all started descending. During this walk, the two woman with us (one was Bruno's mother) proceeded slowly, because of the snow, so they were late; I stopped, waiting for them.

From under the woods near to the castle, I then saw two young men appear, dressed in jackets and short trousers; they are rather small, but sturdy, they were smiling, and one of them supported a bicycle on his shoulders! A bicycle there, in the snow! They were actually walking on the snow, got near to the two women, and told them something, then they proceeded toward the town; later on, Bruno's mother told me they had asked her whether she was Bruno's mother!

At last we got back to our cars and left, although driving was not so easy because of the snow. Once back in Pescara, I returned home by train.

Later on, Sammaciccia told me that the walls, above which the young man had been seen, were 5 meters tall in the inner part; therefore either the man was floating in the air, or he was tall enough. The front door could not have been opened, because a gravitational device was preventing that. About the two young short men, they actually were automata, sent out to thank us. It would have been impossible that they had come from a different path, because the one we used while descending was the only one available. Then too, our presence had acted as a shield against the CTRs, as I had suspected.

172

During 1963 I was in strict contact with my friend Bruno. The Roman newspaper *Il Tempo* presented a long series of articles about UFOs, very well written by Bruno, with many pictures in them. An article appeared in a magazine, about an experience he had during a summer afternoon: he was driving his car along the sea-front, in Montesilvano, when he saw objects approaching quickly from the sea; the first one had a very unusual shape, it was not a disk, but something that looked like a conventional plane, with something similar to a couple of rudders; it penetrated into the sand of the shore, and disappeared. The other objects were all disk-shaped, and behaved as if they were pursuing the first one. Bruno took five B/W pictures of the scene, that showed some kind of energy emanating from the place where the first object had disappeared; it was like some kind of dark smoke arising from the sand. The only picture of the first object shows also an old lady and a boy not far away, who do not seem to be surprised by what is taking place. An interference by the UFOs?

Later on, Bruno told me that after everything was over, he reached the place where the first UFO disappeared, and he found that the sand there was vitrified. He picked up a piece of this substance, and put it in a pocket in his trousers. When he got back home to Rome, he took it out to have a look, and felt his thigh burning, in an area corresponding with the pocket; he found there a reddened area, that was hot to the touch; apparently the sand had become radioactive.

I again got in touch with Giorgio, who had witnessed the "bells" in Rome on June the 24th, 1959. Together we met Bruno one night in summer; we felt rather free, because our wives were on vacations. After a talk that lasted some hours, the three of us went to Teulada St., where the RAI (the Italian national broadcaster) had its headquarters, and waited on the road while Bruno entered the garage to take back his car; when we heard the noise of its motor we noticed that the street-lamp just in front of the garage entrance had switched off. We went a little away; when Bruno, in his car, was getting near to us, the street-lamp suddenly switched on, in a strong violet light. He stopped near to us, to say good-bye, and we told him what had taken place. A bit perplexed, he re-entered the garage, and the light switched off. When he got out a second time, the lamp switched on itself, in a bright violet light. Then Bruno went home, and we did the same, our minds confused, wondering what had taken place. We felt as if someone was watching us, making use of our electric devices, maybe even able to read our thoughts. Anyway, nothing else happened, and in the following days we were left with many unanswered questions.

Although Bruno had returned to northern Italy on vacations, the summer of 1963 was for me a continuous sequence of events, probably because of the presence, at the same time, of both the W56s and the CTRs in Rome.

One week later I passed through Montesilvano with R.C., a friend of mine; we were getting back from Pescara, and I decided to stop at Sammaciccia's. He was home, and I told him what had happened in the previous days. He told me to stop making mental calls, because Rome was under the CTRs control; moreover, the other Bruno had made a betrayal, allying himself with our enemies! Later on, Sammaciccia confirmed that under Monte Mario there was a CTR base, and, what a chance, Bruno was living in P. le Clodio, on the feet of Monte Mario.

My story ends

Some days later, in Rome, I got a telephone call by Giancarlo, one among the friends of Sammaciccia; he asked me to meet him in Ungheria square. He confirmed Bruno's betrayal, telling me to stop any contact with him. I answered:

If Bruno has done something wrong, it is my duty to stay near to him, even if I do not agree with him, because of our mutual friendship. If he is right, I am even more forced to stay on his part, because it is thanks to him that I got my experiences. Moreover, these aliens seem to replicate the state of war that exists on our Earth; I cannot decide which faction is the right one, therefore I'll remain waiting, without allying with any of them.

Giancarlo then left; that night he phoned, telling me that I was going to receive no harm from the W56s.

Gaspare De Lama's Report (from his book "Mass Contacts")

The beginnings

I was fond of UFO's since 1948, I had read one of Perego's books. I wrote him to express my opinion, and the consul phoned me back; later on he came to Milano to meet me (I was living in 19 Giulio Cesare Square). We became friends (I still have a book of his, that he signed for me). We met many times, and he offered for me to become the secretary of CISAER (Author: a private group of UFO scholars, founded by Perego). I declined, in order to remain dedicated to my painting; moreover I should have gone to live in Rome. He never told me about the W56's.

One day I saw, in a magazine, pictures of flying saucers, in an article signed by Bruno Ghibaudi [1]. I wrote him a letter, he phoned me back, and within a few days he too came to meet me. During the conversation, he told me how things actually were. Later on he came again, this time with Bruno Sammaccia, who, in this way, got in touch with me and my family.

Mirella, my wife, was very interested, the same with my mother (then about 70). One day my mother told me that Sammaciccia had come to my house when I was out; she and Bruno remained talking for a while; he had counselled her to push me to give up, because the W56 story could become dangerous for the quietness of my family. My mother answered that I was of age, that she didn't want to interfere in my decisions, and that she would have agreed to anything I was going to do.

The present

Few days later, at night Bruno phoned me (he was already living in Milano, in Capecelatro Street, at those times in the outskirts of the town). He came, and we got out on the street, in order to see a disk that was to pass. Actually it came, at a very low height (we thought some 400 metres); it was larger than the full moon, of a pale orange, shiny, but with definite contours. It was 11 p.m., and nobody was in the street.

Later on, Bruno told me that the W56's had decided to "present" themselves to me. I was to choose a place in the country around Milan (without electric power pylons on it), then buy an 8 mm film. Next day Bruno asked me to take him to the place I had chosen (in the Trenno area), and asked me to insert myself the film into his camera, and started to shoot at an empty sky, while I was near him. He took also some still pictures. When he was over, he asked me to take away the films, and have them developed; next day I went to the Ferrania, in Matteotti Street (Author: a well-known Italian film company). When I got the developed film, I took it home, and my family and I watched it. It lasts a few minutes, and I still have it, although it has been a bit damaged with time. Some of the still pictures Bruno shot in that occasion are actually those presented in the book "Contattismi di massa", from no. 16 up to no. 25, plus someone else's pictures, that I still have.

Author: Let me comment on this strange story: when I read it, at first I didn't believe it, for a very good reason that I will explain. At the end of the 60's, I shot some 20 pictures of a low-flying scout, that actually landed, near Montesilvano (North of Pescara); it was very early in the morning, a misty day; I was in a rather rectangular clearance, surrounded by trees all around. The scout came in from the west, flew a couple of times over the clearance, at tree-top level, tried to land on the north-east corner of the rectangle, then, at the very last instant, its pilot realized that the soil was very rough in that point, rose again, and finally landed on the south-east corner. Later on I gave Bruno both the prints and their negatives, so that he could distribute them among his friends.

When we decided to write down this book, I asked Bruno to give me the pictures he had, in order to insert them into it, but he answered that he had been left with very few of them! Giving them around with liberality, he was now left with very few pictures (in Amicizia times, I had seen literally hundreds of pictures, at Bruno's). So he started looking for pictures among his friends, and a Swiss lady agreed to send us, with a parcel service, the pictures she was keeping in a bank vault (!), requesting that we sent them back as soon as possible in the same way; among these pictures, the ones I present in the photo section, and I was sure they were my pictures; while looking at them, Bruno said something like "treno", that I understood to be the Italian word for "train". I could not see what a train was about with these pictures, but as we were in a hurry, I didn't ask him. When Gaspare made his previous statement, I didn't believe him, because I was sure that I had shot those pictures. Then Gaspare lent me the movie, and I had to realize that the pictures and movie were one and the same thing.

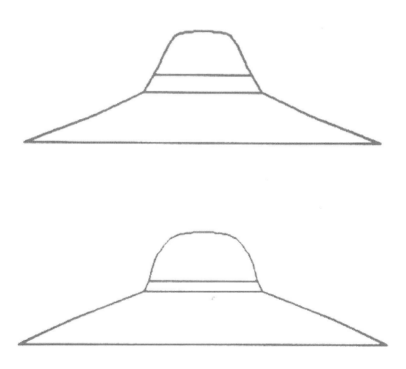

Not yet content, I went on with orthographic analysis of all the pictures, via computer, of course, I have been teaching for years Computer Graphics! So I discovered that they show two different objects; the drawing above presents the shapes of the two scouts, reduced to a same diameter:

Evidently they are slightly different from one another, so, probably, only pictures no. 42, 44, and 49 are of mine (the lower shape), while the others are connected to the Trenno (not "treno", as I had understood!) episode. Probably, while the pictures were being passed from hand to hand, someone made a muddle of the two sequences, losing many pictures in the process, and what the Swiss lady keeps in a vault is actually the mix of two different sets. The surroundings are very similar, therefore it is not so strange that a mixing occurred, but it is symptomatic of the small care taken in preserving such memories. Now that I've explained, I hope, the *quid pro quo*, let's get back to Gaspare:

The phenomena

Both in Milano and Pescara, in Bruno's house in Genova Street, I (and often my wife with me) was with Bruno, and often I have witnessed the following phenomena:

In Montesilvano I have seen (always upon appointment) a disk three different times, with unambiguous movements; in one instance it was moving like this:

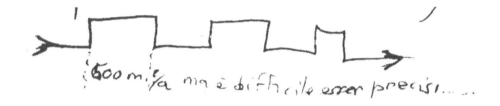

In all evidence, it was making a demonstration!

I've witnessed very many times objects being created from nothing, as if in the final stage of a transmitting process; at times they were appearing near the ceiling, then falling down, other times they were appearing on the ground, then rising quickly, knocking against our chairs. Most times they were movies, or tape recordings with the voices of some W56's in there (Sigir most times), who were giving us some directive, or just greeting us. When I was taking hold of these objects, they were always warm.

At times, blue flashes (2÷3 metres long) were appearing and zigzagging along on the floor, at times passing near to us, but never hitting us. We had been told that they were to put, or to verify, control and defense systems inside the house.

I've witnessed the phenomenon of street lights switching themselves off and then on again when we were passing under them (both walking, or in a car).

One day Bruno asked my mother, my wife and me to look through the eye-piece of a camera, aimed to the sky. "Do you see anything?" he was asking us, but there was nothing to see; then he would say "Look again now", and the camera was now showing a flying saucer; then it would disappear, and another one, may be a larger one, came in its place… it was an amusing show.

I've seen Bruno make telephone calls, with numbers suggested by the W56's, numbers 20 figures long (Author: At those times, with electro-mechanical switches, this was a plain impossibility, but I too tested it, in my case numbers were 30-35 figures long!), getting connected without passing through the telephone switches, and free of charge.

Once I was asked to act as an "aerial" (just to give it a name), I do not remember for what purpose, over the base in Pineto, at night. I was alone, inside a wood, and from time to time flames 30 cm high were lighting up and switching off all around me, some 2 metres away (I was a bit perplexed…), but Sigir, via wireless, told me not to fear anything from the CTR's. Speaking about radio sets, mine had had been organized by the W56's so that, while receiving their messages, changing the tune was not affecting the reception.

Another time, I, together with other persons of our group, were asked to wear pendants down on our necks: they had been made of wood, with small copper nails into them, following their instructions. Bruno had a telepathic conversation with some of the W56's and some guys from another race, friends to them; that lasted half an hour. At the end, we were asked to take our pendants off, and, to our astonishment, we found that the side that had been in touch with our chests was carbonized, although our skins had suffered no damage!

Once Sigir greeted all of us via wireless (we were sitting in circle, my wife was with me), calling each one by name, in the very same order we were sitting, as if he was able to see us; I believe that he was actually looking at us.

One of the best memories I have: I was astonished (by that point nothing was able to amaze us) because of the poetry exhibited. I was standing, leaning against the trunk of a pinaster, on the hill near Pineto, and, through my small radio set, I was in touch with Sigir. It was a sunny afternoon, and I was there to fulfill some of their purposes. Sigir was speaking to me, and at a certain moment he told: "I know, dear Gaspare, that you'd like to be down with us, and embrace us, but you can't imagine how much I'd like to be up there with you, outside this base, in the open under the sun, under that pinaster, where a small bird is now arriving"; and actually I saw a small sparrow flying toward the tree, then stopping on a branch a little over my head, "and now it will start to chirp" and it started chirping, "and now it will happily fly away" – and it flew away toward the sea. I'll never forget that episode.

The end

In Milano I got acquainted also with Giulio, who had been for some time in San Salvador. We became friends, I was feeling well with him. Unfortunately, he went away, after a furious quarrel with Bruno (I know the reasons, but it would be too long to discuss them here). That evening, Raffaella (Bruno's wife) phoned me in agitation, begging me to rush to their home. When I got there, Giulio had already fled, being menaced by Bruno; Raffaella told me that Bruno was going to break a bottle over his head (questioning our Friends was making Bruno go wild…). So I went to Giulio's hotel, and found him upset and weeping. Their friendship was over. Then he went away, and I haven't seen him since them.

One day, we were alone, Bruno and I, and Sigir sent us a wireless message; he was complaining because a "Higher Entity" (UTI, maybe?) had harshly censured what the W56's had done. The words of this censure were very severe. Bruno found them unjust, and that was the only time I've seen him weeping (but for anger); I try to calm him down, I couldn't see him in that state.

Battles between the CTR's and the W56's were now a daily affair; moreover Bruno was exasperated because of the way things were going on inside our group. Unfortunately, I began noticing that Bruno himself had started to backbite about someone in the group, and to relate to me unfair words said against me by others within the group. I could not understand this totally new behaviour, after our Friends had asked us to try to stay together, in harmony, otherwise Uredda would destroy itself. I was disillusioned, disconcerted. Then, once Bruno behaved in a really inhuman way against the architect Walter and his wife Verena (as with Emilio, it was myself who introduced them into the group); Bruno was wrong, in my opinion, but my intercession was to no avail. He dared to rage on them for more than a month (although Walter had done so much for our cause, and Verena was the most beautiful woman – I mean from an interior point of view – I have ever met). Moreover, I repeat, their fault was a minimal one, and unintentional. I was astonished (the W56's had nothing to say on that?).

Other things took place, not so serious, but many of them, and I was affected: I no longer liked such a Bruno. He really trusted me, and was often saying "I'm sure that you'll never betray me", but while he was saying so, something had changed within myself, I was disillusioned by the new Bruno, although I was trying my best to understand his reasons. I had always a kind of love to him, but I was willing to be honest to him, and, above all, to myself. Therefore, I decided to get out.

Via the Judge B. (as Stefano has quoted him) Bruno sent me the tapes recorded by our Friends, who were soliciting me to get back, with moving words. I didn't. Bruno wrote me many letters, very lovely ones, which I always answered; I still keep his letters, and the ones by Verena, who once described how our friends had healed, in an almost miraculous way, her daughter Maja, after an abortion she had suffered.

Years later Bruno came to Milano (he no longer had his house there), phoned me, I went to his hotel, and we had lunch together. I tried to explain him that I still was loving him, that I was grateful for the experiences I could never have had elsewhere, if not for him (which was true). He was looking at me with reproach in his eyes, and I understood that I was to see him no longer. But I still have Bruno in my heart.

Final remarks

I could tell so many other events, and phenomena, that I remember quite well... For instance, the time Bruno told me that the name W56, beyond referring to the starting date of the story, was also meant as an homage to George Washington, who had been the only President of an Earth nation to have got some contacts (I don't know in which way) with the W56's. But I repeat, whatever I could add, would not change too much the history of the W56's.

Post scriptum

My involvement with the W56's lasted from 1960 to 1965.

Damiano D'Alessandro's Report

<u>Author</u>: Damiano is an old friend of mine; we have known each other for many years, because we have been frequenting the same flying club in Preturo (near to L'Aquila), where he was a flight instructor in his spare time; now I let him speak about his experiences:

A strange encounter

On the 25th of February, 2008, around 9:30 A.M., my wife and I were in Rome, walking towards Tiburtina railway station, coming from the bus terminal, on the platform to our right. I had already looked in front of me, without noticing anything strange. A few seconds later, looking again in front of me, I saw a man, a very tall one, about three meters tall, judging from the shelter. He was a very big guy, well-proportioned according to his height, with short, dark hair, obviously big hands and feet; he was carrying a jacket on his right arm, was neat and very erect, almost a statue. He was coming toward us, apparently going to the bus station.

I had him in front of me for some 10-15 seconds, before he went past us, without even looking at us. He seemed to be looking at nobody, his eyes were fixed above the people. I noticed that, within the crowd, nobody looked astonished at the sight of such a big person.

At first, I thought I was dreaming, then, as time went by, I almost forgot this strange encounter. On the 17th of March, 21 days later, I attended a convention in Montesilvano organized by the CUN (Italian Center for UFOs), together with Enrico, a friend of mine, and a member of its local branch. Entering the hall, I noticed a person, one well known to me, whom I had been missing for some time, my old friend Stefano Breccia. My first reaction was to ask him "What are you doing here?" and he answered "What are YOU doing here? Here I am at home!".

So, I sat in the first row, listening carefully to the presentation by Stefano. The convention was centered on the Amicizia case, with Stefano, Gaspare De Lama and Paolo Di Girolamo speaking about their experiences, that were totally new to me. Gaspare spoke about communications he had received via small radio sets, but I was not able to understand who had been sending those messages; the speech by Paolo was barely understandable, because of the low volume of his voice. At the end, a young boy, who had seen me speaking to Stefano, came to me and told me that it was necessary to investigate, because under the Maiella [1] there was a base, inhabited by giants. A bit perplexed, I looked at Enrico, wandering whether the boy was out of mind, but Enrico told me: "Look, that's true, there are giants under the Maiella. Ask Stefano Breccia about them, because he knows everything.". I went to Stefano, and asked him about the giants; he answered that there had been giants in the past, but that now it was over.

In previous years, on many occasions I had flown small planes with Stefano, as we are both private pilots; many times I have towed his glider, but we never spoke about UFOs, therefore I got really curious, and, when the conventions was over, I asked Stefano permission to pay him a visit, to discuss the subject, and he agreed.

On the 19th, I went to his premises, forty km away, and we spent the whole afternoon discussing about the W56s and the Amicizia case. As I have always been sure of the existence of people from other planets, this was very good news; I asked Stefano permission to visit him again in the future, and he answered that I was welcome. Before I left, Stefano presented me with a signed copy of his book. The same night I started reading it, directly from the chapter about Amicizia, and, well in the night, I had not yet finished. As it was late, I jumped directly to the photo section; among them there was one showing a tall man, and the caption told that he was one of the W56s, inside Sammaciccia's garden [2]; at first I did not pay too much attention to it, but all of a sudden I remembered the man I had met at the Tiburtina station in Rome. I went back to that picture, and gazed at it, because that man was almost a brother of the one I had seen in Rome. The simple idea that I could have seen a W56 filled me with joy, not with fear. With some difficulty, I was then able to sleep.

Next morning, at first I did not remember what had passed the night before, but while I was having my breakfast, all of a sudden that picture came back to my mind, as a shock. At once I phoned Stefano, asking him who that man was. He answered that he was one of the W56s, by the name of Kenio, that he was about 3 meters tall, and that probably he had been shot dead during the battle against the CTRs in 1978. I contested: "Stefano, he can't be dead, because I have met him in Rome, together with my wife. Either it was him, or a close relative of his." Stefano told me that we should meet again, so that same afternoon I again travelled all the way to his house.

There I told Stefano about my story; he remained a bit absorbed in deep thought, then told me: "Look, all that has taken place, your meeting in Rome, your attendance at my lecture, your visit yesterday, my book, everything, did not happen just by chance. In all evidence that has been planned by our friends.".

Here I present a reconstruction based on an actual picture of the shelter under which my meeting has taken place, and the Kenio picture, from Stefano's book, reduced in dimensions to agree with my memory:

After Stefano's revelation, I became very excited, although in that day I was still rather ignorant about Amicizia.

Since that day, my life started to change; not long afterwards, I started witnessing unexpected and unexplainable events, beyond our capabilities. I kept Stefano up to date on what was going on, and we have discussed every instance, most times without being able to find a conventional explanation. Now I am going to quote some of the most interesting cases:

Electronic malfunctions

One day, the reception of the TV signal via satellite started fading out, each time for less than a minute, without apparent cause, then, all of a sudden, everything was getting back working correctly, then, a few minutes later, another black-out, and so on. Two days after my mother's funeral, it happened again, again without any apparent cause. Today, my satellite receiver is still working perfectly.

One night I phoned Stefano, but instead of hearing him, I found myself listening, over the phone, to two persons, speaking in English; at the same time Stefano, answering my call, was hearing something similar. I had to shut down the call, and then dial again, this time with success.

Another time I was having a conversation with Enrico, my friend, making use of my mobile telephone, while driving from Raiano to Castelvecchio Subequo; [3] we were speaking about the W56s, and it lasted some 10 minutes. What is strange is that in that peculiar area there is no signal coverage, it is simply impossible to make a call via cellular phone, yet we were able to converse without the least problem!

Some days later, while driving from Chieti to Sulmona, I was again talking to Enrico via cell phone; this time the signal was very strong. But, when I started speaking about the weapons of the W56s, all of a sudden we could no longer hear each other. Yet both devices (mine and Enrico's) were showing a signal intensity near to the maximum possible. Only after some 10 seconds we started hearing each other again.

In October, I was sleeping; I awoke feeling a strong pain in my abdomen, like an intestinal colic; after a while, it went away, and I started to sleep again; next morning, when I awoke, I realized that the chronic pain I was suffering from, due to a lesion to my first lumbar vertebra, had disappeared; during the following couple of weeks, at times I felt as if I had some liquid inside my right ear, and occasional pain. Since then, up to the moment of writing these lines (October 2010), my chronic vertebral pain has totally disappeared.

Other oddities

On Nov 6, 2008, at half past 9 a.m., I was walking along the sea shore in Pescara. When I spotted a sea gull flying nearby; the bird had, on the tip of its right wing, a small red light! Weather was overcast, and no source of light could have generated that effect.

Next day, the 7th, by half past 6 p.m, I was at home, watching a TV program, when all of a sudden the screen got black. At first, I thought that my decoder had broken; any way I switched my computer on, and started a program to see on it the TV broadcast; it was working! I tried to exchange the plugs, but the TV set remained black, while the broadcast was visible on the computer screen. After a while, everything reverted to normality.

A meeting on the sea shore

Next day, the 8th, at 20 past 9 a.m., I was walking along the sea shore in Pescara, southward; 500 metres past the Guerino restaurant [4]; I spotted a girl, who was walking in the opposite direction; she was wearing dark trousers, was some 1.65 tall, dark haired. When we got some 20 metres from each other, I got the impression that her face was a bit unusual, and thought that maybe she was from "elsewhere". So I tried to send her a telepathic message: "Please stop, let's talk". I had already stopped, looking at the sea. She continued walking, passing after me, but stopped some 10 metres later, turning toward the sea, and glancing at me. I though: "Please, get back, and if you like, let's stop and talk". A minute elapsed, then she got back toward me, then going beyond me. When she was some 40 metres away, I thought again "I need another confirmation; please, stop". She did indeed stop, turned again to the sea; after a while, she resumed her walk, and I followed her. After 250 metres, or so, she left the shore, stopping one moment to look at me, then went to a parking site, and entered a grey car, a Seat, while I was leaving the shore in my turn. The parking had two different exits, and she chose the worst suited exit, from her point of view, the one just in front of me, and went away.

That same afternoon Gaspare De Lama phoned me, from Bologna, and I started telling him about that encounter, but all of a sudden he was no longer able to hear me. After a while all got back to normal, and I started telling him again about my encounter, but again he was no longer able to hear me, so I closed the conversation. Then I tried to call him back, but my telephone was showing that the number he had called me from had the Naples area-code! Anyway I tried twice to call that number, without receiving any answer. Then I found that the memory of my telephone had recorded my two tentative calls as if they had been made the day before, the 7th! Later on, I was dining by myself, watching the TV, and with my computer switched on, in stand-by; all of a sudden I heard Gaspare speaking through the computer loudspeakers! I almost choked; I was only able to understand his last word, "second", and that was all.

Strange webcam behaviour

At 9:37, on February the 15th, 2009, as I awoke I switched on my computer, and, through it, I switched on my meteorological station, sitting just outside my house; among its instruments, there was a web cam, receiving images and noises from the street outside; the data are sent automatically through the Internet.

As soon as the station started to operate, I heard strange noises coming from its microphone, different from the usual street noises. At first I thought of some malfunction, so I stopped and restarted the program many times, to no avail. The situation was strange enough, so I phoned Stefano, who was lying in bed because of a flu, and told him what was going on, suggesting to him to connect to the Internet to hear the noises himself. In the meantime I started recording those noises never heard before, at times stopping and restarting the program, without any result. In total, I recorded one hour and a half.

During this recording, I tried to reach the station's microphone, knocking on it with a pencil, but the noise was not transmitted: the microphone had been switched off, and the noises I was hearing were generated somehow inside the unit. At this moment I became sure that the cause had to be looked for "elsewhere". After one hour and a half of recording, I switched the computer off, then started it again. Then I started the program managing my station, and this time the operation worked: my webcam started transmitting the usual street images and sounds.

Some days later, I made use of a peculiar software to analyze those sounds; at a certain point of the recording I noticed an abrupt change in the waveform; listening to that point of the recording, after some trials to centre it exactly, I heard a woman voice saying "OK" several times; I went through that piece of my recording, and was confirmed that there was a woman saying "OK" many times.

At that point, I got curious, and went through the recording; a bit later, I found a man's voice, uttering "Qui sono io" (approx. pronunciation: "Kwee zounau eeoh", meaning "Here I am"), again iterated some times.

Next day I presented my recording to Enrico, my friend, and he too recognized the voices. He asked me for a copy, because he wanted to have his wife listen at those sounds. When the lady listened at the voices, she remained dumbfounded: they were, she told her husband, the very same words that had been recorded on tape 20 years before, by her parents, over a mountain!

Enrico's parents-in-law had a son, who died very young. They never accepted the situation, and would have liked, at any cost, to get in touch with their son, after his death. After many trials, one day a friar suggested them to take a tape recorder to a secluded place, and to have it running in silence. They did as suggested, and indeed they recorded something, that they were not able to understand; they got back to the friar, who said that it looked to be ancient Aramaic, and sent them to an old scholar of this language. The latter, after listening to the tape, said that the words meant "Here I am"!

But that's not all: a few days after my recording, Stefano phoned me; he too had been listening to the sounds, and had made an interesting discovery.

Author: before letting Damiano going on with this episode, it's better that I interrupt him to present a fact that, at first sight, has nothing to do with what follows; on the contrary, as you are going to see, there is a totally unexpected, and unexplainable, connection, a connection that can't but bring to light unsuspected operations on the part of our Friends.

On February 9, 2000, (nine years before this fact) I had given a lecture at my company, the Scuola Superiore Guglielmo Reiss Romoli; the subject was Applications of Fractal Analysis, and the audience consisted in Mathematics professors from the University of Novosibirsk; I had already lectured on Fractal Analysis in that University, the largest in all Russia, so in 2000 I was just giving the last details on this subject, that I had been studying for more than 20 years. One promising application of this relatively new branch of Mathematics is Computer Music Composition, so, in that occasion, I presented the audience also with some passages from music composed by programs I had written. That has been the first, and only, occasion that my music went public, to persons who, a few days later, got back to their University in Siberia. Among other passages, there was this one (just a short excerpt):

This music is identical to a piece inside the webcam recording (only half a tone lower)! What connection could there be between a computer composition presented only once, in 2000, and strange noises generated who knows how by a webcam 9 years later?

Moreover, what's the use of that?

After this comment, let's start listening again to Damiano.

SLI examples

On February, 17, 2010, at half past 8, p.m., I was driving; approaching a street lamp, that was off, I noticed that two metres before reaching it, it suddenly switched on; the same happened with the following lights [5].

Since some time, my son started receiving "their" care; one night, awaking by midnight, he saw a tall figure, near to his small daughter's (9 months old) cradle; the being was curved toward the cradle, as if looking into it. The being was wearing a rather long coat, and was barely visible at the dim light inside the room. It was some 2.5 metres tall. As he noticed that my son had awoken, the being disappeared.

Meetings with Aniae

(Author: before proceeding, it must be said that Damiano divorced from his wife, but in these days they were still frequenting each other).

On Nov 1, 2009, my wife and I have been looking at the movie that Pier Giorgio Caria had made for Voyager (a TV program), and at the end she told me, "They will never broadcast such a movie.

Then we remained talking a bit; since I told her about this reality, her attitudes have changed, which is a bit unusual for her. Anyway, she concluded telling me that she was needing to meet one of Them, in order to be fully sure. "It doesn't depend on me, nor on you; it's up to them" I answered. She went to my sleeping room; after a while, she ran out, frightened, shouting me "What have you put in your room? I have seen two small, bright, white lights. What are they?"

I tried to calm her down, and asked her what had taken place.

"The first one came out from behind your wardrobe, flew just in front of my face, I've seen it quite clearly, then it landed on your bed, and extinguished its light. Immediately another one came out from behind a trunk, flew towards me, turned around me, then went under the bed. I knelt in order to be able to see it, but nothing, there was nothing to be seen! They were as little as pin-heads, and extremely bright, so that they were plainly visible, although the lights were on."

At this point, I understood that she had been confronted with two Aniae [6]; she had asked for some evidence, and has been presented with a small, but still great, evidence. By the way, this fact confirmed the sensation I was feeling for a few days, of not being alone at home, as if someone was spying on me.

A few days later, on Feb 14, 2010, my wife noticed a small blue light under a handkerchief, on her bed; she was looking for her cell-phone, and believed she had found it; but when she took the hanky from the bed, there was nothing under it, neither the light. Probably another ania, this time at her home.

189

A strange picture at the Rocca Pia (Ascoli Piceno)

On Oct 6, 2008, I went to the Rocca Pia together with Stefano Breccia; as usual, we wandered around the old castle, taking pictures of the place; then we stopped where, we had been told, in the past years the W56s used to open a vertical passageway to enter their base under the castle; there Stefano took a picture of me:

Both Stefano and I were in the shadow, therefore there is no possible explanation for the red and green (the original image is in colour) halos visible in the image; even more, having noticed the strangeness of this picture, Stefano shot a second one, say some 30 seconds later, and this new picture resulted to be totally normal. Strange things do happen!

Author's report

After having quoted so many witnesses, maybe it will be interesting to tell something about what happened to myself during the last few years. Of course I am going to present here only the most interesting episodes, forgetting many others that are not so significant.

I have been teaching Algorithms for Computer Graphics at the Engineering Faculty of the University of L'Aquila, for 10 years or so. I was not a formal university professor, I was teaching on the basis of a private contract between the university and myself. My course was among the most Mathematics-intensive in the whole course of degree. My lessons were Power Point presentations, full of FORTRAN programs that I had written, in order to demonstrate something interesting.

One afternoon, the day before a lesson, I had decided to modify my next-day presentation; I made some changes here and there, and added a few programs that I had previously written and, obviously, tested. This work had been made on the computer I am writing these notes on. I tested the presentation, finding that everything was OK, then mastered a CD with it; besides the presentation, the CD contained also the images and the programs involved, both source and executable codes.

Before going on, a note for the readers who are not acquainted with FORTRAN programming; FORTRAN is a very old language (designed, first, in the late '60s), particularly well-suited for mathematical computation; that's why I continue to use it, because I believe that it is the best language for such kind of problems. A FORTRAN program is a text file (source code) that, in order to be executable, must be converted into a binary code (executable code); this job is demanded from another program, a FORTRAN compiler, that translates from source code into executable code. As FORTRAN is nowadays a language for misoneists, it is not so commonly found; I use a compiler designed twenty years ago by DEC Corporation for their Alpha computer. I repeat, programming in FORTRAN means, first, writing the program as a text file, then compiling it in order to get an executable file.

Getting back to that night, I copied the CD into the portable computer that I was going to use next day to make my presentation; then, as I did not feel so confident about Windows portability, I tested my presentation on this second computer, and found that it was wrong: a program simply was not working!

I looked at its source code, and found a major mistake in it: a vital instruction was simply missing. Then I verified the hour its executable code had been generated: it was coincident with the time the CD had been mastered; I verified also the original files, and found them correct.

Just try to imagine what all this means: when I was mastering the CD, using NERO, "someone" had taken the source file of that program, modified then compiled it ("they" should have been in possess of a PC, and of a compiler compatible with mine), generating a wrong executable code, then "they" must have deluded Windows, substituting the two wrong files to the original ones on the way to the CD; moreover, as I always instruct Nero to verify, after having mastered a CD, its contents with the original files, also during this second phase "someone" deluded Nero itself! I still keep the CD as a souvenir...

Of course this has not been the only instance when "someone" tampered with my computers; another strange thing happened not so long ago with eng. Carlo Bolla, a friend of mine with whom I have a continuous e-mail exchange. A few months ago I sent him a mail whose contents have been replaced with the ones of another mail, much older, that I had deleted from my computer!

Then, I believe, many people all around the world have known of the major earthquake that in April 6, 2009, almost destroyed the town of L'Aquila, where Daniele, one of my sons, still lives. Thankfully our house got no damage. Unfortunately, the house where the girl-friend of Daniele was living, was destroyed; the girl was living there with her sister, father and mother; the three women died because of the accident (Daniele's girlfriend after long treatments in various hospitals); the father was ejected, safe but unconscious, into the street; someone found him, and he was taken to a hospital in Rome. More than 300 people died because of that earthquake, and the Italian government decided to organize formal funerals for all them.

Daniele, his brother and his mother with him, that morning were waiting for the ceremony to start, near the coffins of the three women. For various reasons, no direct relatives could attend. As it is usually the case with formal ceremonies, operations were rather turbulent, while waiting for authorities to arrive; during that mess (both my sons, later, and separately from each other, told me), they saw a very tall "priest", wearing a dark soutane, who approached the coffin of Daniele's girl-friend, stop some ten seconds in front of it, as if in prayer, then went away, nowhere to be seen again. My sons reported that he was some 2.5 meters tall, to the point that they asked each other: "What is that?".

I live in the platform of a large house, my sleeping room facing east. One night, not so long ago, I was probably dreaming, and I remember only the end of my dream, when I was asking myself "Who has switched the light on?", then I awoke, and indeed my room was filled with a vivid, but not blinding, white-bluish light. I recognized the kind of light that usually permeates "their" bases, a very typical one, and, who knows why, I convinced myself that just outside my window there should be the device originating the light. Anyway, I took it very calmly: first, I lighted myself a cigarette, then I got up, and walked outside my room; when I was near to its door, the light went off; obviously outside the house there was nothing to be seen.

Then, one morning, I found that during the night before, "someone" had taken my portable computer from my desk, and put it on the floor (who knows why?).

On my desk, typically on the right, a pile of various papers sits, typically 15 cm high; one afternoon (I was outside the room) my wife and I heard a strong clang coming from my cabinet: running into the room, I found that a large crystal ashtray, that was usually resting on my desk, had somehow taken off, flying to the right, had flown over the papers, then had crashed into the ground (a tile still shows the effects of this flight).

Then we had "personal" earthquakes. First, it happened to me; one night I was sitting in my cabinet, when a rather strong quake struck; just imagine that a pendulum clock on the wall had its safety mechanism blocking its operations, plus several other effects. Nobody else in the house noticed anything! A few years later, the opposite took place: in the upper floors they sensed a quake, while I, in the basement, felt nothing. In both instances, the national service taking care of quakes did not report anything in our area.

To the apples we salt we return

This sentence comes from "The Saucers Speak!", by George Hunt Williamson and Alfred C. Bailey; it is a message from one of their interlocutors. It's meaning is a bit obscure, because Williamson never cared to explain it, at least in this book; more information is contained in his following books. His "Friends" were naming "apples" people over this Earth who, for some unknown reasons, had been kept an eye on; what is really strange is that it happens that such a, let's say, surveillance, in many instances has been taking place even before the involved persons had been born!

I have already told of a very strange near-accident where two relatives of mine have been involved (the biplane unusual landing), many years in advance of my birth; then, I may recollect several instances when "something" prevented me from being damaged.

For instance, when I was 5 or 6 years old, one summer afternoon I had found, by chance, a pair of binoculars in my house and, together with a friend of mine, we have been looking all around through them; nothing unusual for two boys. What is really strange is that, at a certain moment, I decided to look at the sun, that was going to set! And, instead of being blinded at once, I saw a strange panorama, much like our Moon, with craters on it, under a yellowish light. Then I handed the binoculars to my friend, telling him what I had seen, and suggesting him to do the same, which he did, seeing roughly the same scene. And we have been looking directly at the sun, without any protection, and we are still able to use our eyes, even to-day! Strange enough, isn't it?

Then there is the story regarding my girlfriend of those days, and the DC-3 accident. She had been prevented from exiting her house, so that she missed the plane, and escaped the bad fate of that flight. And, of course, our Friends told me that they had acted that way as a kindness towards me, who met them, the first time, only some years later!

A crazy adventure

More often than not, the interaction with our Friends was leading to absurd situations; at those times I mostly did not realize the madness of what was taking place, and only years later I started wondering. The following is a classic example of such an event; it must have happened during a Winter, in the late 60's.

One day, very early in the morning, Giancarlo received a telephone call from our Friends: during the night a battle had taken place between them and their "enemy brothers"; three from the W56s had sheltered inside a grotto in the Sila mountains (Calabria region, south-western tip of Italy); could Giancarlo bring them something to eat? Before going on, let's notice a first strangeness: why was Giancarlo's help required? Couldn't our Friends cope directly with the problem?

Anyway, Giancarlo phoned me, inviting me to join the game, and I agreed; so he came to pick me up in his white Giulia (an Alfa Romeo machine), and we started southward. In those days no highway was available, and the only road was a narrow one, passing through almost all the villages on its way. In one of these villages an open-air market was taking place; we stopped to buy a sack of potatoes, and a small, living, piglet, then started our trek again.

We arrived to Calabria late at night, under guidance by our friends via wireless, but also under a heavy snowfall, and started climbing the Sila; at a certain point the poor Giulia refused to proceed further on along a narrow path probably meant for goats only, so we had to continue by foot, the potatoes sack and the piglet with us. Thankfully, the grotto was not far away, so we entered it, and found the three W56s concealed inside.

My first reaction obviously consisted of inviting them to join us in the car, and get back to Pescara, but they declined. So we left the potatoes and the piglet, bade them good luck, got back to the car, and started our way back, alternating at the wheel, and arriving to Pescara the following night.

Mission accomplished, we believed. Far from that! Next morning Giancarlo received another telephone call, a rather angry one, by the way; hadn't he been asked to bring our Friends some food? "Yes – Giancarlo answered – we took them potatoes and a small pig." But he should have been aware that our Friends would never have killed a small pig, even if starving. "But we left them also a sack of potatoes," Giancarlo tried to justify himself. "Yes, but our Brothers gave them to the piglet, which was hungry!"…

I swear that it is not a joke!

The Soviet Academy of Sciences

In this episode, the W56s do not appear directly.

For many years my company worked in cooperation with the Soviet Academy of Sciences, its Moscow branch. In those years Internet had not yet evolved in the West into general use from the old ARPA Net; but in the Soviet Union there was already something quite similar, whose use was widespread among universities. It was called Adonis and was a connection among many computers, based on exchanging files among users. The main difference with the Internet consisted in that messages were not directly sent to a peculiar user: addressing was generated via interest: a message concerning a peculiar topic was automatically sent to all the users who had expressed an interest in it. By the way, when the Chernobyl accident happened, the first ones to notice that something strange was taking place were teachers from the Stanford University, who, via Adonis, alerted their Russian counterparts.

In Europe Adonis reached Vienna, and the STET (the Italian TLC holding of those times) was interested in trying to extend it to Italy, and the job to investigate this possibility had been assigned to my company. So I started working extensively in cooperation with scholars from the Soviet Academy of Sciences, with exchanges of researchers.

One night I had as my guest at dinner Prof. Vladimir Serdjuk, director of the Institut Prikladnikh Avtomatizirovannikh Sistjem; better to say, both of us were guests at my mother's, in Pescara. The old lady was aware of my interactions with the W56s, she had actually met one of them sometimes, and was very proud that her son was involved in such an adventure, although, obviously, she had to keep silent on the whole matter.

That night, as usual, my Russian friend was exalting the Soviet success in many fields, Adonis among them. It was typical of those years: Soviet people were sincerely proud of their achievements, almost to the point of being conceited about them. I was translating from Russian into Italian and back, and my mother was getting tired of listening to that list of Soviet success; at a certain point, she pretended that I translated: "Yes, but you do not even imagine which scientists may be found among my son's friends!"

Perego and Fellini

Frederico Fellini, the well-known film director, was very fond of everything paranormal and, on course, of the Amicizia saga. One night he invited Alberto Perego to have dinner at Cinecittà, the little Italian Hollywood South of Rome. Plenty of actors were present, and, as usual, Alberto was the centre of the attention. He was speaking fluently about our Friends, how superior they were, somebody just short of Angels; in front of him a young actress was sitting, who was literally hanging on his lips, without missing a single word. Then Alberto stopped one moment to eat something, and the girl dared: "Magnificent consul; have you ever met them?" "For sure, my dear; we had also lunch together." "Wonderful, consul, and what have you eaten?" "Lamb and fried potatoes!", at which everybody burst into loud laughter!

Perego had told me that he had already arranged for a meeting between Fellini and one of our Friends.

Notes

The DC-3 Accident

1 ADF means "Automatic Direction Finder".

Unexpected encounter in Heathrow

1 Do not be surprised for my calm answering a call from aliens: I had been conversing with them for years!
2 About *Hydrae*, refer to "Mass contacts".

The witness by Paolo Di Girolamo

1 Bruno is a journalist; as he has signed lots of articles about UFOs on Italian newspapers, even telling of his meetings with the W56s, I believe that here I may say that his family name is Ghibaudi.
2 According to me, this figure is a great underestimation.
3 From my point of view, this name should be written Dimpietro.
4 Aniae were discussed in "Mass Contacts".
5 Also automata have been discussed in "Mass Contacts".
6 I have been reported performing strange activities in Italy while, actually, I was working in Argentina.
7 Their usual way to draw the materials we were collecting for them.
8 The way back.
9 A typical phenomenon, that repeats itself even to-day; people speak of SLI, from "Streetlight Interference".

Gaspare De Lama's Report

1   He is the usual Bruno referred in the previous chapter.

Damiano D'Alessandro's Report

1   The Maiella is a wide mountain group, west of Pescara.
2   This picture appears in my previous books on this subject.
3   Two villages in the general area of L'Aquila, west of Pescara.
4   A very old restaurant, in the centre of the town.
5   A rather common phenomenon that has been named "SLI".
6   Aniae, in this context, are small biological robots, meant to watch what takes place in their environment, and to take some action, if they believe it necessary.

Chapter 9

La Isla Friendship

This is a rather strange case that, it looks, is still taking place; it is difficult to understand whether it has any connection at all with the Amicizia case, apart from its name. It is situated in a remote island on the south-western shores of Chile, which is named "The Island of Friendship".

The first oddity consists in that, in a Spanish-speaking country, the name "Friendship" is in English. Another strange thing is that "Friendship" is not a translation, but the actual name of the island. Then, it is not clear which, among the thousands of small isles along the coast of Chile is indeed La Isla Friendship; many people have tried to find it, to no avail. To add strangeness to strangeness, it has been pretended that Friendship is not the original name of the island; the island got this name only in relatively recent times.

On the Internet there are many reports about La Isla Friendship, but, as it is often the case with the Web, most of them are rubbish. I am in debt to a Chilean scholar, Sergio Alcayaga Chelme, who kindly sent me information that I can't but consider true: it is a bit difficult to investigate something taking place, more or less, at the other side of the world! There are also Italian persons who, in a way or another, have strangely been in touch with this case. Then, of course, I am in debt to the main character, Ernesto De La Fuente, for his own account of his experience.

Foreword

As I have said, the main character in this story, at least the person who appears to have been among the first ones speaking about it, is Eng. Ernesto De La Fuente Gandarillas, who, in his youth, had shown unusual psychic capabilities. Following his tales, this man has been living since Sept, 1983, in Chiloé, a secluded area in south-western Chile, and had to resort to wireless connections to get in touch with the rest of the world. Some of his contacts were living in Santiago, the Chilean capital, and it looks that the first events took place there. But, before the "official" start of this story, Eng. De La Fuente started getting in touch, via wireless, with a group of people operating a station named "Friendship"; this station was apparently situated on an unknown island, belonging to the archipelago De Las Chonos, even more southward. Someone had decided to call the island with the name "Friendship".

A long series of wireless talks started, with not only De La Fuente participating, but also other Chilean hams, and even people from other countries in South America. It looks that the Friendship people owned a boat, named *Mythilus II*, that they were using to travel to other places. One day, when they were on their boat near to the island Caucahué, they called De La Fuente, proposing he meet them in a place named Quemchi, near to Caucahué; this way Ernesto met for his first time the Friendship people.

The following map, taken from Google Earth, shows the two places, Quemchi and Chiloé:

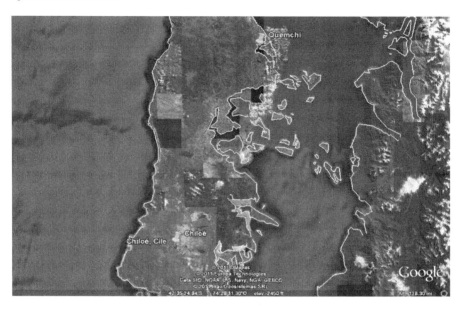

He says that the people were red-haired, a bit taller than usual, with their skin burned by the sun, and clear eyes; Ernesto was especially struck by the strong feeling of peace that was emanating from their persons.

After this first meeting, they started visiting him at his premises, and as Ernesto started getting acquainted with them, he was surprised more than once. Their culture is astonishing, although based on different assumptions. For instance, their arithmetic is using the base 6, at times 60, instead of the base 10 we are used to. I may just remember here that ancient Babylonians were acting in a similar way, using both bases 10 and 60 at the same time. Their medicine is a bit different from ours, because it concentrates on a healthy body, not on diseases. The same with their knowledge about history, anthropology, paleontology, astronomy, physics, and so on.

They presented themselves with "biblical" names, like Ariel, Rafael, Gabriel. When asked where they had got such incredible knowledge, they answered that they are totally ignorant! They are only putting into practice the teachings they had received from the "Angels from God". At first Ernesto had thought that it was some kind of religious concept, but he had to change his mind when one day he was told that "Next Thursday we will not be able to come, because the Angels of God are arriving on our island"; these "Angels" were looking to be very physical people!

Some kind of cooperation started between De La Fuente and the Friendship people; they were helping him in difficulties, and he started helping people who, invited by them, were travelling to La Isla Friendship, typically picking them up with his car at a railway station, and taking them to a harbour, where the Mythilus II was waiting for them. Among these visitors was the Lucero family (this was not their real name, but the name of their wireless station); Octavio, Cristina, his wife, plus three daughters. The visit by the Lucero's has been announced several times, but always cancelled at the very last moment.

Also Ernesto was invited various times to visit La Isla Friendship, but he always refused, because it would have meant spending a couple of weeks only in travel. During one of his trips to Santiago (where his wife and children were living), Ernesto got in touch with the Lucero's, who were living there. Ernesto recalls that the talking had been very funny indeed, because each party was asking the other about who the Friendship people actually were, and at the end they had to confess each other that they hadn't the slightest idea. Anyway, he was told that a group had been created, from radio-hams who were in touch with Friendship on a more or less regular basis, and he joined it. During the first meeting he attended, Ernesto heard unbelievable tales about healings, prophecies, and technical suggestions.

The formal start of the story

The "enigma" began in 1984, when the radio-ham Octavio Ortiz listened from Santiago to an SOS from a ship because of a menacing UFO in the south of Chile. That very day, after listening to the complete account of the incident, including people whose skin was burnt, Ortiz received a call from "Alberto" who claimed to have witnessed, from another ship, the whole phenomenon. Between Ortiz and Alberto a friendship developed. After disappearing for a short period of time, Alberto returned to narrate that he had met some "strange" people living on an island, to where he would be sending some equipment and other materials, by ship. Soon after, in May 1985, and through Alberto, Ortiz got in touch with Ariel, one of the Friendship people.

The image above shows De La Fuente and Ortiz.

Then, on the afternoon of Saturday 17 August 1985, in Santiago de Chile, at about 4:00 p.m., thousands of people began to observe the passage of a strange object over the city. The event was so spectacular that the news department of Television Nacional de Chile, channel 7, used a special camera to record the object on videotape. It must be noted that, later on, someone pretended to have ascertained that the object had been a French stratospheric balloon, but that looks a bit difficult to believe, because interactions took place with witnesses during the sighting.

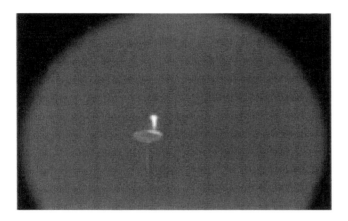

According to wireless talks between Ernesto and Cristina, it looks that it all started with Cristina talking via radio to Ariel, and inviting him to Santiago; she got the answer "We are already here!" When she tried to give him some indications about how to get to her house, she was answered "No need for that. Go, and look through the window." She looked, and saw a grey object, just over her house, that was sparkling in various colours. In that moment Octavio, her husband, arrived, and started recording the conversation. The object remained over Santiago for a long time, and was seen by thousands of people, and recorded by some TV channels. The image above was taken through a telescope. Later on the recording of the talks with Ariel was posted on the Internet, so that many people all around the world could hear it.

Editor's note: As the Isla Friendship claims began emerging in Chile just a few years after the official end of the Italian Amicizia experience, it is tempting to think of them as a new attempt by the Akrij aliens to establish their concepts among humans. There are numerous parallels. However, as with Amicizia, the whole story has remained largely hidden behind rumours, claims and counterclaims. Until its participants come forth with a coherent account, judgment must be suspended.

The photograph above is a perfect example; while it purports to show the craft mentioned in the previous paragraph, in all likelihood it is indeed a French MIR long-duration stratospheric balloon. However, this image does

201

not conform to the description of the craft near her house given by Cristina. Nor does it match the description given by other witnesses or a photograph purportedly taken by another witness south of Santiago.

Two different phenomena ensued: from his part, Ernesto, who was very sceptical about UFOs, started looking for advice from different people, most of the time with funny results. At the same time the story became widespread all around the world (Author: I must confess that I heard nothing about it in those years), with international journalists going to Santiago to interview the various witnesses.

To keep it brief, after a while Eng. Ernesto became convinced that he was having some business with extraterrestrials, so he started enquiring of them, always via wireless, about the big problems, but he was always answered that his culture could not allow him to understand the true situation. For instance:

"Where are you from?"

"From the universe."

"But which part of the universe?"

"Do you know how the universe is made?"

and so on… At the same time, Ernesto was the object of harsh jokes on the part of some people in Santiago who evidently did not believe a word of the story. Ernesto was trying to find skilled people, in diverse disciplines, who could discuss the subject, most of the time to no avail. Thankfully there were some exceptions.

For instance, an Electronic Engineer from Santiago, Daniel Morales, started enquiring about telepathy, and was instructed how to build an aerial that could be able to receive telepathic messages; unfortunately, the instructions were coming at a very low pace, so that Morales decided to complete it based upon his technical skills; something went wrong, and he was struck by a strong electric discharge, coming apparently from nowhere. Just after that the aerial collapsed, destroying part of the roof of his house. Shocked by that, Morales went to live in southern Chile, waiting for a call from the Friendship people, a call that never arrived.

Other similar things took place, often with not such destructive results. For instance, a dentist experimented with success some idea from the Friendship people, but then got afraid of what his colleagues could say, so that he returned to more mundane practices.

In the meantime, Ernesto had got back to his resort in Chiloé, and the usual activity of cooperation with the Friendship people started again. He was always talking with them via wireless, most of the time to no avail, because their answers were difficult to understand, or elusive. For instance, to the question "Are you extraterrestrials" the answer was "No, you are confused. We, from the

Congregation, have all been born from women." (after all, this sentence may have a different meaning, as we will see shortly).

The other, obvious, question was "Who are the God's angels?", to which "Ernesto, we have invited you many times to come here to meet them." Another time he asked Ariel what was his job before entering the Friendship group, and was answered "You would not believe it, but I was serving in the army ... Then one day I saw the Light ...". "What is this Light?". "You are going to see it one day or another."

After some questioning, Ernesto got to these conclusions: Ariel had been a war pilot, in a period when aircraft had no hydraulic systems; he had been based on Fort Lauderdale, therefore he was from the States; when he "saw the Light" he was 25, and the WWII had not started yet. That means that now he should be about 90, although he looks much younger. Similar conclusions have been reached about other members of the group.

Among such "young" elderly people, there is an Italian scientist, Andrea Nisbetti, who is said to have worked together with Wernher Von Braun in 1937, to have been the technical director in Kumersdorf, and to have disappeared after the bombing of Peenemünde, just to reappear, years later, in the States, working for the NASA. (Author: I have not been able to find anything about Mr. Nisbetti). There were many others with such inconsistencies between apparent and real age.

The ultimate goal of Friendship people

Once, in 1989, Ernesto hosted a meeting with some Friendship people at his premises in Santiago. The talk went as follows:

"We are happy that you ask this, we had been waiting for it."

"Why?"

"Because you have understood that knowledge, by itself, means nothing, if you do not have a goal; it only leads to corruption."

"And what is this goal?"

"The Angels of God are waiting for you."

"And why?"

"In order that you help us in our job, to establish a way of communication between them and ourselves."

"Should I be a sorcerer to do so?"

"Not so, but certain capabilities are required to communicate with them, and for the moment we are the only ones able to do so."

"And why do they not speak our language?"

"Ernesto, you are behaving like most people over this planet, with an unbelievable haughtiness."

"And why?"

"North Americans pretend that everybody speak to them in English, French farmers expect that inter-stellar travellers address them in their language, and Chileans wait to hear the ugly Spanish they speak. Don't you believe that they all expect too much?"

"And so, let's choose a language that we both may be able to speak."

"Speaking? Do you believe that, as you are used to communicate through articulated sounds, that all the dwellers of this galaxy, and others, behave the same way?"

"I've never thought about that."

"Look – said Gabriel, pointing to a line of ants over a wall – Do you believe that they communicate with each other?"

"I think so."

"And how?"

"I do not know."

"Through tactile vibrations, that they perceive thanks to their aerials. Did you ever try to communicate with them?"

"Never."

"Nor did we. Anyway, they constitute an organized society, that has been living since millennia together with humans, on the same planet, without any communications."

"I do not believe it is so much important."

"Other beings, much more evolved than you, could think the same about ourselves, don't you think so?"

"There is so great a difference?"

"Much more than you could imagine. Think how much humanity has changed in the last few years. Think of the difference in terms of 5,000 years. Right now we are beginning to understand the human genome. Think of what we'll be 10,000 years from now."

"We'll be able to clone living beings?"

"Much more than that, things you've never heard about."

"When will this happen?"

"When it will be possible to develop computer-based algorithms to communicate with them. It is similar to the problem with ants. The communication system the God's Angels use is as different from ours as ours is from that of the ants or bees. Maybe you could get in touch with them via telepathy, but you could never be sure of the fidelity of what you've received. Even ourselves, from the Congregation, are not yet able to understand everything, because of different ways of thoughts, that you cannot understand, because you have already organized it in your head. You may understand that a mistake in understanding a scientific concept could result in chaos."

"What can be done, then?"

"Only one thing: to make our computers able to communicate with theirs."

"And why this is not accomplished yet?"

"Because the technological difference between their computers and ours is too great."

"What might be done, then?"

"What we are already doing. Helping mankind to develop better computers, and   trying to take theirs to our level."

"Where is this action taking place?"

"All over the world. Do you believe that this sudden explosion in computer sciences has been by chance?"

Lung cancer

Jumping over years of strange happenings, one day Ernesto discovered he had developed a cancer in his lungs. This time he accepted the umpteenth invitation to La Isla Friendship, because they had promised him they could cure his disease.

So Ernesto was taken to the island, entered its underground facilities, and lived there for four days. During his stay, he had the occasion to talk to many of the "Friendship" people, normal earthlings engaged in scientific research beyond Ernesto's capability of understanding. The environment was a very technological one, again difficult for him to understand.

Of course, this is the most interesting part of Ernesto's tale, starting with the trip itself, with intelligent dolphins escorting the boat, and the last stretch under remote control from the island itself. Then the underground facilities, full of technological wonders. A first oddity consists in the length of Ernesto staying in the island: he states that his memory is rather blurred, but estimations vary from one day to four or five days, up to some months! Ernesto in those times was living by himself, so there is no witness available to give a final answer.

The "Friendship people" were apparently normal Earthlings who, after some exceptional experience, had migrated to the island; among them Ernesto found a lady whose activity consisted in training dolphins, on a parity bases; other people were studying the Bible, the Pentateuch, directly in Hebrew, in order to find messages concealed within the text. There were a few sick persons, waiting to be healed, among them the lady Ernesto was to marry years later!

The cancer treatment was explained to Ernesto, although it looks that their point of view differs strongly from ours; the treatment itself consisted in inoculating him with a liquid, partly organic and partly inorganic, followed by the generation of a field with the aim of refrigerating the liquid down to nearly absolute zero, and that is all!

The number of experiences Ernesto had while on the island makes us think of a duration much longer than just a few days, but his memory is still full of gaps.

Then, a funny mistake of mine: while listening to an interview, I believed that Ernesto said: "fumaban puros" (= "they were smoking cigars"), and in a lecture I underlined that the Friendship people were also smokers, like our W56s; however, listening later on to a better recording, I found out that Ernesto had been saying "...el aire puro" (= "clean air")...

Other voices

As often happens, when strange things are taking place, every kind of rumour arises; of course the evergreen story of Nazi survivors was recalled, who at times are said to have escaped to South America, together with their Vril weapons, and the whole lore associated with them; but also silly charges of theft, of deceit, of abuse, even of murder! Almost surely there is nothing true behind such charges, but it is a pity that most people, when they aren't able to understand something, resort to such silliness. Also in Italy, when Amicizia was at its full, similar rumours were circulating.

Recent developments

At the beginning of 2011 a Chilean girl was able to arrange a meeting with the Friendship people; once again, she was invited to join them, but she refused.

Recently, Sergio Alcayaga gave this enigmatic answer to an interviewer:

"Yes, I am going to meet them; not necessarily extraterrestrials, but local scientists... I believe it will take place within a couple of years. There are meetings with key witnesses, that make me believe that some of them have got in touch with alien technology, but also, maybe, with religious movements."

Some pictures

I am indebted to Eng. De La Fuente for the following images. Let's start with a picture taken by a sergeant of the Carabineros (police) near to the Tenencia Freirina:

I was asked to analyze this image, and made use of a fractal algorithm I had invented several years ago:

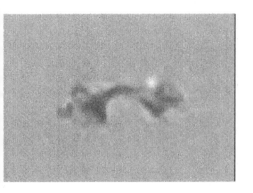 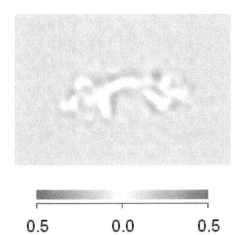

0.5   0.0   0.5

On the left the object, converted to B/W; on the right what I call its fractal transform; my program computes, in every pixel, the fractal dimension of the image, then takes into account only the fractional part of this number (that therefore goes from 0.5 to 0.99, to 0.0, to 0.5 again). I found that artificial objects tend to have values near to 0.0 (in my image, almost white areas), while natural objects have values near to 0.5; in this case, my analysis shows that the object is an artificial one.

Then a night-time image, really wonderful when it is seen in colour:

Another image comes from the Huasco Valley; there is a UFO in its upper right hand portion, unfortunately not so evident in this B/W version:

Once again, the fractal transform underlines that this object is of artificial nature:

 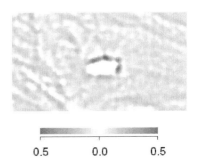

0.5   0.0   0.5

And so on, and so forth. As usual, pictures are no evidence at all; but, anyway, they are often interesting. To end this chapter, Ernesto De La Fuente has been so kind to send me the following comment on it:

Stefano Breccia tuvo la gentileza y buena educación de enviarme el capítulo de su nuevo libro en que se refiere a mí, lo que dice mucho de su calidad humana. Uno de los errores que mas se confabulan para desprestigiar el fenómeno Ovni, es la excesiva fantasía y la desinformación de muchos comunicadores, es por eso que me permito felicitar a Stefano Breccia por su veraz transcripción de los fenómenos que a mi atañen y espero pronto tener en mis manos el libro completo.

Ernesto de la Fuente Gandarillas
Freirina, Norte de Chile, Noviembre de 2011

It reads:

"Stefano Breccia has been so kind and well-mannered to send me the chapter of his new book that refers to me; that says so much about his human qualities. One of the most common mistakes, that devalues the UFO phenomenon, is due to the excessive imagination and lack of information on the part of many researchers. Therefore, I am glad to congratulate Stefano Breccia on his faithful transcription of the phenomena that concern me, and I'm longing to have in my hands the finished book."

Ernesto de la Fuente Gandarillas
Freirina, Northern Chile, November 2011.

Chapter 10

Enlarging our horizons in a cosmic environment

Carlo Bolla

After having finished reading this book, we are faced with a tale difficult to dismiss as merely novel: humans meeting face-to-face with anthropoid beings from outside, trips inside space ships, visits to huge underground bases, and so on and so forth. In this appendix I am just going to add something to this pattern, I will just try to give the reader some basic tools to try to understand. I want to ask whether such stories are really as absurd as they may appear to many readers; such a reaction is to be expected, when faced with things so far from our everyday way of life.

Much among what I'm going to write will appear obvious, already heard of, but it is necessary to go through such concepts, because thinking through them will help us. Let's start, for instance, with our planet: Earth, a rocky sphere about 12,745 km in diameter, luxuriant with life and abundant water, orbiting our star, the sun, that in its turn orbits the centre of our galaxy, that comprises at least 240 billions of other stars. Almost all of us are aware of that, but how many stop and think for one moment about that? Very few, for sure, because such a phenomenon does not affect in any sensible way our daily way of living, yet it constitutes an important part of our reality.

I want to enlarge our usual points of view, beyond our daily miseries. Philosophy and science go in this direction, trying to understand and give a meaning to what exists, although often going through different paths. And they are both necessary to understand our world. So, let's start listening to science, particularly to that branch that is devoted to studying our universe, that is astronomy.

What does Astronomy state about the existence of life in the universe? A scientist would say that an answer may be just probabilistic in nature, because up till now no dweller of other planets has revealed himself to earth mankind. But let's go by steps. Up to some decades ago science maintained that other planets were an exception; it was thought improbable that other stars had planets orbiting them; in the same way, our earth's huge amount of water (essential to life) was to be considered an exception; then, earth life itself was a lucky improbability.

Well, today, thanks to new methodologies and instrumentations, science gives different answers: other planets seem to be the rule, not the exception; up to now, over **1100** planets orbiting other stars have been discovered **and even some**

planets floating freely in space; water exists in great quantities all over the universe, in the inter-stellar clouds where stars are born, and therefore also within the proto-planetary disks that surround such stars; moreover, now it is believed that life is a rather common phenomenon.

Not a negligible change, after all, and in a rather short time. Science renews itself day after day: it is not so seldom that things considered impossible up to a few days before, become a truth; it's a rather common phenomenon in science's history.

I have not listed all the possible examples; anyway what this tells us is that it is very probable that, throughout the whole universe, things follow similar patterns, maybe the very same ones. Of course this is but a simple hypothesis, at least until we are able to move away from here and verify what actually takes place elsewhere. We stepped on our Moon, and sent probes to near planetary bodies, but that is not enough to confirm, or reject, our previous hypothesis.

Everything within our universe supposedly derives from that Big Bang that astrophysics places 15 billion years ago; therefore, if it contained a development program for every particle created in those tiny instants of explosion, it is plausible that such plots are still followed almost everywhere, here and in nearby galaxies. Exo-biologists themselves have found out via spectroscopy that hydrogen, carbon, nitrogen and oxygen are found everywhere within the universe, and organic molecules, the basis of life as we know it, are composed of such substances. In short, everything makes us believe that life is widespread.

We may only rely on the concept of life, as we know it; maybe elsewhere it takes forms quite different from what we are used to, but for now we can't state anything on that. But any scientist will agree that the humanoid form is probably the best suited: a trunk supported by two legs, two limbs with prehensile terminations, a head supported by a neck, with the various receptive organs in it (eyes, ears, nose, mouth) ready to acquire information from the environment. Other details (skin colour, height, somatic aspects) are probably of secondary importance, dependant on environmental conditions. The same scientist would reinforce such considerations underlying the fact that on our earth only man, among the many life forms, resulted a winner, because best suited to his goals.

Indeed, aside from its intelligence, our species could not have evolved, if our body was sensibly different. Other life forms (dogs, dolphins) show an interesting level of intelligence, but their bodies are not suited to put into practice anything but the simplest actions, they are not able to "make" things. After all, if we had only two phalanxes per finger, or were we missing an opposable thumb, it would be very difficult, if not actually impossible, to perform most of our common actions. That means that the human body is very suited to its goals, and that is true for the whole of it. It seems as though intelligence and anatomy develop together, and so our previous scientist imagines a humanoid structure for an advanced being. Therefore, when we reach another planet where an intelligent species dwells, we should not be astonished to find that they have an anthropomorphic structure, differing perhaps only in secondary details.

Another consideration, again deriving from paleontology, reveals that the "material" that living organisms are made of tend to get more and more refined as new species are generated, like a painter who returns many times to his work, each time embellishing and refining it. If we take a look to the animals that appeared 300 million years ago, or even more, arachnoids and reptiles, we see that they have primitive bodies, as if made of raw material. Later on, the birds (that come from reptiles, according to our science), when they appear, show an evident superiority, at least from an aesthetic point of view. The same with marine races, if we compare the first sponges and the first fishes to the most recent ones. Well if that is true elsewhere, we should not expect evolved beings showing a primitive structure because intellectual evolution must be matched by an efficient body. Our reptiles have remained reptiles, and did not evolve towards a higher status; at most, some among them evolved to birds. In the same way, if we accept the hypothesis that we descend from apes, our differences do not consist simply in phonation organs, but in a global better build.

Hypothesizing a race that evolves keeping its exterior aspect the same is nonsense from the point of view of evolution.

Of course we must accept the possibility of a *de*volution, when a race down-grades to lower levels, but that's another question. So, let's start from the hypothesis that extraterrestrial beings might be humanoid in shape. They will enjoy a superior mind and conscious thought, so that sooner or later they will start with the usual questions: "Where did we come from?" "What are we?" "Where are we going?" and so on, questions that they will try to answer, in a way or another. Some societies probably will proceed in a way similar to the one suggested by our philosophy, other could resort to spiritual media, and so on. But, when attempting to understand how our universe works, it is mandatory to resort to scientific research. First natural laws (physics and chemistry) must be understood, then ways must be developed to implement such discoveries. Such a process does not leave out the others quoted before, on the contrary, a synergy would be ideal, a situation that on our Earth is far from having been reached.

Aside from the push to discovery, we ought to say some words on the volume of space occupied by a generic civilization, remaining always on the field of comparative analysis and logic extension. We are all aware that, as a civilization grows from a technologic point of view, it enlarges its borders, so that the space it occupies gets wider.

As an example, let's consider a tribe, the initial aggregation stage of a human society; they do not know the wheel, so that the space they may travel is limited; what lies behind a far-away mountain is an almost unreachable aim; symmetrically, to the members of a tribe, it is simply unconceivable that someone may reach them from so far away. When they discover the wheel, their borders wide a bit; now they are able to reach places rather far away, in a rather comfortable way, for instance in order to look for food. If they live on the shore of a lake, or of sea, it will be the development of boats that offers them wider living environments, plus the possibility of fishing.

The history of mankind tells us that the development of transportation media involves two major consequences: the exploration of new territories and their conquest, meaning their annexation to previously occupied lands. Of course, another people may already be dwelling there, so that conflicts may arise, or, on the contrary, pacific cohabitation, in accordance with the respective levels of civilization.

In short, the development of wheel based media, drawn by animals, allowed past civilizations to expand their borders up to a level simply unthinkable before (suffice to remember the Roman Empire), although travel times were nevertheless not to be neglected. Later on, thanks to science, other media were developed (engines, railroads, planes), and travel times were greatly reduced, and the universe began to "shrink", so that far away places became familiar.

Electricity greatly enhanced all that, allowing levels that a few centuries before would have looked totally utopian. Then too, electronics and telecommunications have in practice totally cancelled distances all over our planet. In a not so far future, we'll be able to reach every point of Earth in even less time, and the world will become a single, wide, country. In the Middle Ages going from one town to another required an effort greater than going today from Rome to New York. So, from this point of view, our "province" has enlarged many times.

What has all that to do with the UFO problem? Very much, indeed!
When we speak of other civilizations, we refer to people able to travel through space, people whose technical achievements have allowed them to consider several star groups as a "single country"! Our technological level allows us only flights to our Moon; these days a trip to Mars and back is under study, but looks to be impracticable because of the many problems it presents.

Because of the many difficulties presented by space travel, even on a short scale like our solar system, interstellar travels look just like a mirage. How many times have we heard astronomers stating that a flight to the nearest star (Proxima Centauri) should require four years travel time, even moving at the speed of light (300,000 km/sec)? But with our present means, and the ones we may suppose, such a trip should last thousands of years!

So, is interstellar travel impossible?

Once again, we should reflect a moment, and imagine we have in our hands a book about the history of science. We could verify that, up to a few moments before their implementation, many of our discoveries have been considered as impossibilities, often because of physical problems.

214

For instance:

The theory of relativity is just as unacceptable to me as, say, the existence of the atom or other such dogmas. (Ernst Mach)

Blood circulation is impossible, useless, incomprehensible, absurd for the life of people.
(Guy Papin)

It is unlikely that anyone could find hitherto unknown lands of any value.
(Report of the committee organized in 1492 by Queen Isabella of Spain)

I even think that in the distant future the submarine may be the cause of bringing battle to a stoppage altogether, for fleets will become useless, and as other war material continues to improve, war will become impossible. (Richard Van Der Riet Wooley)

Space travel is utter bilge!
(Richard Van Der Riet Wooley)

There is a young madman proposing to light the streets of London - with what do you suppose —with smoke!
(Sir Walter Scott (1771-1832), on a proposal to light cities with gaslight)

That the automobile has practically reached the limit of its development is suggested by the fact that during the past year no improvements of a radical nature have been introduced. (Scientific American, Jan. 2, 1909)

Men might as well project a voyage to the Moon as attempt to employ steam navigation against the stormy North Atlantic Ocean.
(Dr. Dionysus Lardner, Professor of Natural Philosophy and Astronomy at University College, London, 1838)

That is the biggest fool thing we have ever done. The atomic bomb will never go off, and I speak as an expert in explosives. (Admiral William Leahy, 1945)

There is not the slightest indication that [nuclear energy] will ever be obtainable. It would mean that the atom would have to be shattered at will.
(Albert Einstein, 1932)

Too often, achieving "impossibility" has been just a matter of time. Today, interstellar travel (or, to say it better, space travel that does not require tens of thousands of years, a time scale that would force us to use little independent worlds as spaceships) is considered just such an impossibility.

What if, once again, this is only an *apparent* impossibility? A scientist would answer that the speed of light represents an insurmountable limit, and even if a spacecraft could reach that speed, it would face the effects on mass and time described by Einstein's Relativity. But general physics speaks also of the possibility of movement from a point to another by bending the space-time lattice. That is, through a process that we might theoretically envisage, it should be possible to make the initial and final points coincide, so that the path is of nill length, and, more important, no relativistic side effects arise. So, at least at a theoretical level, the huge distances should be no longer a problem. Of course, we are not able, at the moment, to realize how that could be done.

Is it possible that someone else in the universe has already achieved this goal? Everything makes us believe that it is definitely possible. Astrophysics tells us that there are many stars older than our sun, so that eventual civilizations developed there must be much older than ours, also in their technology. We cannot even imagine what results they might have achieved, surely including also quick trips over large distances.

Therefore, whoever states that interstellar trips are impossible is apparently unable to conceive of something beyond the trivial uses, and has learnt nothing from the book of the history of science. Science is very young, a daughter of that Galileo who, in 1609, watched the night sky with a telescope that he himself had built. Who can imagine the goals achieved by someone who has an history thousands of years long?

In spite of the many progresses since then, which might make us believe we have reached the topmost knowledge, we must convince ourselves that we are still in an embryo status. When, some centuries from now, our posterity will read back the statements by our scientists, they will smile, just as we smile at some peremptory assertion of the past, even the recent past, that we now know to be groundless in spite of the seriousness they were made with.

The ability of building interstellar spacecraft will represent the "wheel" of our future. Once again history will repeat itself, our borders will get wider, we'll reach new lands (planets), that maybe we'll colonize, or maybe we'll interact with their local dwellers, in a process that will repeat itself, but on a wider scale.

Then, if we think back to the great number of space civilizations that must exist, we'll understand that many people must be spread all around, and that, therefore, the space is full of intelligent life.

But where are all those other people? Why don't they get in touch with us?

These obvious questions are now famously named after Enrico Fermi, who looks to have been the first one to ask them. [1] Let's try to find an answer, or a sign of a possible solution.

Today a scientist would answer that the question does not hint that life is rare (science itself no longer believes that), but rather that interstellar communications aren't so easy, and, as usual, that interstellar travel is simply impossible; all of that should justify the apparent loneliness we are experiencing. But we believe that this is not the right answer, because it is a consequence of the wrong way of thinking we have already discussed.

We believe that the answer is an easy one, although multi-faceted. Fermi's paradox implies that, if someone comes here from far away, he would necessarily reveal himself and get in touch with us; this seems obvious if we consider the effort of making such a trip, that otherwise would look useless. But are we really sure of that?

Let's try to put ourselves in their place: let's think that we arrive on a planet where a population dwells that has not yet achieved space travel. Would we really land immediately and get in touch with them? Probably, on the contrary, we should wait and see, remaining concealed, before forcing this population to such an event as the first contact with people from far away.

Probably our analysis would find out a primitive, barbarous society, although already developed a bit from a technological point of view. In this case, probably we would refuse any contact. Changing roles, this could be our present situation with respect to visitors from outside. They would have their UFOs, and wonder why the aliens do not get in touch with them.

Our anthropological pride does not allow us to accept the idea that someone might have got here already, without getting in touch with us. Yet we do not look so desirable: wars, killings, drug smuggling, corruption at every level, injustice of every kind. How could a space visitor desire to get in touch with people like us?

Let's change roles once again, and put ourselves in the place of our space visitors who have just found a rather barbaric society on this small planet. It may be that, nevertheless, both ourselves and our planet may be of interest to them, although such interest does not imply a formal contact. In this case, our best strategy would consist of moving inside their environment, concealed from them, a bit like our film directors when they produce a movie on a secluded and barbarian tribe lost somewhere in the Amazon jungle. How many science fiction tales have shown us such a situation? If the atmosphere and the physical aspect are suitable for us, it would not be too difficult to us to mingle with them, unnoticed. We believe that this should be the right strategy.

Let's change roles: what if some aliens are already walking our streets, obviously concealed to our sight? Some would reject such an idea but, thinking a bit about it, it is the most plausible one. This would be our conduct, if we were the visitors; why shouldn't they behave the same way? The more so if we remember that we are speaking about civilization much older than ourselves.

Then let's remember that, in the same way that we have laws preventing some kind of interaction with primitive Amazon tribes, probably it's the same with them, and that is probably true at every level (let's remember, for instance, the huge spacecrafts the W56s were encountering at times in space, their own UFOs, probably belonging to even more civilized people, so that no contact was possible).

Nevertheless, few are ready to accept this possibility, and that's because of our pride. We remain convinced that we are the center of the universe, although our sun is a small star near the edge of a galaxy composed by more than 240 billions stars, and our galaxy is but one among one hundred billion similar ones.

Let's remember the *Star Trek* saga; it shows us a universe crowded with many intelligent races, that cooperate, make federations, fight their enemies, go exploring, and so on, and that's a magnificent scenario. Yet, in the stories if is often the earthlings who solve the most difficult problems of other people, regardless of their level of science, as if earthlings are some cosmic panacea! Such a point of view is far from plausible, because it again stems from our pride.

On the opposite side, the scientific one, when the topic of life in the universe is addressed, usually statistics are quoted, so that intelligent life is considered highly probable. But, most of the time anyway, our science speaks of civilizations at a level lesser or equal to ours. Very seldom science speaks of civilizations at a much higher level than us, not because there is no proof, but because of our pride. Yet, it is science itself that speaks of extremely old stars, whose planets must have been inhabited well before our Earth.

Anyway, to our scientists the speed of light constitutes a limit that makes interstellar communications and travels extremely difficult, if not impossible at all. Therefore the UFO problem is considered little more than a day-dream. Very few scientists dare to show some interest in this subject, while others prefer to remain in the shadows.

Let's get back to Fermi's Paradox, (if aliens exist, where are they?). UFO scholars are often questioned "If indeed they come here, why do aliens not get in touch with us?" We have already given an answer, to which another consideration should now be added, the principle of non-interference (the "First Directive" in the Star Trek saga). This is well known among UFO scholars since the very beginning of this phenomenon (1947), thanks to many communications allegedly of alien origin, according to which no civilization is allowed to interfere with a less evolved one. This principle is a must, because otherwise the lower civilization would suffer drawbacks from the contact; and also because a civilization has to be able to dig its road by itself on a social, technological and spiritual scale (Author: a concept underlined many times by the W56s). Only in this way successes can contribute to increasing the maturity of their authors, and the wisdom obtained this way greatly helps in every aspect of life, even on a cosmic scale.

Thanks to the non-interference principle, contactees all around the world have received from supposed aliens only simple but incisive admonitions, being left free to follow them or not.

Indeed, if we think of the various myths of the past that recount alleged deeds by aliens that had been considered gods by primitive earthlings, we have the unpleasant feeling that this principle has been broken many times by those who have underlined its importance. This has taken place when our remote ancestors have been subdued by their "gods", or have suffered unpleasant consequences in a way or another. At times the relationships went on in a benign way, with the "gods" teaching agriculture, astronomy and science. Unfortunately, there have been also negative drawbacks, often starting new religions, that still survive today, or generating wars, struggles, conflicts between ethnic races, whose consequences we are still suffering in the Third Millennium, and that have heavily influenced people. That underlines the necessity of non-interference.

If so, why are we receiving messages today of a different kind? It's difficult to give an answer. Maybe, "in the sky", someone decided to change the approach, after the mistakes made by his ancestors. Or maybe our planet has since become a kind of protectorate by someone who takes care of it. Or whatever else. What is evident is that, since a certain moment, the presence of "gods" has become much less evident, and the present human civilization has developed since then, seemingly without any interference. In fact, it looks that even now some interference has taken place, here and there, in a very soft way (my friend Stefano Breccia has well underlined this phenomenon in his presentation titled "Discrete Influences"). Actually it is a bit difficult to believe in a drastic change of attitude on their part. Probably what they have done has been to render themselves less visible (although their craft continue to move in our skies), maybe adopting a long-term strategy that we can't even imagine.

Since the 40s of the last century, the trend looks to have reversed itself. Those who in the past were traveling on chariots of fire now show themselves in flying saucers, Unidentified Flying Objects. But their strategy has been different, based on evasiveness, in a cat and mouse game. This evasiveness is probably part of a program aimed at awakening the masses to their presence. And that would agree with the non-interference principle. It would not be a good idea to present a fleet of spaceships over our major towns: panic, suicides and people going mad would be the obvious result of such action, even with the assurance of good-will on their part. Decades of UFOs have accustomed people to the alien presence in our skies, while astronomy has got more and more sure of life beyond our planet. The synergy between these facts, plus the de-classification of UFO-related documents by many governments recently has accustomed people to the UFO question, in numbers that will increase with time.

Contactee-ism started together with the UFO phenomenon, in the '40s: many people claimed to have met the pilots of flying saucers and to have contacts with them on a more or less regular basis. Such pilots are always described in the same way: anthropomorphous beings, maybe with unusual heights, skin color, building, different from us just as one race differs from another, but usually looking to be an improved version of humans in ethical, physical and spiritual aspects.

Such anthropomorphic descriptions agree with the hypothesis of humanoid morphology that is presented by our exo-biology. We find the same concept in the "gods" on their chariots of fire, superior beings with different attitudes toward us.

A large literature exists on the identity between such "gods" and today's aliens, so that it will be useless to discuss it here, aside from considering that such an identity is the only explanation of many strange facts from the past.

Among the most eccentric aspect of these early "gods" consists in their down-to-earth behavior: jealousy, vengeances, love affairs, and the like. Most mythologies tell of such qualities that one should not expect from a god, to the point that one wonders how superior beings could behave this way. The answer is probably that they, although superior, remain human, with characteristics that are probably universal in nature. Independently from their skills and knowledge, the drive to have amusements, to explore, to acquire life's pleasures remain unchanged, because they are written in our DNA. At most they may manifest themselves in different ways, above all depending on their interior evolution.

Yet we find it difficult to accept such behaviors, probably because we have been used to think of "aliens" as serious and solemn beings, and it is not easy to retrench an image so well rooted in our minds.

In the same way, we may find it difficult to accept the idea that people from other worlds live among us, inside our social lattice, evidently with a precise strategy in mind. Why? Leaving aside our pride that we have already discussed, probably the reason consists in that we believe that aliens descending on our planet should exhibit the noble attitude our movies have accustomed us to, with the magnificence apparently required by the circumstances. Obviously also our scientists think the same way. Once again, it is a mental habit difficult to eradicate.

The more so if we agree with the theory that most science fiction movies have been made in order to convey true concepts. And the well-disposed aliens of the Star Trek saga have been replaced, in recent times, by monstrous and destructive beings. Of course it is fanciful to believe that all movies carry some truth in them, but one wonders whether there is a precise plot beyond all that. But this problem is beyond our scope.

Getting back to aliens living within our society, this may look to be a case of the reality going beyond imagination for they have been here for a long time. Astronomy has been looking for them, for instance with the SETI project, with a lot of effort and expense, while all the time they were already here, intermingled with us; as they probably show no marked difference from us (too tall or too short, for instance) they are able to live at ease without being recognized as something different. Amicizia is but one story depicting such a situation, together with who knows how many untold stories (and Amicizia has been kept a secret for more than 50 years!) that many people live confidentially. It is unnecessary to say that these stories are the most interesting ones.

Someone could object that the idea of aliens living with us is improbable, a bit like tourists visiting another country, but it makes sense for anyone whose scientific and technological achievements have "shrunk" their universe, and for them far-away planets became just near-by countries. One day we too shall be able to do so, but a long time is needed.

With these basis concepts in mind I hope that the reader starts thinking in a "cosmic sense", helped in that process by the contents of this book. That means removing ourselves mentally from time to time from our usual routine, and thinking a bit "outside" our box. It helps to widen one's horizons, and to prime the spark that forces us to ask many questions and to wonder about the universe and life beyond our planet, questions that we cannot remain ignorant of any longer.

Although today an official, open, meeting with the pilots of flying saucers is considered improbable, one day or another it will have to take place, because such an alien evasiveness cannot last forever. My opinion is that a mind accustomed to think about the universe, and its inhabitants, automatically prepares to meet anyone who pays us a visit on board their flying saucers. It is not too short a process, probably it has already started, as youngsters are being attracted by the UFO phenomenon, but probably that is not enough. History teaches us that goals are never reached when in a hurry.

At this point, allow me to open a parenthesis that goes beyond the "enlightenment" aspect of this appendix, and is directed to those who think in a more natural way, and that derives from the many conversations I have for many years with my friend Gaspare De Lama and Mirella, his wife, who have been initiated by the mystic Osho. Swiss psychologist Carl Gustav Jung spoke, in his time, about the "collective unconscious", according to which everything, in the universe, is connected with everything else. "If you hurt a blade of grass, you'll hurt a star," teaches Osho. This way aliens, because of a qualitative divine law, would meet us only if they find in us a true aspiration wanting to meet them. Gaspare states that they already have the ability to measure the critical mass of the earth population feeling such a desire. According to the cosmic unconscious, the evolution of aliens themselves should be helped by efforts from our part in the same direction. Probably the information we are receiving since the beginning of the UFO phenomenon might be due to such considerations.

The importance of a collective thought, positive and permeating, may be reflected by the concept of Uredda's welfare, that was at the basis of the relationships between earthlings and W56s. Uredda, in Stefano's words, is a true entity that operates on people, on situations, on everything. This entity has to be kept alive by a sincere friendship feeling among earthlings and between them and the W56s. This way the W56s were granted a shield against their enemies, and the

221

"power source" for their devices, a shield that went missing at their final defeat. Uredda is extremely important, as another Amicizia participant, Emilio, underlines; he felt a strong affinity to the Uredda of a particular W56.

Now let's get back to the original subject about widening our perception horizons. Such a cosmic thought must take place with great care, without withdrawing from reality, a danger that is always present in such circumstances. We have to reason with our own brain, without indulging in sectarianism, without being influenced by those who make a religion of UFOs. Beyond being dangerous, such concepts should play absolutely no role in this Third Millennium.

NOTES

1 - Author: It looks as though Fermi's paradox derived from a conversation between Enrico Fermi and Leó Szilard, at Los Alamos, in 1950:

> EF: *Do you believe extraterrestrials exist?*
> LS: *Yes.*
>
> EF: *Do you think they have ever visited Earth?*
> LS: *Yes.*
>
> EF: *If they are visiting Earth, where are they?*
> LS: *They are among us, but they call themselves Hungarians.*

Chapter 11

What begins must finish

Up to now we have examined in some detail the saga of Amicizia, plus some other stories, similar to it. We have seen how they started but, up to now, did not see how they ended. Yet all of them have come to an end, in different ways. So probably this is the right moment to do so.

My experience with the W56s started when I was an university student, then it went on after I graduated, after I served in the army, and after I got a job and started working. Useless to say, it has been a fascinating experience, that allowed me to satisfy many curiosities, especially in the field of physics and astronomy, but, above all, to become friend to magnificent people, assimilating their points of view and their morality, on a basis to which I still adhere strictly.

Yet, keeping the contact with entities from outside is not as easy a task as it may look at first sight. On the contrary, it is extremely demanding, both in terms of time, of money, and of willingness; by the way, I had also got married, with two sons, and the negative side-effects of such a situation were making me more and more worried; please remember that some people involved in one way or another have been killed.

Moreover, I started having a very busy professional life, where the place left for the W56s was becoming shorter and shorter. Briefly, the situation was becoming no longer bearable, so one day I said to my Friends that probably the best decision was to stop our liaison, and they agreed without any comment. This happened in the late 80s.

Since then, they have always found the way to let me feel their presence around me, mostly with "tricks" and "jokes" of various kind, always harmless (the last one just a few days ago), a reassuring feeling, after all.

So, only my direct involvement came to an end, but they are still around.

The situation was drastically different with Bruno Sammaciccia and his group (to which, remember, I always remained external). The internal cohesion started to deteriorate, because of a woman, Bruno told me. In this way the support to Uredda was decreasing, to the point that our Friends decided to interrupt the contact. They did so in a rather spectacular way, pretending to have been engaged in a furious battle by the CTRs.

Indeed, in the last months of 1978 the waters of the Adriatico Sea went mad, with hundreds of sightings of UFOs, both over the sea and over land. They pretended to have been defeated, to the point of being forced to evacuate our Earth, which they apparently did, in front of Bruno and his wife, to their dismay.

They had promised to get back in the first years of the new century, but Bruno died without meeting them again. In the meantime, Bruno's group disintegrated.

Also in this case, anyway, they remained present; one winter afternoon Bruno asked me to take him on the shore of Montesilvano. Of course, due to the season, there was nobody around. When we arrived to the shore, we found the word "Benvenuti" (= "welcome") written on the sand with letters one meter high, without any footprints around! Bruno was a bit comforted.

In Germany the contacts went on for a longer period; anyway, when I met in Novosibirsk one of the German engineers, he told me that everything was over also from his point of view, again because of a decision from his part.

So probably everybody from the old guard of Amicizia broke the connection, in one way or another. Consul Alberto Perego had passed away and Bruno Ghibaudi told me that everything was over also for him, and so on.

In Chile, the experience of Ernesto De La Fuente came to a stalemate some years ago; here is what he has written me about the situation:

The communication was partially interrupted after I came back from the island, mainly because of my fault; I was too busy getting married and enjoying my new health condition.
Anyway, the contact has always been the same; they contact me whenever they want, but I have no way of contacting them. The last communication was something like six month ago.
I got sick and I thought that I was going to die, then I received a phone call from Ariel telling me that I was not going to die because before passing away I had to meet personally the "Ángeles del Señor". I am still waiting.

Also Howard Menger in the US took the decision to interrupt his contacts, for reasons similar to mine; Connie, his widow, has written me:

You are correct. The communications on a working basis between Howard and the "visitors" did mutually come to an end. It was Howard's choice. He chose to stay here with me for the benefit of raising our two children. Originally, according to Howard we were brought together for that purpose of having certain genetically and spiritually oriented souls enter this plane. He could have been free and chosen to go on working and serving his non-terrestrial friends, but our love for one another precluded that arrangement. I am sure, occasionally, he did see one or two of them, but it was only on a personal and private basis and was not public. For thirty five years we maintained our silence and concentrated on our sign advertising business and our family. Family is very important to us.

What I may say is that Amicizia (or something like it) is still active; I know some people are still involved with it, either in a full way as in our times, or in a softer way. The Work is still in progress!

Chapter 12

Some pictures

Now let me present some pictures; almost all of them have never been shown before. Let's start with a formation of six flying saucers over the Adriatic Sea; the picture has been taken *from above*. This image was already presented in "Mass Contacts," p. 362:

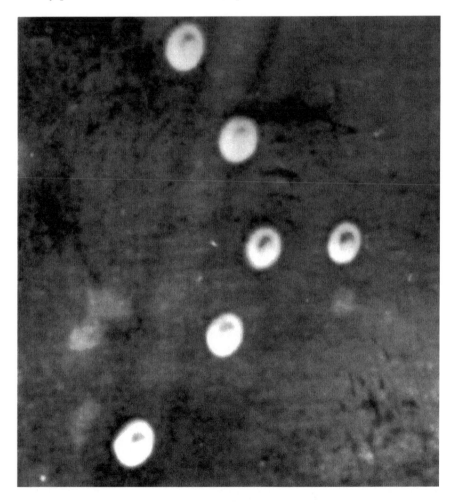

It may be seen that the light comes from the lower margin of the image. Unfortunately, I do not know when it has been shot, but I know the name of the photographer.

This picture was shot in Roseto (20 km north of Pescara) on Sept 29, 1960:

I shot this picture at the building of my company (under construction):

Coppito, 22–12–76 ore 13 ca.

As the caption reads, it has been shot on Dec 22, 1976, around 1 p.m.

Then, a sequence of a scout flying away; the images are still frames taken from an 8 mm film. The place is Trenno, near to Milano:

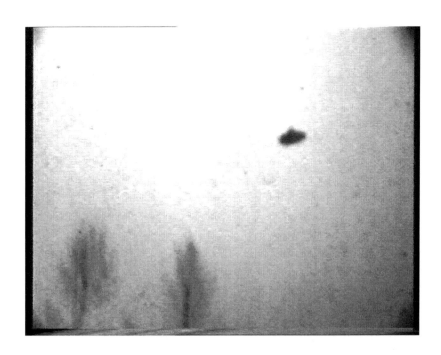

While flying around randomly, the scout went behind a group of trees.

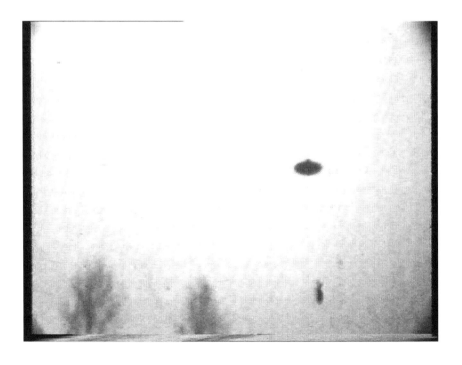

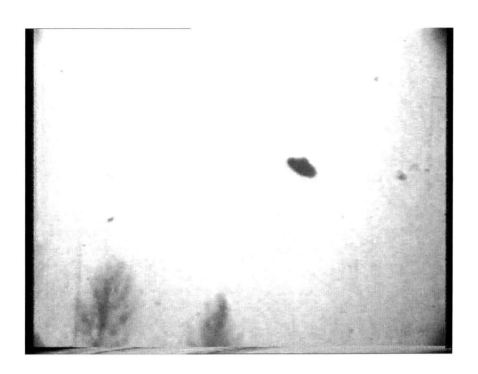

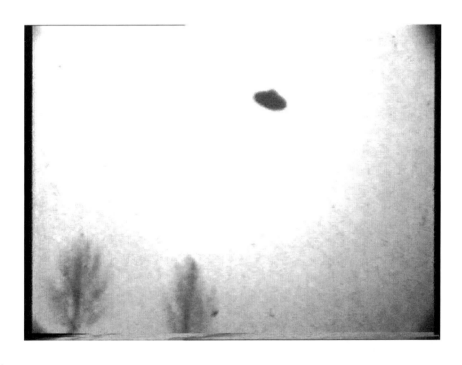

232

A scout flying over L'Aquila:

Then our W56 friend Kenio, about whom so much has been debated:

At the end, three more images of the W56 skin-diver who appeared on the cover of "Mass Contacts". These images are made on glass negatives (a rather old technique, not in use for many years); this particular plate was broken.

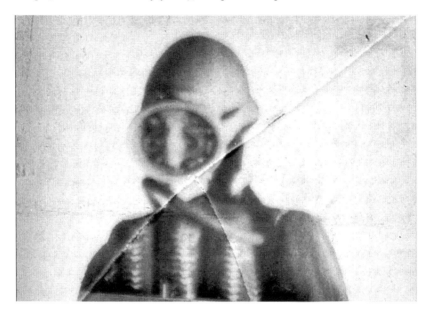

As I told in "Mass Contacts", some of the original pictures, who knows why, have been cut in halves, then the two parts recomposed at random; this photo indeed shows a W56 with three arms! Its upper portion is the same as the previous image.

The white circles are the result of a CTR weapon.

Chapter 13

Conclusions

Anthropocentrism is a hard nut to crack! Not so many years ago we believed that our Earth was the centre of the universe. Now, about UFOnauts, we call them "extraterrestrials", that are "not from this Earth". The same principle is contained in the equivalent Russian word "инопланетяне", that is "from other planets". Once again, it is "we" vs. "others". A bit of megalomania, isn't it?

We wonder why "they" do, or do not do, something, and it is always "they", someone different from ourselves. How mistaken may we be! There is no antinomy, they pretend that "I am everybody, and everybody is me". Maybe we, Earthlings, are only their small brethren, but altogether we ("we" and "they") are a single, very wide family.

What our Friends have taught us is that the concept of native place is quite irrelevant. One of them would say "My home is wherever I dwell". Many of them feel themselves as being "terrestrial", simply because they are living here, although they were born elsewhere. Then, many others of them have actually been born here!

Mankind is universal, and the place of birth does not mean too much. Different aspects should be taken into account, the major among them being the level of evolution. And, on this scale, the "we vs. others" does not play too much in our favour. I do not mean here evolution in technology, the mastering of biology, and the like. Sooner or later, when our scientists will be able of spoiling themselves with their pride, and the global economy will stop fighting against it, we could hope to get to similar results. What I mean here is the lack of individualism, the ability of being friends to all, their spontaneity in calling the CTRs "our enemy brothers".

I am not a man to deliver sermons. *Qui sine peccato est vestrum, primus in illam lapidem mittat* = *He that is without sin among you, let him first cast a stone at her* (St. John, 8, 7). I am not intending to convince anybody. But Franco Saija was saying: "Only one thing is possible to the ones who have seen and understood something: to witness!"

And therefore I am testifying here that I believe firmly in what I have written, and that I have written it in the hope that my poor words, in rough English, may make someone think about himself, first, then about the night sky full of stars, in order to be able to perceive

the love that moves the sun and the other stars.

or, if you prefer:

любовь, что движет солнце и другие звезды.

or, to say it in the best way:

l'amor che move 'l cielo e l'altre stelle.

(Dante Alighieri: Commedia, Paradiso, XXXIII, 145)

The End

Bibliography

Books:
- Tullio Bosco: "Accadeva a Pescara" – Arte della stampa, Pescara, 1992.
- Stefano Breccia: "Contattismi di Massa" – Nexus, Battaglia Terme (PD), 2007.
- Stefano Breccia: "Mass Contacts" – AuthorHouse, Bloomington, 2009.
- Ivan Ceci: "Alberto Perego" – TuttiAutori, Milano, 2010.
- John Robert Colombo: "The UFO Quote Book" – Colombo & Company, Toronto, 1999.
- Timothy Good: "Alien Earth: An Extraterrestrial Enterprise" – in press.
- Jimmy Guieu: "L'homme de l'espace" – Fleuve Noir, Paris, 1954.
- Alberto Perego: "Svelato il mistero dei dischi volanti" – La Tipografica, Roma, 1957.
- Alberto Perego: "Sono extraterrestri" – Alper, Roma, 1958.
- Alberto Perego: "L'aviazione di altri pianeti opera tra noi" – CISAER, Roma, 1963.
- Alberto Perego: "Gli extraterrestri sono tornati" – CISEAR, Roma, 1970.
- Roberto Pinotti: "UFO: Scacchiere Italia" – Arnoldo Mondatori, Milano, 1992.
- Roberto Pinotti: "UFO: Il fattore contatto" – Arnoldo Mondatori, Milano, 2007.
- Roberto Pinotti: "Alieni: Un incontro annunciato" – Arnoldo Mondatori, Milano, 2009.
- Solomon Shulma. "Инопланетане Над Россией" – Ермитаж, 1985.

DVDs:
- Piergiorgio Caria: "Il caso Amicizia" – Studio 3TV, Porto Sant'Elpidio (AP), 2010.
- Michael E. Salla (Ed.): "Mass Contact in Italy" – Kealakekua, Hawaii, 2010.

Articles:
- Warren P. Aston: "Amicizia: Alien Encounters in Italy" – NEXUS, Aug/Sep, 2010.
- Warren P. Aston: "Contato Directo: Caso Amicizia: Uma extraordinária história de relaciamento e amizada com alienígena" 171 – Revista UFO, Brazil, Nov, 2010.
- Warren P. Aston: "Amicizia: Mass alien contact in Europe from 1956 onwards" - UFOlogist magazine, Australia, Nov/Dec, 2010.
- Warren P. Aston: "Contatti alieni in Italia: il caso Amicizia" – NEXUS New Times, Italy, Feb/Mar, 2011.
- Warren P. Aston: "Inside a Flying Saucer: Photographs inside an Akrij craft" - UFOlogist magazine, Australia, May/Jun, 2011.
- Warren P. Aston: "Dentro de uma nave" 191 - Revista UFO, Brazil, Aug, 2012.

- Enrico Baccarini: "Amicizia; la storia di un sodalizio" – Lux Terrae, Sept/Oct 2010.
- Teresa Barbatelli: "Un Report sullo sconvolgente Contattismi di Massa" – Area 51, Jul 2007.
- Teresa Barbatelli: "Eppure c'è" – Notiziario UFO, no. 171, Sept. 2009.
- Stefano Breccia: "Dalla Luna a Marte" – Achab, XII, 1990.
- Stefano Breccia: "Contattismi di massa" – Notiziario UFO, no. 66, Dec 2006/Jan 2007.
- Stefano Breccia: "Evviva Internet – Notiziario UFO, no. 69, Jun/Jul 2007.
- Stefano Breccia: "Amicizia: A Story of Friendship in Italy"– Journal of Abduction-Encounter Research, JAR 8, Oct 2009.
- Harry Challenger: "Mass Contacts" – Flying Saucers Review, Vol. 54/1, Spring 2009.
- Giulio Perrone: "1956-57: Una strana storia a Pescara" – Notiziario UFO, no. 71, Oct/Nov 2007.
- Roberto Pinotti: "Italia 1956 – Contattiamo di massa occulto" – Notiziario UFO, no. 65, Oct/Nov 2006.
- Roberto Pinotti: "Il CUN incontra Amicizia" – UFO Magazine, no. 6, May 2010.
- Fabio Siciliano: "Gli alieni di Amicizia" – Area 51, Oct 2007.
- Fabio Siciliano: "Alieni infiltrati in Italia" – Area 51, Oct 2007.
- Fabio Siciliano: "In cerca dei creatori" – Area 51, Dec 2007.
- Umberto Visani: "The Friendship Affair" – the Australasian Ufologist, Jul-Aug 2010.

The witness of Paolo Di Girolamo
- Paolo Di Girolamo: "Noi e loro" – Nexus, Battaglia Terme (PD), 2008.
- Hilary Evans: "Sliders" – Anomalist Books, New York, 2010.

Gaspare De Lama
- Stefano Breccia: "Mass Contacts" – AuthorHouse, Bloomington, 2009.
- Gaspare De Lama: "Con gli alieni in Italia c'ero anch'io" – Notiziario UFO, no. 69, Jun/Jul 2007.

The Concept of Reality
- Father Luciano Canonici o.f.m. (comm.): "Scritti di S. Francesco e di S. Chiara" – Porziuncola, S. Maria degli Angeli (Assisi), 1982 (sponsored by Bruno Sammaciccia).
- Sadi Marhaba: "La via della realtà" – Porziuncola, S. Maria degli Angeli (Assisi), 1975.
- Swami Chinmayananda (comm.): "The Holy Geeta" – Central Chinmaya Mission Trust, Bombay.
- Bruno Sammaciccia: "Alla ricerca di Dio" – Porziuncola, S. Maria degli Angeli (Assisi), 1976.
- Bruno Sammaciccia: "Meditazioni" – Fabiani, Pescara, 1979.
- Sushil Kumar De (Ed.): "Mahabharata" – Bhandarkar Oriental Research Institute, Poona, 1958.
- Swami Satya Prakash Sarasvati, Satyakam Vidyalankar: "RgVeda Samhita" –

Vedi Pratishthana, Delhi, 1977.

Their Behaviour
- Giuseppe Lazzari: "UFO Operazione Terra" – SIAD Ed., Milano, 1980.
- Robert Salas, James Klotz: "Faded Giant" – Privately Published, CUFON, 2004.
- Robert Hasting: "UFOs and Nukes" – AuthorHouse, Bloomington, 2008.
- Richard L. Thompson: "Alien Identities" – Govardhan hill Publ. San Diego, 1993.

Amicizia and the Alien Receptiveness Program
- Howard Menger: "From Outer Space to You" – Saucerian Books, Clarksburg, 1959.
- Howard and Connie Menger: "The High Bridge Incident" – privately published, 1991.

The Genesis of Mankind
- Pushpa M. Bhargava: "Mathematics, Astronomy and Biology in Indian Tradition" – Kailash, Delhi, 1995.
- Mauro Biglino: "Il libro che cambierà per sempre le nostre idée sulla Bibbia" – Infinito Ed., Milano, 2010.
- Mauro Biglino: "Il dio alieno della Bibbia" – Infinito Ed., Milano, 2011.
- Jean Baptiste Biot: "Études sur l'astronomie indenne et sur l'astronomie chinoise" – Blanchard, Paris, 1969.
- Stefano Breccia: "I numeri nella storia dell'umanità" – SSGRR, L'Aquila, 1995.
- Stefano Breccia: "Il mito di Fetente" – Società dell'informazione, Fall 1995.
- Jean Bottéro: "La religione babilonese" – Sansoni, Firenze, 1961.
- M. Rampolla del Tindaro: "Lingua sanscrita" – Typographica Senatus, Roma, 1936.
- E. S. Drower: "Mandaeans of Iraq and Iran" – Brill, Leiden, 1962.
- Krshna Dvaipayana Vyasa: "Shrimad Bhagavatam" – Bhaktivedanta, Delhi, 1977.
- Raymond O. Faulkner: "The Ancient Egyptian Pyramid Texts" – Oxford University Press, Oxford, 1969.
- Richard J. Gillings: "Mathematics in the Time of the Pharaohs" – Dover, New York, 1972.
- Henri Frankfort: "Kingship and the Gods" – Chicago University Press, Chicago, 1948.
- Michael A. Hoffman: "Egypt before the Pharaohs" – Alfred Knpof, New York, 1979.
- Thorkild Jacobsen: "The Sumerian King List" – Chicago Universityt Press, Chicago, 1939.
- Leonard William King (Ed.): "Enuma Elish" – Lozac & Co., London, 1902.
- Samuel Noah Kramer: "L'Histoire commence à Sumer" – Librairie Arthaud, Paris, 1975.
- François Martin: "Le livre d'Hénoch" – Archè, Paris, 1975.
- George Michanowsky: "Le retour de l'étoile de Sumer" – Albin Michel, Paris, 1980.
- Otto Neugebauer: "Le scienze estate nell'antichità" – Feltrinelli, Milano, 1974.

- Christian O'Brien: "The Genius of the Few" – Turnstone Press Ltd, Wellingborough, 1985.
- André Parrot: "Déluge et Arche de Noé" – Delachaux et Niestlé, Neuchâtel, 1954.
- A. Pohl, R. Follet: "Codex Hammurabi" – Pontificium Institutum Biblicum, Romae, 1950.
- Robert Thomas Rundle Clark: "Myth and Symbol in Ancient Egypt" – Thames and Hudson Inc., New York, 1959.
- Biagio Russo: "Schiavi degli dei" – Drakon, Pescara, 2010.
- Rev. Archibald H. Sayce: "Astronomy and Astrology of the Babylonians" – Wizards Bookshelf, San Diego, 1981.
- Gay Robins, Charles Shute: "The Rhind Mathematical Papyrus" – The Trustees of the British Museum, London, 1987.
- G. B. Roggia: "L'epopea di Gilgamesh" – F.lli Bocca, Milano, 1944.
- Gary V. Smith: "The Concepì of God; the Gods as King in the Ancient Near East and the Bible" – Trinity Journal 3 NS, 1982.
- George Smith: "The Chaldean Account of Genesis" – Wizard Bookshelf, Minneapolis, 1977.
- Vishnu S. Sukthankar (Ed.): "The Mahabharata" – Bandarkar Oriental Research Institute, Poona, 1958.
- Bardo Thödol: "Le livre des morts tibétain" – Adrien Maisonneuve, Paris, 1933.
- Richard L. Thomson: "Vedic Cosmography and Astronomy" – Bhaktivedanta, Delhi, 1989.
- Veeravalli S. Varadarajan: "Algebra in Ancient and Modern Times" – the American Mathematical Society, Providence, 1998.
- Ganesh Vasuedo Tagare (Transl.): "The Kurma Purana" – Motilal Banarsidass, Delhi, 1981.
- Sir Ernest Alfred Wallis Budge: "The Egyptian Book of the Dead" – Dover, New York, 1967.
- Sir Ernest Alfred Wallis Budge: "The Gods of the Egyptians" – Dover, New York, 1969.
- Sir Ernest Alfred Wallis Budge: "Osiris" – Dover, New York, 1973.

The CTRs
- Kenneth Arnold, Ray Palmer: "The Coming of the Saucers" – privately published, Boise, 1952.
- John Robert Colombo: "The UFO Quote Book" – Colombo & Co, Toronto, 1999.
- Roberto Pinotti, Alfredo Lissoni: "Gli X-Files del Nazifascismo" – Idealibri, Rimini, 2001.
- Roberto Pinotti, Alfredo Dissoni: "Luci nel cielo" – Mondatori, Milano, 2011.

Other Presences
- Filippo e Giorgio Bongiovanni: "Eugenio Siragusa: Il contattato" – Giannone, Palermo, 1989.
- Maria Antonietta De Muro, Orazio Valenti: "I Giganti del cielo" – Internet e-book, care of http://www.edicolaweb.net

La Isla Friendship

- Stefano Breccia: "I numeri nella storia dell'umanità" – SSGRR, L'Aquila, 1995.
- Ernesto De La Fuente Gandarillas: "La Isla Friendship" – Privately Published.
- Teresa Barbatelli: "E ora salta fuori un'altra Amicizia" – Notiziario UFO no. 169, Jun 2009.
- Nicolás Sánchez: "Isla Friendship: ¿Lugar de encuentros cercanos en el sur de Chile?" – "Nos sur", May 2011.
- Noticiero ufologico autonomo no. 12, XII 2011.

Printed in Great Britain
by Amazon